THE ANCIENT
ROMAN
— WORLD —

TEACHING GUIDE

OXFORD

UNIVERSITY PRESS

OXFORD
UNIVERSITY PRESS

Oxford University Press, Inc., publishes works that
further Oxford University's objective of excellence
in research, scholarship, and education.

Oxford   New York
Auckland   Cape Town   Dar es Salaam   Hong Kong   Karachi
Kuala Lumpur   Madrid   Melbourne   Mexico City   Nairobi
New Delhi   Shanghai   Taipei   Toronto

With offices in
Argentina   Austria   Brazil   Chile   Czech Republic   France   Greece
Guatemala   Hungary   Italy   Japan   Poland   Portugal   Singapore
South Korea   Switzerland   Thailand   Turkey   Ukraine   Vietnam

Copyright © 2005 by Oxford University Press, Inc.

Published by Oxford University Press, Inc.
198 Madison Avenue, New York, NY, 10016
www.oup.com

Writer/Editor: Robert Weisser
Project Editor: Lelia Mander
Project Director: Jacqueline A. Ball
Education Consultant: Diane L. Brooks, Ed.D.
Design: designlabnyc

Casper Grathwohl, Publisher

ISBN-13: 978-0-19-522284-5 (California edition)   ISBN-13: 978-0-19-517895-1

Printed in the United States
on acid-free paper

CONTENTS

NOTE TO THE TEACHER

Dear Educator:

You probably love history. You read historical novels, watch documentaries, and enjoy (and, as a history teacher, no doubt criticize) Hollywood's attempts to recreate the past. So why don't most kids love history too? We think it might be because of the tone of the history books they are assigned. Many textbook authors seem to assume that the sole goal of teaching history is to make sure the students memorize innumerable facts. So, innumerable facts are crammed onto the pages, facts without context, as thrilling to read as names in a phone book.

Real history, however, is not just facts; it's the story of real people who cared deeply about the events and controversies of their times. And learning real history is essential. It helps children to understand the events that brought the world to where they find it now. It helps them distrust stereotypes of other cultures. It helps them read critically. (It also helps them succeed in standardized assessments of their reading skills.) We, like you, find history positively addictive. Students can feel the same way. (Can you imagine a child reading a history book with a flashlight after lights out, just because it is so interesting?)

The World in Ancient Times books reveal ancient history to be a great story—a whole bunch of great stories—some of which have been known for centuries, but some of which are just being discovered. Each book in the series is written by a team of two writers: a scholar who is working in the field of ancient history and knows what is new and exciting, and a well-known children's book author who knows how to communicate these ideas to kids. The teams have come up with books that are historically accurate and up to date as well as beautifully written. They also feature magnificent illustrations of real artifacts, archaeological sites, and works of art, along with maps and timelines to allow readers to get a sense of where events are set in place and time. Etymologies from the *Oxford English Dictionary*, noted in the margins, help to expand students' vocabulary by identifying the ancient roots, along with the meanings, of English words.

The authors of our books use vivid language to describe what we know and to present the evidence for *how* we know what we know. We let the readers puzzle right along with the historians and archaeologists. The evidence comes in the form of primary sources, not only in the illustrations but especially in the documents written in ancient times, which are quoted extensively.

You can integrate these primary sources into lessons with your students. When they read a document or look at an artifact or building in the illustrations they can pose questions and make hypotheses about the culture it came from. Why was a king shown as much larger than his attendants in an Egyptian relief sculpture? Why was Pliny unsure about what to do with accused Christians in his letter to the emperor? In this way, students can think like historians.

The series provides a complete narrative for a yearlong course on ancient history. You might choose to have your students read all eight narrative books as they learn about each of the civilizations in turn (or fewer than eight, depending on the ancient civilizations covered in your school's curriculum). Or you might choose to highlight certain chapters in each of the books, and use the others for extended activities or research projects. Since each chapter is written to stand on its own, the students will not be confused if you don't assign all of them. The *Primary Sources and Reference Volume* provides longer primary sources than are available in the other books, allowing students to make their own interpretations and comparisons across cultures.

The ancient world was the stage on which many institutions that we think of as modern were first played out: law, cities, legitimate government, technology, and so on. The major world religions all had their origins long ago, before 600 CE, as did many of the great cities of the world. *The World in Ancient Times* presents this ancient past in a new way—new not just to young adults, but to any audience. The scholarship is top-notch and the telling will catch you up in the thrill of exploration and discovery.

Amanda H. Podany and Ronald Mellor
General Editors, *The World in Ancient Times*

THE WORLD IN ANCIENT TIMES PROGRAM

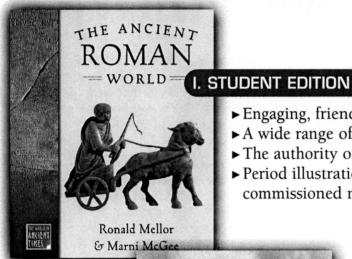

I. STUDENT EDITION

► Engaging, friendly narrative
► A wide range of primary sources in every chapter
► The authority of Oxford scholarship
► Period illustrations and specially commissioned maps

II. TEACHING GUIDE

► Wide range of activities and classroom approaches
► Strategies for universal access and improving literacy (ELL, struggling readers, advanced learners)
► Multiple assessment tools

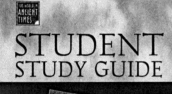

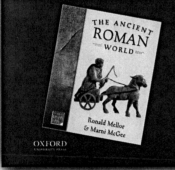

III. STUDENT STUDY GUIDE

► Exercises correlated to Student Edition and Teaching Guide
► Portfolio approach
► Activities for every level of learning
► Literacy through reading and writing

PRIMARY SOURCES AND REFERENCE VOLUME

► Broad selection of primary sources in each subject area
► Ideal resource for in-class exercises and unit projects

TEACHING GUIDE: **KEY FEATURES**

The Teaching Guides organize each *The World in Ancient Times* book into units, usually of three or four chapters each. The chapters in each unit cover a key span of time or have a common theme, such as a civilization's origins, government, religion, economy, and daily life.

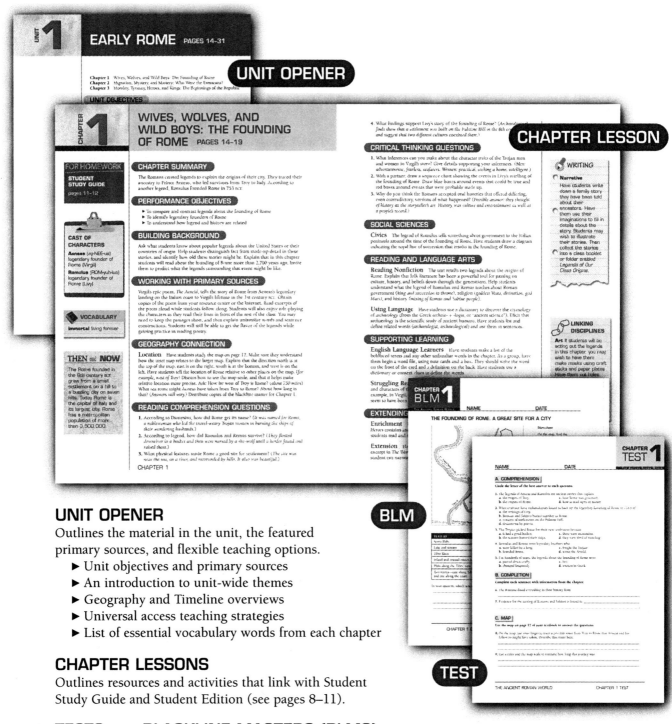

UNIT OPENER

Outlines the material in the unit, the featured primary sources, and flexible teaching options.

- ▶ Unit objectives and primary sources
- ▶ An introduction to unit-wide themes
- ▶ Geography and Timeline overviews
- ▶ Universal access teaching strategies
- ▶ List of essential vocabulary words from each chapter

CHAPTER LESSONS

Outlines resources and activities that link with Student Study Guide and Student Edition (see pages 8–11).

TESTS AND BLACKLINE MASTERS (BLMS)

Reproducible tests and exercises for assessment, homework, or classroom projects

Organized so that you can easily find the information you need.

CHAPTER SUMMARY AND PERFORMANCE OBJECTIVES

The Chapter Summary gives an overview of the information in the chapter. The Performance Objectives are the three or four important goals students should achieve in the chapter. Accomplishing these goals will help students master the information in the book.

BUILDING BACKGROUND

This section connects students to the chapter they are about to read. Students may be asked to use what they know to make predictions about the text, preview the images in the chapter, or connect modern life with the ancient subject matter.

WORKING WITH PRIMARY SOURCES

A major feature of *The World in Ancient Times* is having students read about history through the words and images of the people who lived it. Each book includes excerpts from the best sources from these ancient civilizations, giving the narrative an immediacy that is difficult to match in secondary sources. Students can read further in these sources on their own or in small groups using the accompanying *The World in Ancient Times Primary Sources and Reference Volume.* The Teaching Guide recommends activities so students of all skill levels can appreciate the ways people from the past saw themselves, their ideas and values, and their fears and dreams.

CHAPTER **1**

WIVES, WOLVES, AND WILD BOYS: THE FOUNDING OF ROME PAGES 14–19

FOR HOMEWORK

STUDENT STUDY GUIDE
pages 11–12

CAST OF CHARACTERS

Aeneas (ay-NEE-us) legendary founder of Rome (Virgil)

Romulus (ROM-yuh-lus) legendary founder of Rome (Livy)

 VOCABULARY

immortal living forever

THEN and **NOW**
The Rome founded in the 9th century BCE grew from a small settlement on a hill to a bustling city on seven hills. Today Rome is the capital of Italy and its largest city. Rome has a metropolitan population of more than 3,500,000.

CHAPTER SUMMARY

The Romans created legends to explain the origins of their city. They traced their ancestry to Prince Aeneas, who led survivors from Troy to Italy. According to another legend, Romulus founded Rome in 753 BCE.

PERFORMANCE OBJECTIVES

▶ To compare and contrast legends about the founding of Rome
▶ To identify legendary founders of Rome
▶ To understand how legend and history are related

BUILDING BACKGROUND

Ask what students know about popular legends about the United States or their countries of origin. Help students distinguish fact from made-up detail in these stories, and identify how old these stories might be. Explain that in this chapter students will read about the founding of Rome more than 2,700 years ago. Invite them to predict what the legends surrounding that event might be like.

WORKING WITH PRIMARY SOURCES

Virgil's epic poem, *The Aeneid*, tells the story of Rome from Aeneas's legendary landing on the Italian coast to Virgil's lifetime in the 1st century BCE. Obtain copies of the poem from your resource center or the Internet. Read excerpts of the poem aloud while students follow along. Students will also enjoy role-playing the characters as they read their lines in front of the rest of the class. You may need to keep the passages short, and then explain unfamiliar words and sentence constructions. Students will still be able to get the flavor of the legends while gaining practice in reading poetry.

GEOGRAPHY CONNECTION

Location Have students study the map on page 17. Make sure they understand how the inset map relates to the larger map. Explain that the direction north is at the top of the map, east is on the right, south is at the bottom, and west is on the left. Have students tell the location of Rome relative to other places on the map. (*for example, west of Troy*) Discuss how to use the map scale, and that it helps make relative location more precise. Ask: How far west of Troy is Rome? (*about 750 miles*) What sea route might Aeneas have taken from Troy to Rome? About how long is that? (*Answers will vary.*) Distribute copies of the blackline master for Chapter 1.

READING COMPREHENSION QUESTIONS

1. According to Dionysius, how did Rome get its name? (*It was named for Roma, a noblewoman who led the travel-weary Trojan women in burning the ships of their wandering husbands.*)
2. According to legend, how did Romulus and Remus survive? (*They floated downriver in a basket and then were nursed by a she-wolf until a herder found and raised them.*)
3. What physical features made Rome a good site for settlement? (*The site was near the sea, on a river, and surrounded by hills. It also was beautiful.*)

CHAPTER 1

GEOGRAPHY CONNECTION

Each chapter has a Geography Connection to strengthen students' map skills as well as their understanding of how geography affects human civilization. One of the five themes of geography (Location, Interaction, Movement, Place, and Regions) is highlighted in each chapter. Map skills such as reading physical, political, and historical maps; using latitude and longitude to find locations; and using the features of a map (mileage scale, legend) are taught throughout the book and reinforced in blackline masters.

4. What findings support Livy's story of the founding of Rome? (*Archaeological finds show that a settlement was built on the Palatine Hill in the 8th century BCE and suggest that two different cultures coexisted there.*)

CRITICAL THINKING QUESTIONS

1. What inferences can you make about the character traits of the Trojan men and women in Virgil's story? Give details supporting your inferences. (*Men: adventuresome, fearless, seafarers. Women: practical, seeking a home, intelligent.*)
2. With a partner, draw a sequence chart showing the events in Livy's retelling of the founding of Rome. Draw blue boxes around events that could be true and red boxes around events that were probably made up.
3. Why do you think the Romans accepted oral histories that offered differing, even contradictory, versions of what happened? (*Possible answer: they thought of history as the storyteller's art. History was culture and entertainment as well as a people's record.*)

SOCIAL SCIENCES

Civics The legend of Romulus tells something about government in the Italian peninsula around the time of the founding of Rome. Have students draw a diagram indicating the royal line of succession that results in the founding of Rome.

READING AND LANGUAGE ARTS

Reading Nonfiction The text retells two legends about the origins of Rome. Explain that folk literature has been a powerful tool for passing on culture, history, and beliefs down through the generations. Help students understand what the legend of Romulus and Remus teaches about Roman government (*king and succession to throne*), religion (*goddess Vesta, divination, god Mars*), and history (*mixing of Roman and Sabine people*).

Using Language Have students use a dictionary to discover the etymology of *archaeology* (from the Greek *archaio-* + *-logia*, or "ancient science"). Elicit that archaeology is the scientific study of ancient humans. Have students list and define related words (*archaeologist, archaeological*) and use them in sentences.

SUPPORTING LEARNING

English Language Learners Have students make a list of the boldfaced terms and any other unfamiliar words in the chapter. As a group, have them begin a word file, using note cards and a box. They should write the word on the front of the card and a definition on the back. Have students use a dictionary or context clues to define the words.

Struggling Readers Have students make a chart comparing the events and characters of the two legends. Then help students draw conclusions: for example, in Virgil, the founders of Rome came from Troy; in Livy, the founders seem to have been living in Italy already.

EXTENDING LEARNING

Enrichment Edith Hamilton's book *Mythology: Timeless Tales of Gods and Heroes* contains another myth about the founding of Rome by Aeneas. Have students read and summarize this myth for the class.

Extension Have student groups act out scenes from *The Aeneid*, from the excerpt in *The World in Ancient Times Primary Sources and Reference Volume*. One student can narrate while the others take the parts of the characters involved.

THE ANCIENT ROMAN WORLD

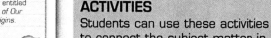

WRITING

Narrative
Have students write down a family story they have been told about their ancestors. Have them use their imaginations to fill in details about the story. Students may wish to illustrate their stories. Then collect the stories into a class booklet or folder entitled *Legends of Our Class Origins*.

LINKING DISCIPLINES

Art If students will be acting out the legends in this chapter, you may wish to have them make masks using craft sticks and paper plates. Have them cut holes for eyes and mouth. They can model their characters' features after the pictures of Roman men and women in Chapters 1–3.

READING COMPREHENSION AND CRITICAL THINKING QUESTIONS
The reading comprehension questions are general enough to allow free-flowing class or small group discussion, yet specific enough to be used for oral or written assessment of students' grasp of the important information. The critical thinking questions are intended to engage students in a deeper analysis of the text and can also be used for oral or written assessment.

SOCIAL SCIENCES ACTIVITIES
Students can use these activities to connect the subject matter in the Student Edition with other areas in the social sciences: economics, civics, and science, technology, and society.

READING AND LANGUAGE ARTS
These activities serve a twofold purpose: Some are designed to facilitate the development of nonfiction reading strategies. Others can be used to help students' appreciation of fiction and poetry, as well as nonfiction, by dealing with concepts such as word choice, description, and figurative language.

SUPPORTING LEARNING AND EXTENDING LEARNING
Each chapter gives suggestions for students of varying abilities and learning styles; for example, advanced learners, below-level readers, auditory/visual/tactile learners, and English language learners. These may be individual, partner, or group activities, and may or may not require your ongoing supervision.
(For more on Supporting or Extending Learning sections, see pages 16–19.)

TEACHING GUIDE: **CHAPTER SIDEBARS**

Icons quickly help to identify key concepts, facts, activities, and assessment activities in the sidebars.

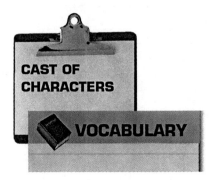

▶ Cast of Characters/Vocabulary

These sidebars point out and identify bolded, curriculum-specific vocabulary words and significant personalities in the chapter. Pronunciation guides are included where necessary. Additional important vocabulary words are listed in each unit opener.

▶ Writing

Each chapter has a suggestion for a specific writing assignment. You can make these assignments as you see fit—to help students meet state requirements in writing as well as to help individual students improve their skills. Areas of writing covered include the following:

Description	Personal writing (journal/diary)
Narration	News article (print and electronic)
Explanation	Dialogue
Persuasion	Interview
Composition	Poetry

▶ Then and Now

This feature provides interesting facts and ideas about the ancient civilization and relates it to the modern world. This may be an aspect of government that we still use today, word origins of common modern expressions, physical reminders of the past that are still evident, and other features. You can use this item simply to promote interest in the subject matter or as a springboard to other research.

▶ Linking Disciplines

This feature offers opportunities to investigate other subject areas that relate to the material in the Student Edition: math, science, arts, and health. Specific areas of these subjects are emphasized: **Math** (arithmetic, algebra, geometry, data, statistics); **Science** (life science, earth science, physical science); **Arts** (music, arts, dance, drama, architecture); **Health** (personal health, world health).

▶ For Homework

A quick glance links you to additional activities in the Student Study Guide that can be assigned as homework.

ASSESSMENT

The World in Ancient Times program intentionally omits from the Student Edition the kinds of section, chapter, and unit questions that are used to review and assess learning in standard textbooks. It is the purpose of the series to engage readers in learning—and loving—history written as good literature. Rather than interrupting student reading, and enjoyment, all assessment instruments for the series have been placed in the Teaching Guides.

▶ CHAPTER TESTS

A reproducible chapter test follows each chapter in this Teaching Guide. These tests will help you assess students' mastery of the content standards addressed in each chapter. These tests measure a variety of cognitive and analytical skills, particularly comprehension, critical thinking, and expository writing, through multiple choice, short answer, and essay questions.
An answer key for the chapter tests is provided at the end of the Teaching Guide.

▶ WRAP-UP TEST

After the last chapter test you will find a wrap-up test consisting of 10 essay questions that evaluate students' ability to synthesize and express what they've learned about the ancient civilization under study.

▶ RUBRICS

The rubrics at the back of this Teaching Guide will help you assess students' written work, oral presentations, and group projects. They include a Scoring Rubric, based on the California State Public School standards for good writing and effective cooperative learning. In addition, a simplified hand-out is provided, plus a form for evaluating group projects and a Library/Media Center Research Log to help students focus and evaluate their research. Students can also evaluate their own work using these rubrics.

▶ BLACKLINE MASTERS (BLMs)

A blackline master follows each chapter in the Teaching Guide. These BLMs are reproducible pages for you to use as in-class activities or homework exercises. They can also be used for assessment as needed.

▶ ADDITIONAL ASSESSMENT ACTIVITIES

Each unit opener includes suggestions for using one or more unit projects for assessment. These points, and the rubrics provided, will help you evaluate how your students are progressing towards meeting the unit objectives.

USING THE STUDENT STUDY GUIDE FOR ASSESSMENT

▶ Study Guide Activities
Assignments in the Student Study Guide correspond with those in the Teaching Guide. If needed, these Student Study Guide activities can be used for assessment.

▶ Portfolio Approach
Student Study Guide pages can be removed from the workbook and turned in for grading. When the pages are returned, they can be part of the students' individual history journals. Have students keep a 3-ring binder portfolio of Study Guide pages, alongside writing projects and other activities.

The Student Study Guide works as both standalone instructional material and as a support to the Student Edition and this Teaching Guide. Certain activities encourage informal small-group or family participation. These features make it an effective teaching tool:

Flexibility

You can use the Study Guide in the classroom, with individuals or small groups, or send it home for homework. You can distribute the entire guide to students; however, the pages are perforated so you can remove and distribute only the pertinent lessons.

A page on reports and special projects in the front of the Study Guide directs students to the Further Reading resource in the student edition. This feature gives students general guidance on doing research and devising independent study projects of their own.

FACSIMILE SPREAD

The Study Guide begins with a facsimile spread from the Student Edition. This spread gives reading strategies and highlights key features: captions, primary sources, sidebars, headings, etymologies. The spread supplies the contextualization students need to fully understand the material.

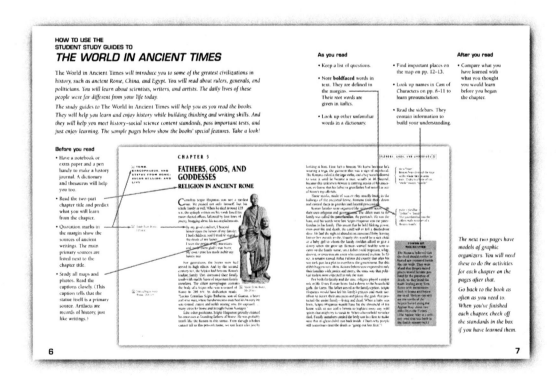

Portfolio Approach

The Study Guide pages are three-hole-punched so they can be integrated with notebook paper in a looseleaf binder. This history journal or portfolio can become both a record of content mastery and an outlet for each student's unique creative expression. Responding to prompts, students can write poetry or songs, plays and character sketches, create storyboards or cartoons, or construct multi-layered timelines.

The portfolio approach gives students unlimited opportunities for practice in areas that need strengthening. Students cam share their journals and compare their work. And the Study Guide pages in the portfolio make a valuable assessment tool for you. It is an ongoing record of performance that can be reviewed and graded periodically.

GRAPHIC ORGANIZERS

This feature contains reduced models of seven graphic organizers referenced frequently in the guide. Using these devices will help students organize the material so it is meaningful to them. (Full-size reproducibles of each graphic organizer are provided at the back of this Teaching Guide.) These graphic organizers include: outline, main idea map, K-W-L chart (What I Know, What I Want to Know, What I Learned), Venn diagram, timeline, sequence of events chart, and T-chart.

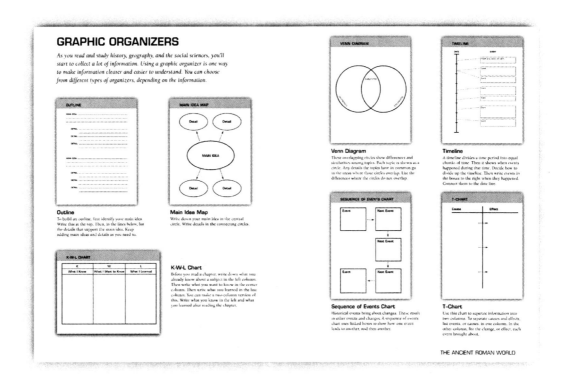

STUDENT STUDY GUIDE: **CHAPTER LESSONS**

Each chapter lesson is designed to draw students into the subject matter. Recurring features and exercises challenge their knowledge and allow them to practice valuable analysis skills. Activities in the Teaching Guide and Student Study Guide complement but do not duplicate each other. Together they offer a wide range of class work, group projects, and opportunities for further study and assessment that can be tailored to all ability levels.

CHAPTER SUMMARY
briefly reviews big ideas from the chapter.

ACCESS
invites students into the content by building background, tapping prior knowledge, or visual note-taking.

ADDITIONAL VOCABULARY
Additional vocabulary words important to accessing student book content are listed on page 10 of every Student Study Guide.

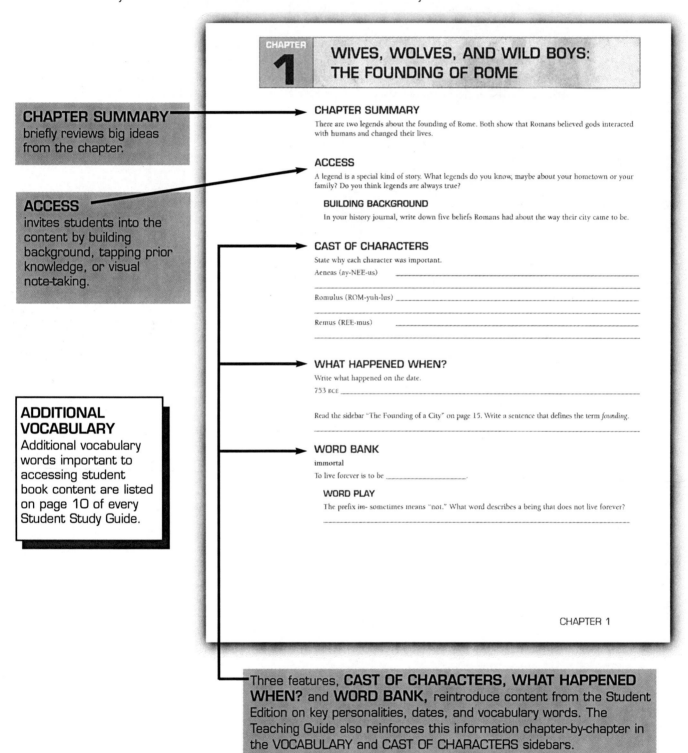

CHAPTER 1

WIVES, WOLVES, AND WILD BOYS: THE FOUNDING OF ROME

CHAPTER SUMMARY
There are two legends about the founding of Rome. Both show that Romans believed gods interacted with humans and changed their lives.

ACCESS
A legend is a special kind of story. What legends do you know, maybe about your hometown or your family? Do you think legends are always true?

BUILDING BACKGROUND
In your history journal, write down five beliefs Romans had about the way their city came to be.

CAST OF CHARACTERS
State why each character was important.
Aeneas (ay-NEE-us) _____

Romulus (ROM-yuh-lus) _____

Remus (REE-mus) _____

WHAT HAPPENED WHEN?
Write what happened on the date.
753 BCE _____

Read the sidebar "The Founding of a City" on page 15. Write a sentence that defines the term *founding*.

WORD BANK
immortal
To live forever is to be _____.

WORD PLAY
The prefix *im-* sometimes means "not." What word describes a being that does not live forever?
_____

CHAPTER 1

Three features, **CAST OF CHARACTERS, WHAT HAPPENED WHEN?** and **WORD BANK,** reintroduce content from the Student Edition on key personalities, dates, and vocabulary words. The Teaching Guide also reinforces this information chapter-by-chapter in the VOCABULARY and CAST OF CHARACTERS sidebars.

CRITICAL THINKING
CAUSE AND EFFECT

Draw a line from each cause and connect it to the result, or effect. (There is one extra effect.)

CAUSE	EFFECT
1. Amulius feared he would be overthrown,	a. they floated down the river and were saved by a she-wolf.
2. Rhea Silvia broke her vows,	b. the Romans and Sabines went to war.
3. A servant couldn't kill the babies,	c. Romulus killed Remus.
4. Remus made fun of Romulus,	d. Romans and Sabines called a truce
5. Romulus's men kidnapped Sabine women,	e. Romulus and Remus were born.
6. The Sabine women ran onto the battlefield,	f. he forced Rhea Silvia to join the Vestal Virgins.
	g. Remus killed Romulus.

WITH A PARENT OR PARTNER

When you have completed the chart, read aloud each cause-and-effect pairing to a parent or partner. Use the word "so" to connect each cause with each effect.

WRITE ABOUT IT

The Trojan women were *appalled* that Aeneas and the Trojan men were planning another journey after they reached the mouth of the Tiber River. To be *appalled* means to be

a) happy.

b) excited.

c) shocked.

Circle your answer.

In your history journal, write a short dialogue or a descriptive scene between the Trojan men and women about making this second journey. Why were the women appalled? How did the men respond?

WORKING WITH PRIMARY SOURCES

The image at left is an ancient Roman coin. It shows an image of a Roman god. Think about what we can learn about ancient cultures through artifacts like this one. Answer the following questions in your history journal.

1. Why do you think the figure is wearing an olive wreath?

2. Why would the Romans put a god on their coins?

3. What famous people do we use on coins today? (It's okay to take a peek at your pocket change!)

4. If people found your coins hundreds of years from now, what conclusions might they draw about your culture?

5. Think up a design for your own coin and draw it in your history journal.

THE ANCIENT ROMAN WORLD

CRITICAL THINKING exercises draw on such thinking skills as establishing cause and effect, making inferences, drawing conclusions, determining sequence of events, comparing and contrasting, identifying main ideas and details, and other analytical process.

WRITE ABOUT IT gives students writing suggestions drawn from the material. A writing assignment may stem from a vocabulary word, a historical event, or a reading of a primary source. The assignment can take any number of forms: newspaper article, letter, short essay, a scene with dialogue, a diary entry.

WORKING WITH PRIMARY SOURCES invites students to read primary sources closely. Exercises include answering comprehension questions, evaluating point of view, and writing and other forms of creative expression, including music, art, and design. "In Your Own Words" writing activities ask students to paraphrase a primary source.

IMPROVING LITERACY WITH THE WORLD IN ANCIENT TIMES

The books in this series are written in a lively, narrative style to inspire a love of reading history–social science. English language learners and struggling readers are given special consideration within the program's exercises and activities. And students who love to read and learn will also benefit from the program's rich and varied material. Following are strategies to make sure each and every student gets the most out of the subjects you will teach through *The World in Ancient Times*.

ENGLISH LANGUAGE LEARNERS

For English learners to achieve academic success, the instructional considerations for teachers include two mandates:

- Help them attain grade level, content area knowledge, and academic language.
- Provide for the development of English language proficiency.

To accomplish these goals, you should plan lessons that reflect the student's level of English proficiency. Students progress through five developmental levels as they increase in language proficiency:

Beginning and Early Intermediate (*grade level material will be mostly incomprehensible, students need a great deal of teacher support*)

Intermediate (*grade level work will be a challenge*)

Early Advanced and Advanced (*close to grade level reading and writing, students continue to need support*)

The books in this program are written at the intermediate level. However, you can still use the lesson plans for students of different levels by using the strategies below:

Tap Prior Knowledge
What students know about the topic will help determine your next steps for instruction. Using K-W-L charts, brainstorming, and making lists are ways to find out what they know. English learners bring a rich cultural diversity into the classroom. By sharing what they know, students can connect their knowledge and experiences to the course.

Set the Context
Use different tools to make new information understandable. These can be images, artifacts, maps, timelines, illustrations, charts, videos, or graphic organizers. Techniques such as role-playing and story-boarding can also be helpful. Speak in shorter sentences, with careful enunciation, expanded explanations, repetitions, and paraphrasing. Use fewer idiomatic expressions.

Show—Don't Just Tell
English learners often get lost as they listen to directions, explanations, lectures, and discussions. By showing students what is expected, you can help them participate more fully in classroom activities. Students need to be shown how to use the graphic organizers in this guide and the mini versions in the student study guide, as well as other blackline masters for note-taking and practice. An overhead transparency with whole or small groups is also effective.

Use the Text

Because of unfamiliar words, students will need help. Teach them to preview the chapter using text features (headings, bold print, sidebars, italics). See the suggestions in the facsimile of the Student Edition, shown on pages 6–7 of the Student Study Guide. Show students organizing structures such as cause and effect or comparing and contrasting. Have students read to each other in pairs. Encourage them to share their history journals with each other. Use Read Aloud/Think Aloud, perhaps with an overhead transparency. Help them create word banks, charts, and graphic organizers. Discuss the main idea after reading.

Check for Understanding

Rather than simply ask students if they understand, stop frequently and ask them to paraphrase or expand on what you just said. Such techniques will give you a much clearer assessment of their understanding.

Provide for Interaction

As students interact with the information and speak their thoughts, their content knowledge and academic language skills improve. Increase interaction in the classroom through cooperative learning, small group work, and partner share. By working and talking with others, students can practice asking and answering questions.

Use Appropriate Assessment

When modifying the instruction, you will also need to modify the assessment. Multiple choice, true and false, and other criterion reference tests are suitable, but consider changing test format and structure. English learners are constantly improving their language proficiency in their oral and written responses, but they are often grammatically incorrect. Remember to be thoughtful and fair about giving students credit for their content knowledge and use of academic language, even if their English isn't perfect.

STRUGGLING READERS

Some students struggle to understand the information presented in a textbook. The following strategies for content-area reading can help students improve their ability to make comparisons, sequence events, determine importance, summarize, evaluate, synthesize, analyze, and solve problems.

Build Knowledge of Genre

Both the fiction and narrative nonfiction genres are incorporated into *The World in Ancient Times*. This combination of genres makes the text interesting and engaging. But teachers must be sure students can identify and use the organizational structures of both genres.

Fiction	Nonfiction
Each chapter is a story	Content: historical information
Setting: historical time and place	Organizational structure: cause/effect, sequence of events, problem/solution
Characters: historical figures	Other features: maps, timelines, sidebars, photographs, primary sources
Plot: problems, roadblocks, and resolutions	

In addition, the textbook has a wealth of the text features of nonfiction: bold and italic print, sidebars, headings and subheadings, labels, captions, and "signal words" such as *first*, *next*, and *finally*. Teaching these organizational structures and text features is essential for struggling readers.

Build Background

Having background information about a topic makes reading about it so much easier. When students lack background information, teachers can preteach or "front load" concepts and vocabulary, using a variety of instructional techniques. Conduct a chapter or book walk, looking at titles, headings, and other text features to develop a big picture of the content. Focus on new vocabulary words during the "walk" and create a word bank with illustrations for future reference. Read aloud key passages and discuss the meaning. Focus on the timeline and maps to help students develop a sense of time and place. Show a video, go to a website, and have trade books and magazines on the topic available for student exploration.

Comprehension Strategies

While reading, successful readers are predicting, making connections, monitoring, visualizing, questioning, inferring, and summarizing. Struggling readers have a harder time with these "in the head" processes. The following strategies will help these students construct meaning from the text until they are able to do it on their own.

PREDICT: Before reading, conduct a picture and text feature "tour" of the chapter to make predictions. Ask students if they remember if this has ever happened before, to predict what might happen this time.

MAKE CONNECTIONS: Help students relate content to their background (text to text, text to self, and text to the world).

MONITOR AND CONFIRM: Encourage students to stop reading when they come across an unknown word, phrase, or concept. In their notebooks, have them make a note of text they don't understand and ask for clarification or figure it out. While this activity slows down reading at first, it is effective in improving skills over time.

VISUALIZE: Students benefit from imagining the events described in a story. Sketching scenes, story-boarding, role-playing, and looking for sensory details all help students with this strategy.

INFER: Help students look beyond the literal meaning of a text to understand deeper meanings. Graphic organizers and discussions provide opportunities to broaden their understanding. Looking closely at the "why" of historical events helps students infer.

QUESTION AND DISCUSS: Have students jot down their questions as they read, and then share them during discussions. Or have students come up with the type of questions they think a teacher would ask. Over time students will develop more complex inferential questions, which lead to group discussions. Questioning and discussing also helps students see ideas from multiple perspectives and draw conclusions, both critical skills for understanding history.

DETERMINE IMPORTANCE: Teach students how to decide what is most important from all the facts and details in nonfiction. After reading for an overall understanding, they can go back to highlight important ideas, words, and phrases. Clues for determining importance include bold or italic print, signal words, and other text features. A graphic organizer such as a main idea map also helps.

Teach and Practice Decoding Strategies

Rather than simply defining an unfamiliar word, teach struggling readers decoding strategies:

- Have them look at the prefix, suffix, and root to help figure out the new word.

- Look for words they know within the word.

- Use the context for clues, and read further or reread.

ADVANCED LEARNERS

Every classroom has students who finish the required assignments and then want additional challenges. Fortunately, the very nature of history and social science offers a wide range of opportunities for students to explore topics in greater depth. Encourage them to come up with their own ideas for an additional assignment. Determine the final product, its presentation, and a timeline for completion.

▶ Research

Students can develop in-depth understanding through seeking information, exploring ideas, asking and answering questions, making judgments, considering points of view, and evaluating actions and events. They will need access to a wide range of resource materials: the Internet, maps, encyclopedias, trade books, magazines, dictionaries, artifacts, newspapers, museum catalogues, brochures, and the library. See the Further Reading section at the end of the Student Edition for good jumping-off points.

▶ Projects

You can encourage students to capitalize on their strengths as learners (visual, verbal, kinesthetic, or musical) or to try a new way of responding. Students can prepare a debate or write a persuasive paper, play, skit, poem, song, dance, game, puzzle, or biography. They can create an alphabet book on the topic, film a video, do a book talk, or illustrate a book. They can render charts, graphs, or other visual representations. Allow for creativity and support students' thinking.

Cheryl A. Caldera, M.A.
Literacy Coach

1

EARLY ROME PAGES 14–31

Chapter 1 Wives, Wolves, and Wild Boys: The Founding of Rome
Chapter 2 Migration, Mystery, and Mastery: Who Were the Etruscans?
Chapter 3 Morality, Tyranny, Heroes, and Kings: The Beginnings of the Republic

UNIT OBJECTIVES

Unit 1 covers the period from the founding of Rome in 753 BCE to the beginning of the Roman Republic in 509 BCE. In this unit, your students will learn

▶ the importance of oral history in understanding ancient civilizations.
▶ how and when Rome was founded.
▶ the impact that the Etruscan civilization had on the development of Rome.
▶ the origins of the Roman Republic.

PRIMARY SOURCES

Unit 1 includes excerpts from the following primary sources:

▶ Virgil, *The Aeneid*
▶ Dionysius of Halicarnassus, *Roman Antiquities*
▶ Livy, *From the Founding of the City*
▶ Herodotus, *Histories*

Pictures of artifacts from the earliest Roman times can also be analyzed as primary sources:

▶ Bronze sculpture of wolf feeding Romulus and Remus
▶ Ruins of Temple of Vesta
▶ Etruscan wall painting, jewelry, sarcophagus, and relief sculpture
▶ Bronze bust of Brutus
▶ Ruins of Roman Forum

BIG IDEAS IN UNIT 1

Movement, conflict, and **exchange** are the big ideas presented in Unit 1. The unit discusses where the people of the Italian peninsula came from, how Rome grew to dominate the peninsula, and the cultural exchange that went on between Etruscans, Romans, and Greeks.

One way to introduce these ideas is to have students look at the map on page 20 of their books. Explain that each of the three groups on the map came from elsewhere—north of Italy (Etruscans), across the Adriatic Sea (Italic peoples), and Greece. Elicit from students what happens when peoples from different regions or heritages bump up against each other: trade, cultural exchange, conflict.

GEOGRAPHY CONNECTION

The movement of peoples into the Italian peninsula and the gradual dominance of the region by Rome is the major geographic element of this unit. You can relate this to the North American experience: first the land was dominated by

Native Americans, then Europeans came and pushed the Native Americans aside, then the Europeans competed for supremacy on the continent. Students should understand that such movement and mixing of peoples continues to this day, although in the more subtle form of government-controlled immigration in some countries.

If possible, have students look at a physical map of Italy. Have them tell the dimensions of the peninsula, where its mountains and plains are, and how long its rivers are. Have them identify the location of Rome on the map, and tell what physical features are in that area.

TIMELINE

1000 BCE	Italic peoples arrive on Italian peninsula
900 BCE	Etruscans living in central Italy
753 BCE	Traditional date for founding of Rome
750 BCE	Greek colonies founded in southern Italy
616 BCE	Etruscan kings rule Rome
509 BCE	Roman army expels last Etruscan king
475 BCE	Etruscans attack Rome
458 BCE	Cincinnatus named dictator; defeats Aequi
266 BCE	Rome controls entire Italian peninsula

UNIT PROJECTS

Drama

Invite interested students to work together to write a script and design costumes for a play about Horatius Cocles's act of bravery. Suggest that group members compile their ideas and work with a recorder, who writes the script. Allow the group time to prepare and present their play.

Chronology

Students can create a class timeline to show the sequence of events in this unit. The concentration should not necessarily be on dates, but rather on the cause-and-effect chain of events that makes up history. You may want to hang up a 12-inch-wide banner (to represent the centuries) to which students will attach large index cards (use different colored cards for each region of the ancient world) noting each event in the appropriate place on the banner. You can use clothespins or tape to attach the cards. You may want to refresh the timeline as you continue through the book.

Artwork

Interested students can duplicate the artwork they see in the unit, plus other art work they find through outside research. Students might sketch the statues if they cannot create three-dimensional works. You might have one corner of your classroom be a "Roman Art Center," whose exhibits would change throughout your course of study of Rome.

Research Report

Small groups of students can investigate subjects of their choice to bring more information back to the rest of the class. Possible subjects include the legends of the founding of Rome, the government of the Republic, and individuals in the text. Have students ask for recommendations for sources to use from your school resource center. Groups can create a panel discussion or a visual display to explain the information to the class.

ADDITIONAL ASSESSMENT

For Unit 1, divide the class into groups and have them all undertake the Research Report. In particular, note how students' reports explain the origins of the Roman Republic and the importance of different kinds of sources (oral, mythological) in understanding the past. Use the scoring rubric at the back of this guide to assess students' work, and have students rate their own work with the self-assessment rubric. Be sure to distribute the library/media center research log (see rubric at the back of this guide) to help students evaluate their sources as they conduct their research.

LITERATURE CONNECTION

The great literary work dealing with the founding and early years of Rome is the *Aeneid* by Virgil. There are numerous translations of this work, and many of them are tailored to fit the reading level of your students. A full text copy of the epic poem is available at *http://classics.mit.edu/Virgil/aeneid.html*.

Another great work about ancient Rome is the play *Coriolanus*, by William Shakespeare. The story chronicles this Roman leader's rise and fall as Rome develops into a republic.

There are numerous books that students can enjoy, which will broaden their knowledge of early Rome and increase their understanding of how civilizations develop. Students will learn from reading both fiction and nonfiction. They should know the difference between these formats. (You may want to advise students that historical fiction is not always accurate in its details.) Suggest some of the following books to students:

▶ James, Simon. *Ancient Rome* (Eyewitness Books). New York: Dorling Kindersley, 2000. Nonfiction. EASY
▶ Jay, David. *Ancient Rome*. Brookfield, CT: Millbrook Press, 2000. Nonfiction. AVERAGE
▶ Lively, Penelope. *In Search of a Homeland: The Story of the Aeneid*. New York: Delacorte, 2001. Fiction. AVERAGE
▶ Moatti, Claude. *Search for Ancient Rome* (Discoveries Series). New York: Harry N. Abrams, 1993. Nonfiction. ADVANCED

UNIVERSAL ACCESS

The exciting narrative of *The Ancient Roman World* will hold students' interest and encourage all students to enjoy learning about ancient Rome. The following strategies are designed to cover a range of learning styles and reading, language, and skill levels. This section includes suggestions to help differentiate instruction to meet the needs of a diverse student population. You may find that individual students need different types of strategies for different information or concepts. Select the most appropriate activities for the needs of the students in your class.

Reading Strategies

▶ To facilitate reading, point out features such as punctuation and literary references that students will encounter as they read. For example, in Chapter 1, explain that ellipses (...), as in the extract from the *Aeneid* on page 14, are used to indicate that some text is not included.

▶ There will be many unfamiliar names of people and places in these chapters. Make students aware of the Cast of Characters in the front of their book. If a name doesn't appear there, suggest the pronunciation yourself or have the class come to a consensus about it. Say each name several times and then write it on the board. Help students associate the spoken word with the written word.

▶ Have partners read the text together. Suggest that one student read a section aloud, and then the other paraphrase the reading.

Writing Strategies

▶ Have students make a three-column chart for the unit with the headings *Movement*, *Conflict*, and *Exchange*. Have them list details from their reading that tell about each big idea.

▶ The first three chapters tell stories about the founding and development of Rome from the third-person point of view. Have students rewrite the legends from the first-person point of view in which they are participants.

▶ Encourage students to write short essays analyzing one of the legends in this section. Ask them to draw conclusions about the legend in terms of its believability, the moral lesson it teaches, and the event or events it explains.

Listening and Speaking Strategies

▶ To spark students' interest, read aloud the title and first paragraph of each chapter. Use the reading as a springboard for predicting what the chapter is about. Record and review students' predictions. When students have finished reading the chapter, ask whether their predictions were correct.

▶ Encourage a group of students to prepare a dramatic reading of a section of a chapter or of an extract from one of the primary sources used in the chapter. They might use props and/or actions to help dramatize the events. The group can present their dramatization to the class.

UNIT VOCABULARY LIST

The following words that appear in Unit 1 are important for your students' understanding of the social studies content as well as for development of literacy. Use these words for vocabulary study or to reinforce language arts skills (e.g., synonyms, compound words, prefixes and suffixes, and related words). The words are listed below in the order in which they appear in the chapters.

Chapter 1	**Chapter 2**	**Chapter 3**
divine	immigrants	ruthless
voyage	metalworkers	solemn
appalled	interconnecting	condemn
abandoned	afterlife	exile
divination	colony	arrogant
legend	discoloration	magistrate
eventually	sacrifice	congratulate
truce		
contradictory		
mingling		
cremate		
archaeology		
foundation		

WIVES, WOLVES, AND WILD BOYS: THE FOUNDING OF ROME
PAGES 14–19

FOR HOMEWORK

STUDENT STUDY GUIDE

pages 11–12

CAST OF CHARACTERS

Aeneas (ay-NEE-us) legendary founder of Rome (Virgil)

Romulus (ROM-yuh-lus) legendary founder of Rome (Livy)

VOCABULARY

immortal living forever

THEN and NOW

The Rome founded in the 8th century BCE grew from a small settlement on a hill to a bustling city on seven hills. Today Rome is the capital of Italy and its largest city. Rome has a metropolitan population of more than 3,500,000.

CHAPTER SUMMARY

The Romans created legends to explain the origins of their city. They traced their ancestry to Prince Aeneas, who led survivors from Troy to Italy. According to another legend, Romulus founded Rome in 753 BCE.

PERFORMANCE OBJECTIVES

► To compare and contrast legends about the founding of Rome
► To identify legendary founders of Rome
► To understand how legend and history are related

BUILDING BACKGROUND

Ask what students know about popular legends about the United States or their countries of origin. Help students distinguish fact from made-up detail in these stories, and identify how old these stories might be. Explain that in this chapter students will read about the founding of Rome more than 2,700 years ago. Invite them to predict what the legends surrounding that event might be like.

WORKING WITH PRIMARY SOURCES

Virgil's epic poem, *The Aeneid*, tells the story of Aeneas's legendary landing on the Italian coast. Obtain copies of the poem from your resource center or the Internet. Read excerpts of the poem aloud while students follow along. Students will also enjoy role-playing the characters as they read their lines in front of the rest of the class. You may need to keep the passages short, and then explain unfamiliar words and sentence constructions. Students will still be able to get the flavor of the legends while gaining practice in reading poetry.

GEOGRAPHY CONNECTION

Location Have students study the map on page 17. Make sure they understand how the inset map relates to the larger map. Explain that the direction north is at the top of the map, east is on the right, south is at the bottom, and west is on the left. Have students tell the location of Rome relative to other places on the map. (*for example, west of Troy*) Discuss how to use the map scale, and that it helps make relative location more precise. Ask: How far west of Troy is Rome? (*about 750 miles*) What sea route might Aeneas have taken from Troy to Rome? About how long is that? (*Answers will vary.*) Distribute copies of the blackline master for Chapter 1.

READING COMPREHENSION QUESTIONS

1. According to Dionysius, how did Rome get its name? (*It was named for Roma, a noblewoman who led the travel-weary Trojan women in burning the ships of their wandering husbands.*)
2. According to legend, how did Romulus and Remus survive? (*They floated downriver in a basket and then were nursed by a she-wolf until a herder found and raised them.*)
3. What physical features made Rome a good site for settlement? (*The site was near the sea, on a river, and surrounded by hills. It also was beautiful.*)

4. What findings support Livy's story of the founding of Rome? (*Archaeological finds show that a settlement was built on the Palatine Hill in the 8th century BCE and suggest that two different cultures coexisted there.*)

CRITICAL THINKING QUESTIONS

1. What inferences can you make about the character traits of the Trojan men and women in Virgil's story? Give details supporting your inferences. (*Men: adventuresome, fearless, seafarers. Women: practical, seeking a home, intelligent.*)

2. With a partner, draw a sequence chart showing the events in Livy's retelling of the founding of Rome. Draw blue boxes around events that could be true and red boxes around events that were probably made up.

3. Why do you think the Romans accepted oral histories that offered differing, even contradictory, versions of what happened? (*Possible answer: they thought of history as the storyteller's art. History was culture and entertainment as well as a people's record.*)

SOCIAL SCIENCES

Civics   The legend of Romulus tells something about government in the Italian peninsula around the time of the founding of Rome. Have students draw a diagram indicating the royal line of succession that results in the founding of Rome.

READING AND LANGUAGE ARTS

Reading Nonfiction   The text retells two legends about the origins of Rome. Explain that folk literature has been a powerful tool for passing on culture, history, and beliefs down through the generations. Help students understand what the legend of Romulus and Remus teaches about Roman government (*king and succession to throne*), religion (*goddess Vesta, divination, god Mars*), and history (*mixing of Roman and Sabine people*).

Using Language   Have students use a dictionary to discover the etymology of *archaeology* (from the Greek *archaio-* + *-logia*, or "ancient science"). Elicit that archaeology is the scientific study of ancient humans. Have students list and define related words (*archaeologist, archaeological*) and use them in sentences.

SUPPORTING LEARNING

English Language Learners   Have students make a list of the boldfaced terms and any other unfamiliar words in the chapter. As a group, have them begin a word file, using note cards and a box. They should write the word on the front of the card and a definition on the back. Have students use a dictionary or context clues to define the words.

Struggling Readers   Have students make a chart comparing the events and characters of the two legends. Then help students draw conclusions: for example, in Virgil, the founders of Rome came from Troy; in Livy, the founders seem to have been living in Italy already.

EXTENDING LEARNING

Enrichment   Edith Hamilton's book *Mythology: Timeless Tales of Gods and Heroes* contains another myth about the founding of Rome by Aeneas. Have students read and summarize this myth for the class.

Extension   Have student groups act out scenes from *The Aeneid,* from the excerpt in *The World in Ancient Times Primary Sources and Reference Volume.* One student can narrate while the others take the parts of the characters involved.

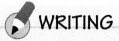 **WRITING**

Narrative
Have students write down a family story they have been told about their ancestors. Have them use their imaginations to fill in details about the story. Students may wish to illustrate their stories. Then collect the stories into a class booklet or folder entitled *Legends of Our Class Origins.*

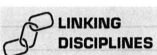 **LINKING DISCIPLINES**

Art If students will be acting out the legends in this chapter, you may wish to have them make masks using craft sticks and paper plates. Have them cut holes for eyes and mouth. They can model their characters' features after the pictures of Roman men and women in Chapters 1–3.

THE FOUNDING OF ROME: A GREAT SITE FOR A CITY

Directions

On the map, find the features listed in the left column below. Then decide how each of these features benefited trade, defense, or transportation in Rome. List the benefits in the right column with a brief explanation. (A feature can have more than one benefit.)

FEATURE	BENEFIT
Seven Hills	
Lake and stream	
Tiber River	
Inland and coastal routes nearby	
Plain along the Tiber, near ford	
Two routes—one along Tiber and one along the coast	

In your opinion, which was the most important of these features for the future of the city? Why?

_____

_____

_____

_____

NAME _____   **DATE** _____

A. MULTIPLE CHOICE

Circle the letter of the best answer for each question.

1. The legends of Aeneas and Romulus are ancient stories that explain
   a. the origins of Troy.   **c.** how Rome was governed.
   b. the origins of Rome.   **d.** how to read signs in nature.

2. What evidence have archaeologists found to back up the legendary founding of Rome in 753 BCE?
   a. the writings of Livy
   b. Romans and Sabines buried together in Rome
   c. remains of settlements on the Palatine Hill
   d. divinations by priests

3. The Trojans picked Rome for their new settlement because
   a. it had a good harbor.   **c.** there were mountains.
   b. the women burned their ships. **d.** they were tired of traveling.

4. Romulus and Remus were legendary brothers who
   a. were killed by a king.   **c.** fought the Trojans.
   b. founded Rome.   **d.** wrote the _Aeneid._

5. For hundreds of years, the legends about the founding of Rome were
   a. passed down orally.   **c.** lost.
   b. changed frequently.   **d.** written in Greek.

B. SHORT ANSWER

Write one or two sentences to answer each question.

6. How did the Romans date everything in their history?

_____

_____

7. What evidence has been found for the mixing of the Roman and Sabine people?

_____

_____

8. According to the oldest Roman stories, why did the gods care so much about Rome?

_____

_____

C. ESSAY

On a separate sheet of paper, write an essay comparing and contrasting the legends of Aeneas and Romulus. Include details about the characters in the stories, the personalities of those characters, and the major events.

CHAPTER 2

MIGRATION, MYSTERY, AND MASTERY: WHO WERE THE ETRUSCANS? PAGES 20-25

CAST OF CHARACTERS

Dionysius (DIE-un-ISH-ee-us) **of Halicarnassus** (HAL-I-kar-NA-sus) 1st-century BCE Greek historian

Herodotus (huh-RAH-duh-tus) 5th-century BCE Greek historian; "Father of History"

 **VOCABULARY**

peninsula land bounded on three sides by water

THEN and NOW

Today, Latin is considered a "dead" language because it is no longer spoken. However, it continues to exist in the Romance languages—including Spanish, Italian, Portuguese, French, and Romanian.

CHAPTER SUMMARY

Other people besides Romans lived in Italy—Greeks in the south and Etruscans in the north. Both had a great effect on Rome. It was from the Etruscans that the Romans adapted their alphabet, elements of their religion, and their engineering skills.

PERFORMANCE OBJECTIVES

▶ To understand why ancient peoples came to the Italian peninsula
▶ To identify achievements, religious beliefs, and social customs of Etruscan civilization
▶ To understand the lasting impact of the Etruscans on Roman architecture, art, and ideas

BUILDING BACKGROUND

Refer students to the pictures of Roman buildings on pages 121 and 148. Elicit what these structures are and express their size. (The Colosseum held up to 50,000 people. Aqueducts like the one shown here were up to 57 miles long and carried up to 50 million gallons of water a day.) Tell students that the Romans got the skills needed to build such structures from the people they will study in this chapter.

WORKING WITH PRIMARY SOURCES

Help students understand that just because a primary source is created soon after an event does not mean that it is more truthful than a later account. Ask: Why is Dionysius's account, which is more distant in time from the Etruscans than Herodotus's account, now considered to be the more truthful? (*Recent archaeological research supports Dionysius's evaluation that the Etruscans were not like the Lydians.*)

GEOGRAPHY CONNECTION

Ask students for examples of how humans have changed the environment in their area; for example, a tunnel built through a mountain, land cleared for farming, bridges over rivers. Tell them that in this chapter they will read about the Etruscans, who were famous for their building projects. As students read, have them take special note of how the Etruscans changed the land for their purposes (page 23).

READING COMPREHENSION QUESTIONS

1. Why did early peoples immigrate to the Italian peninsula? (*to escape war; to seek land and wealth through trade*)
2. According to Herodotus, where did the Etruscans come from? Why did Dionysius of Halicarnassus disagree? (*Herodotus said they came from Lydia. Dionysius disagreed because the language, gods, laws, and institutions of the Lydians were not like those of the Etruscans.*)
3. How did the Etruscans change the land to suit their needs? (*They drained marshy land to make it suitable for farming and grazing. They dug canals and drains to channel extra water into reservoirs. They paved over land to make the Forum.*)

4. What do the wall paintings in Etruscan tombs tell us about these people? (*They tell about Etruscans' everyday life, how men and women related to each other, their work and recreation, their religious rituals, and their musical instruments.*)

CRITICAL THINKING QUESTIONS

1. What set the Etruscans apart from the other cultures in Italy at that time? (*Possible answers: their architecture was brilliant: while others lived in villages, the Etruscans had walled cities and elaborate temples. Their art and jewelry was of high quality. Their government was complex and allowed for cities joining forces.*)

2. How did Etruscan talents help shape Rome? (*Rome learned city planning, engineering, and waterworks from the Etruscans, and applied these advances to the building of Roman arenas, roads, and waterways. The Romans also took elements of their religion—the gods Jupiter, Juno, and Minerva—from the Etruscans.*)

SOCIAL SCIENCES

Science, Technology, and Society   Etruscan inventions in architecture and civil engineering made it possible for them to create the most advanced society of their time in Italy. Have students investigate the arch and the vault and prepare a report on why these innovations helped advance ancient architecture.

READING AND LANGUAGE ARTS

Reading Nonfiction   As students read the text, have them copy words and phrases that show sequence. Then have them summarize the events in the chapter using these and other sequence words.

Using Language   Help students recognize that the following words all end with *-an: Etruscan, Roman, Lydian.* Elicit that *-an* shows that a person is "of a place." Tell students that *Etruscan* means "person of Etruria," the ancient name of the Etruscan region. Have students define the other two terms. (*"person of Rome," "person of Lydia"*) Then ask them to name other examples. (*American, Italian, Mexican, Russian, and so on*)

SUPPORTING LEARNING

English Language Learners   Help students recognize adjectives and their placement before nouns. Using the paragraphs describing the Etruscans on pages 22–23, identify nouns for students, and have them write the adjectives that describe the nouns. Students can explain how each adjective defines its noun, and how all of the adjectives together give a more complete picture of the Etruscans.

Struggling Readers   Have students use the main idea map graphic organizer found in the back of this teaching guide to analyze Etruscan civilization. They might write *The Etruscans had an advanced civilization* in the central circle, and the headings *Art, Architecture, Engineering,* and *Burial Tombs* in the surrounding circles. Students should then add details from the chapter for each category.

EXTENDING LEARNING

Enrichment   Have small groups find pictures of modern examples of arches: in bridges, overpasses, buildings. Students can make a display of the pictures, labeling the arches and telling what the structure is.

Extension   Ask students to act out certain scenes in the text. For example, a group can act out the description of the burial tomb on page 23 while another student narrates.

WRITING

Dialogue

Have students write a short conversation between two Etruscan priests, including details about sacrifices, omens, and what the gods are planning. Writing dialogue may be difficult for some students. Suggest they write sentences, read them aloud, and rewrite the dialogue so that it sounds like natural speech.

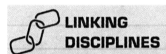

LINKING DISCIPLINES

Music Refer students to the picture of the young Etruscan playing a double flute on page 21. Have students find out more about the musical instruments played by Romans. One useful website for information is *www. personal.psu.edu/ users/w/x/wxk116/ muse/.*

CLOACA MAXIMA: ETRUSCAN ENGINEERING ADOPTED BY ROMANS

Directions

Read the following information about the *Cloaca Maxima,* using the map to locate its route. Then answer the questions on a separate sheet of paper.

Draining the Marsh

The Forum was originally a marshy valley between the Capitoline and Palatine Hills. The ground was fed by a stream and was much too wet to build on. The superior engineering skills of the Etruscans solved this problem around 625 BCE. Archaeologists have discovered evidence of a network of channels that made it possible for the Etruscans to drain and pave the area. The stream that separated the two hills was redirected, and its banks were lined with stones. The redirected stream was known as the *Cloaca Maxima,* or the "great drain." It became Rome's sewer. It flowed into the Tiber River and then out to sea. The Romans expanded the sewer system and hundreds of years later covered it over.

"In Praise of the Roman Sewer System" (from *Natural History,* Pliny the Elder)

Frequently praise is given to the great sewer system of Rome. There are seven "rivers" made to flow, by artificial channels, beneath the city. Rushing onward like so many impetuous torrents, they are compelled to carry off and sweep away all the sewerage; and swollen as they are by . . . rain water, they reverberate against the sides and bottoms of their channels.

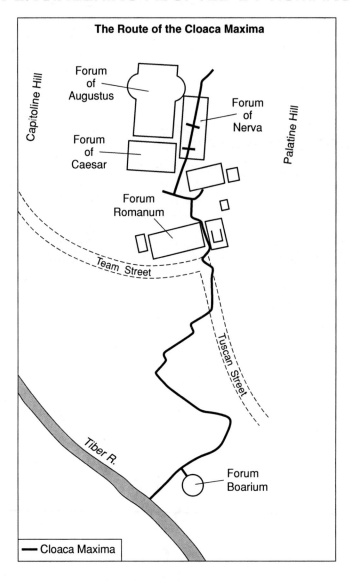

The Route of the Cloaca Maxima

Capitoline Hill

Forum of Augustus

Forum of Caesar

Forum of Nerva

Palatine Hill

Forum Romanum

Team Street

Tuscan Street

Tiber R.

Forum Boarium

— Cloaca Maxima

Occasionally too the Tiber, overflowing, is thrown backward in its course, and discharges itself by these outlets. Obstinate is the struggle that ensues between the meeting tides, but so firm and solid is the masonry that it is able to offer an effectual resistance. Enormous as are the accumulations that are carried along above, the work of the channels never gives way. Houses falling spontaneously to ruins, or leveled with the ground by conflagrations are continually battering against them; now and then the ground is shaken by earthquakes, and yet—built as they were . . . seven hundred years ago—these constructions have survived, all but unharmed.

1. What was the result of draining the marsh between the Capitoline and Palatine Hills?

2. What examples does Pliny give to show how well built the sewers were?

3. What would cause the Tiber River to back up into the sewer system?

NAME _____ **DATE** _____

A. MULTIPLE CHOICE

Circle the letter of the best answer for each question.

1. The Italian peninsula is bordered by all of these bodies of water except the
   a. Mediterranean Sea.   **c.** Adriatic Sea.
   b. Atlantic Ocean.   **d.** Tyrrhenian Sea.

2. Besides the early Romans, Italy was occupied by
   a. French and Etruscans.   **c.** Greeks and Etruscans.
   b. Greeks and Lydians.   **d.** Africans and Asians.

3. Archaeologists have shown that the Etruscans used arches and vaults in their buildings. This shows that they were brilliant
   a. seafarers.   **c.** architects.
   b. city-dwellers.   **d.** traders.

4. In the Etruscan religion, the gods
   a. were not interested in humans.   **c.** were not immortal.
   b. ruled the world.   **d.** could not be understood by humans.

5. By 600 BCE, the Etruscans
   a. dominated the Italian peninsula.   **c.** had been defeated by the Romans.
   b. were a forgotten civilization.   **d.** were living in small, unwalled villages.

B. SHORT ANSWER

Write one or two sentences to answer each question.

6. How did the role of women in Etruscan society compare to the role of women in ancient Greece?

_____

_____

7. How did the Etruscans govern themselves? _____

_____

8. What did the Etruscans believe about their gods?

_____

_____

C. ESSAY

Write an essay on a separate sheet of paper discussing the Etruscan influences on Rome. Include details about religion, engineering, and rulers.

MORALITY, TYRANNY, HEROES, AND KINGS: THE BEGINNINGS OF THE REPUBLIC   PAGES 26–31

CAST OF CHARACTERS

Lucretia (loo-KREE-shuh) legendary figure known for her virtue

Tarquinius (tar-KWIN-ee-us) **Sextus** legendary prince whose actions led Romans to depose King Tarquin

Tarquin last king of Rome, about 500 BCE

Horatius Roman soldier famed for bravery

Cincinnatus Roman dictator who defeated the Aequi, 458 BCE

LINKING DISCIPLINES

Math Rome at its height was the largest city in the world, with 1 million inhabitants. Have students prepare a graph to show the population growth of Rome and its empire over time. Then use the websites listed in the book or an encyclopedia to research this data.

CHAPTER SUMMARY

When the Romans cast out the Etruscan kings in 509 BCE, they established a republic with elected officials. Romans liked to tell stories of the early republican heroes to teach moral lessons: the virtue of Lucretia, the courage of Horatius, and the patriotism of Coriolanus.

PERFORMANCE OBJECTIVES

▶ To explain events leading to the establishment of the Roman Republic
▶ To identify and describe the functions of the Roman Senate and Assembly
▶ To understand the purpose of stories about famous Romans
▶ To outline major events in the early centuries of the Republic

BUILDING BACKGROUND

Elicit from students that the United States is a republic—power comes from the people, who elect representatives to make laws. Ask: What is the difference between this kind of government and a monarchy? Tell them that in this chapter, they will learn why and how Rome changed from a monarchy to a republic.

WORKING WITH PRIMARY SOURCES

Livy's account of the end of the Roman monarchy is a *legend*—a story from the past that may be historical but cannot be verified. Sometimes legends provide moral lessons as well as explanations for events. Have students reread the legend of Lucretia. Ask what the fates of Lucretia, Sextus, and Tarquin the Proud teach about Roman morals as well as Roman history.

GEOGRAPHY CONNECTION

Have students reread the story of Horatius, and then look at the map on page 20. Elicit that a major river like the Tiber is a natural line of defense, since it can only be crossed on bridges in a few places. Help students realize how important Horatius's defense of the bridge was by pointing out on the map how close the Tiber is to Rome.

READING COMPREHENSION QUESTIONS

1. What connection was there between the Roman Republic and the monarchy before it? (*In both governments, the Senate—a group of wealthy, landowning men—held great power. Under the monarchy, they chose the king. Under the Republic, they took control of the government.*)

2. In the early Republic, who handled the business of running the government? How did this change over the years? (*In the beginning, two elected consuls handled most things. As the Republic grew, more officials were needed to handle different jobs. Praetors judged lawsuits, aediles managed road-building projects.*)

3. Why was the Roman army so active during the 500 years of the Republic? (*Rome was growing fast and had to conquer its neighbors to gain control of the Italian peninsula. It also had to defend itself from its neighbors, such as the Etruscans and the Aequi.*)

4. How did Romans make sure they would have a strong leader in times of trouble? (*In times of crisis, the Senate could appoint a dictator, who had absolute power for up to six months.*)

CRITICAL THINKING QUESTIONS

1. The Romans had a bad experience with a tyrant king. How did the Republic guard against a leader becoming a tyrant? (*The Senate shared power with the Assembly so no senator could become too powerful. The Assembly appointed the consuls. Consuls could not serve for two years in a row. No public money could be spent without the Senate's approval.*)

2. What important ideal is illustrated by the story of Cincinnatus? (*Possible answer: A true Roman does his duty with quiet determination; he does not take advantage of the situation to seize power.*)

3. Distribute copies of the blackline master for Chapter 3. Have students complete the activity to get a better idea of what Rome was like at this time.

SOCIAL SCIENCES

Civics   Praetors and aediles were forerunners of today's judges, public works officials, and police. Encourage students to read more about the organization of Rome's government. Have them make a chart to compare then and now.

READING AND LANGUAGE ARTS

Reading Nonfiction   Explain that the chapter is organized into two sections: Rome before and Rome after kings were banished. Have students compare and contrast the government of Rome in these two periods. Make a two-column chart with the headings *Kingship* and *Republic* to list students' points about the two types of government.

Using Language   Many English words came from Latin and Greek. For example, *magistrate* is based on the Latin root *magister*, meaning "master." Encourage students to use a dictionary to find the origin of common English words such as *popular, democracy, justice, auditorium,* and *library*.

SUPPORTING LEARNING

English Language Learners   Ask students to compare the legend of Lucretia or Horatius with legends from their countries of origin. They can ask members of their families for information. Have them prepare a short oral report comparing the legends, to be presented to the class or a small group.

Struggling Readers   Have students complete the main idea map found in the back of this book to illustrate the powers of the Senate. Have them write Senate in the central circle, and its powers in the surrounding circles (*appoint consuls, approve spending, investigate major crimes,* and so on).

EXTENDING LEARNING

Enrichment   Have groups of students learn more about the kings of Rome, the revolt against Tarquin, and the early Republic. Refer them to the Illustrated History of the Roman Empire website listed on the Websites page of their book. Have groups present oral reports about their topic.

Extension   Have interested students read the play *Coriolanus* by William Shakespeare (see Literature Connection on page 26 of this guide). Assign them the task of presenting an oral synopsis of the play to the class and of acting out a crucial scene.

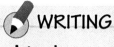

WRITING

Interview

Ask students to imagine they are reporters assigned to interview Cincinnatus after he defeated the Aequi. Have them write *who, what, when, where, why,* and *how* questions they would ask him. Then using what they have learned about Roman government and ideals, have them write the answers he might give.

VOCABULARY

Senate group of wealthy men who dominated Rome's political life

republic government in which power is held by voters

Assembly law-making body made up of all Roman voters

consul highest government official in Roman Republic

dictator official given absolute power in time of crisis

aedile (EE-dile) official in charge of road-building and city markets

magistrate government official

praetor (PREE-tur) official who judged lawsuits

WALKING THROUGH REPUBLICAN ROME

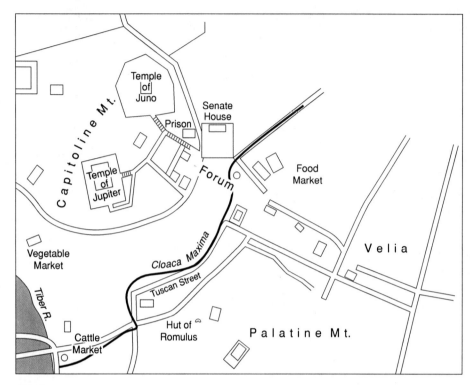

Directions

Use the map to trace a walk through Rome from the Temple of Juno to the Cattle Market, passing through the Forum. On Tuscan Street, you will be next to Rome's ancient sewer, the *Cloaca Maxima*. It has been covered over, but it is still noticeable! Then use the chart below to organize a description of the sights, smells, and sounds you experience along the way.

LANDMARK	SIGHTS, SOUNDS, AND SMELLS
Temple of Juno	
Senate House	
Prison	
Forum	
Food Market	
Tuscan Street	
Cloaca Maxima	
Cattle Market	
Tiber River	

NAME _____ **DATE** _____

A. MULTIPLE CHOICE

Circle the letter of the best answer for each question.

1. The last king of Rome was
   a. Brutus.
   b. Sextus.
   c. Lucretia.
   d. Tarquin.

2. In the republic established by the Romans, the highest power belonged to
   a. military commanders.
   b. citizens.
   c. senators.
   d. praetors.

3. Which group dominated Rome's political life?
   a. Assembly
   b. Senate
   c. praetors
   d. magistrates

4. When could the Senate appoint a dictator?
   a. whenever it wished
   b. in times of drought
   c. in times of great crisis
   d. when the Aequi attacked

5. From legends written down by Livy and others, we can tell that Romans valued
   a. rule by foreigners.
   b. courage and faithfulness.
   c. money above all else.
   d. attacking other people.

B. SHORT ANSWER

Write one or two sentences to answer each question.

6. Who made up the membership of the Assembly?

_____

_____

7. Why was the Senate the most powerful group of people in Rome?

_____

_____

8. Judging by the story of Cincinnatus, how long were dictators supposed to keep their power?

_____

_____

C. ESSAY

Write an essay on a separate sheet of paper explaining why Horatius Cocles was honored by a statue. Use details from the chapter to support your main idea.

LIFE IN THE ROMAN REPUBLIC

PAGES 32-46

Chapter 4 The Rebellion of the Poor: Class Conflict and the Twelve Tables
Chapter 5 Fathers, Gods, and Goddesses: Religion in Ancient Rome
Chapter 6 Hannibal, Rome's Worst Enemy: The Battle for the Mediterranean

UNIT OBJECTIVES

Unit 2 covers events in the Italian peninsula and the Mediterranean from about 493 BCE until the end of the Punic Wars in 146 BCE. In this unit, your students will learn

▶ the structure of Roman society under the Republic.
▶ how a rebellion of the poor made Roman society more just.
▶ the interrelatedness of family, religion, and state in Rome.
▶ the greatest threat to Roman dominance of the Mediterranean region.

PRIMARY SOURCES

Unit 2 includes excerpts from the following primary sources:

▶ Livy, *From the Founding of the City*
▶ Euripides, *The Suppliants*
▶ Aulus Gellius, *Attic Nights*

Pictures of artifacts from the earliest Roman times can also be analyzed as primary sources:

▶ Mosaic of farm worker
▶ Tombstone of craftsman
▶ Scales for medical prescriptions
▶ Statue of Roman citizen
▶ Household shrine
▶ Bust of Scipio Africanus

BIG IDEAS IN UNIT 2

Conflict, justice, religion, and **change** are the big ideas presented in Unit 2. The unit discusses conflict not only between Romans and other peoples, but between classes of Romans as well. It details how Roman society slowly changed because of this class conflict into a society where everyone, rich or poor, could get justice. It also explains the intertwining of the gods, family, and government in Rome. Finally, it tells about the greatest conflict of Republican times—the three wars against Carthage that made Rome ruler of the western Mediterranean world.

Introduce these ideas by eliciting what students know about the Roman gods—their names, their powers, and so on. Explain that the Romans believed the gods controlled all aspects of life, and that this relationship was echoed in the state and in the family. Then explain how Rome eventually grew to be perhaps the greatest empire of its time, and that such growth does not come without conflict and change. Discuss the kinds of conflicts and changes that might occur in such a situation.

GEOGRAPHY CONNECTION

The movement of military forces in the western Mediterranean region is important for understanding the events in this unit. Refer students to the map on page 42 for an overview of these movements. Provide more detailed maps of the military movements of the three Punic Wars so students can follow the complicated events.

TIMELINE

493 BCE	First plebeian rebellion
450 BCE	Second plebeian rebellion; Twelve Tables written
396 BCE	Romans battle Etruscans at Veii
264 BCE	Start of First Punic War
218 BCE	Start of Second Punic War
217 BCE	Hannibal's army invades Italian peninsula
216 BCE	Hannibal defeats Romans at Cannae
202 BCE	Scipio Africanus defeats Hannibal at Zama
146 BCE	Start of Third Punic War; Romans destroy Carthage

UNIT PROJECTS

Military Strategy

The Battle of Cannae is one of the classic battles still written about and studied today. Have volunteers research the battle, the strategies of the opponents, and the course of the battle. They can draw diagrams of the battle's beginning, middle, and end, showing the successful Carthaginian strategy. The diagrams should be labeled, have a legend and a distance scale, and use symbols to represent the opposing forces.

Chronology

Help students draw connections between events that are relatively close in time. For example, the first rebellion of the plebeians took place only about 16 years after King Tarquin was deposed and the Roman Republic was founded. How are these related? Additionally, the Italic people who founded Rome arrived in Italy about the same time as the Phoenicians arrived in Carthage. What was happening in the Mediterranean region that caused the large-scale movement of people? Small groups can create charts showing the related events and the conclusions they draw about their causes.

Calendar

Have a small group investigate the development of the calendar from early Roman times through the Julian calendar up to modern times. They should find out why early people needed calendars, how the division into months came to be, when the year "started," and why adjustments to calendars were needed over the years. The group can make a display or give an oral report to the rest of the class.

Artwork

Have pairs of students investigate the Roman gods and goddesses and how Roman belief in the gods affected everyday life. Tell them to examine one deity, and learn about his or her powers, origins, and style of worship. Students can copy pictures of the deities onto large index cards and write facts about the gods on the back of the cards. Create a classroom deck of cards for the Roman gods.

ADDITIONAL ASSESSMENT

For Unit 2, divide the class into groups and have them all undertake the Chronology project so you can assess their understanding of the interrelatedness of events in history. Use the scoring rubric at the back of this guide to assess students' work, and have students rate their own work with the self-assessment rubric.

LITERATURE CONNECTION

There are numerous books that students can enjoy that will broaden their knowledge of early Rome and increase their understanding of how civilizations develop. You might suggest some of the following to students:

▶ Craft, Elisabeth Roberts. *A Spy for Hannibal: A Novel of Carthage.* Silver Spring, MD: Bartleby Press, 1996. Fiction. AVERAGE

▶ Hamilton, Edith. *Mythology: Timeless Tales of Gods and Heroes.* New York: Warner Books, 1999. Fiction. EASY

▶ Mantin, Peter, and Richard Pulley. *The Roman World: From Republic to Empire.* Cambridge, UK: Cambridge University Press, 1991. Nonfiction. ADVANCED

UNIVERSAL ACCESS

The following strategies are designed to cover a range of learning styles and reading, language, and skill levels.

Reading Strategies

▶ To facilitate reading, point out features such as notes and definitions in the side columns that students will encounter as they read. For example, in Chapter 4, point out the definition of *plebeian* on page 32. Show students that these definitions might tell what the word means, how it was used in ancient times and how it is used today, and the word origins.

▶ There will be many unfamiliar words in these chapters. Before reading a chapter, point out potentially difficult words and ask volunteers how to say them and to define them. Say each name several times and then write it on the board. Help students associate the spoken word with the written word.

▶ Call on students to read quotations from the primary sources aloud. Encourage them to make their voices expressive and to use hand gestures where appropriate. Fit the reading passage to the abilities of each student.

Writing Strategies

▶ Have partners make a four-column chart with headings for each of the unit's big ideas. Partners should get together after reading each chapter to jot down their observations in each category.

▶ Have students imagine what it would be like if America had a religion similar to that of ancient Rome. Have them create a list of modern American "gods." Students should name them, tell their powers, and tell how the gods should be worshiped.

▶ Encourage students to write an essay comparing and contrasting the standing of the plebeians before and after their rebellions and the governmental reforms.

Listening and Speaking Strategies

▶ To spark students' interest, read aloud the boldface vocabulary terms from the chapters. Have volunteers use the words in sentences with a modern setting.

▶ As you read portions of the chapters, call on volunteers to describe what they think the scenes looked like. For example, students may describe Menenius talking to the plebeians on the Sacred Mount. They should strike a pose that they think Menenius might have taken and use hand motions and expressions to show how they think he appeared.

UNIT VOCABULARY LIST

The following words that appear in Unit 2 are important for your students' understanding of the social studies content as well as for development of literacy. Use these words for vocabulary study or to reinforce language arts skills (e.g., synonyms, compound words, prefixes and suffixes, and related words). The words are listed below in the order in which they appear in the chapters.

Chapter 4	Chapter 5	Chapter 6
nourishment	bust	seafaring
status quo	sarcophagus	titanic
discontented	hostage	grappling
decreed	ancestral	siege
	procession	demolish

THE REBELLION OF THE POOR: CLASS CONFLICT AND THE TWELVE TABLES   PAGES 32–35

CAST OF CHARACTERS

Agrippa (uh-GRIP-uh)
Menenius
(men-EN-ee-us)
patrician who ended
plebeian rebellion in
493 BCE

VOCABULARY

plebeian (pluh-BEE-un)
Roman worker

patrician wealthy
Roman landowner

veto power to stop
something

THEN and NOW

Each of the Twelve Tables
included numerous
laws—up to 26 in copies
of the laws that have
survived. Although this
seems like a lot, it is
miniscule when
compared to the law
books of a modern small
city in the United States.

CHAPTER SUMMARY

Ongoing tension existed between the patricians who controlled Rome and the plebeians who did the hard work. Plebeian rebellions caused the patricians to share power and to provide the Twelve Tables—written laws that allowed rich and poor to get justice.

PERFORMANCE OBJECTIVES

► To explain how poor Romans gained greater justice under the law
► To understand symbolism in a parable
► To identify and describe Rome's first written code of laws

BUILDING BACKGROUND

Ask students what *equality* means to them. Then have them imagine what life would be like in the United States if there were no written laws and a few wealthy people and their friends made decisions for everybody on legal matters. Tell students they will read about how poor Romans found a way to gain fairer treatment from the rich.

WORKING WITH PRIMARY SOURCES

Reread the quote from Euripides on page 35: "When laws are written, rich and poor get equal justice." Remind students that if a Roman citizen wanted to seek justice, he himself would go before the Senate or a magistrate and argue his case. Have students evaluate this statement in the context of the modern United States and come up with a revised statement that reflects today's situation.

GEOGRAPHY CONNECTION

The Twelve Tables were placed in the Forum in Rome. Help students understand that, in an age of slow communication, the effects of the laws might not be felt by plebeians who farmed the land far from Rome.

READING COMPREHENSION QUESTIONS

1. Compare and contrast the Roman patricians and plebeians. (*Patricians were wealthy landowners who controlled the government of the Republic. Plebeians were the workers—farmers, craftsmen, traders—who supported the patricians.*)
2. When did the plebeians begin to demand fair treatment? (*after they moved to the city to become craftsmen and traders, and were no longer dependent on the land-owning patricians for their survival*)
3. Why were the patricians panicked when the plebeians left Rome in 493 BCE? (*The patricians needed the plebeians. Without the plebeians, there would be no army for the patricians to lead in case of war. There would be nobody to do all the tasks that kept Rome running.*)
4. What steps were taken to resolve this class conflict? (*The Senate voted to give the plebeians an assembly of their own and tribunes that had the right to veto decrees of the Senate. The Senate also created the Twelve Tables. These put the laws of Rome in writing so that all citizens, rich or poor, could get justice in the courts.*)

CRITICAL THINKING QUESTIONS

1. What is the point of Menenius's story? Is it still true today? (*Possible answer: The Roman "body" could survive only if all of its parts—patrician and plebeian—worked together. This is still true today—if a country's groups don't work together, the country can be torn apart.*)

2. How did the reforms after the plebeian rebellions make life fairer in Rome? (*Possible answer: The plebeians were no longer at the mercy of the patricians. They could create laws through their assembly. Their tribunes could watch out for unfair laws passed by the Senate. Having written laws meant that patrician judges could not make special rulings to protect other patricians.*)

3. Which reform do you think was the most important? Why? (*Possible answer: The Twelve Tables: once written down, the laws could be understood, debated, and even changed. Moreover, the people could see whether judges enforced the laws fairly.*)

SOCIAL SCIENCES

Economics   Any society depends upon a wide range of workers to function. In a timed session, have small groups of students brainstorm and list as many jobs as they can think of. You may want to help groups by explaining different categories of jobs, such as manufacturing, service, and government. To illustrate the complexity of any society's economy, bring the class together to find out how many jobs the groups listed.

READING AND LANGUAGE ARTS

Reading Nonfiction   Have students create a sequence of events chart to show how Rome gradually moved toward a more democratic government in which power was distributed among the various classes of society.

Using Language   Explain to students that Menenius's story is an *allegory*—it uses symbolic characters and events to make a point. Have partners write their own allegories about issues that are important to them.

SUPPORTING LEARNING

English Language Learners   Help students recognize the purpose of special type and formatting. Reinforce that words in boldface in the text (*plebeians, patricians, veto*) are important words to know in understanding the content. Have students identify the side column definitions of these words.

Struggling Readers   Draw a simple diagram of the body. Use the diagram to reinforce what would happen to the body if the stomach did not get any food: nothing would be digested, no nutrients would reach the rest of the body, the body would have no energy and would eventually die.

EXTENDING LEARNING

Enrichment   Students can use Internet sources to learn more about the Twelve Tables. One list can be found at *http://ragz-international.com/Twelve%20Tables.htm*. Have students categorize the laws by the areas of Roman life they controlled, and display them on a chart.

Extension   Students can act out the confrontation between patricians and plebeians, set in modern times. One small group could be the owners of a company, while the larger group would be striking workers. After both parties express their views, they will come to an agreement.

 **WRITING**

Persuasion

Have students reread the section describing the Twelve Tables. Ask them to choose one law that seems unfair and write a letter to the Roman Senate explaining why and how it should be changed.

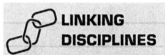 **LINKING DISCIPLINES**

Art Listen to and discuss protest songs such as "We Shall Overcome" and "Blowin' in the Wind." Invite students to write a protest song the plebeians might have sung on the Sacred Mount.

THE TWELVE TABLES

Directions

Each of the Twelve Tables contained a series of laws. Read the following excerpts from the Twelve Tables. Then answer the questions on a separate sheet of paper.

Table 1: If anyone summons a man before the magistrate, he must go. If the man summoned does not go, let the one summoning him call the bystanders to witness and then take him by force.

Table 2: He whose witness has failed to appear may summon him by loud calls before his house every third day.

Table 3: One who has confessed a debt . . . shall have thirty days to pay it in. . . .

Table 4: A dreadfully deformed child shall be quickly killed.

Table 5: Females should remain in guardianship even when they have attained their majority.

Table 6: A beam that is built into a house or a vineyard trellis one may not take from its place.

Table 7: Should a tree on a neighbor's farm be bent crooked by the wind and lean over your farm, you may take legal action for removal of that tree.

Table 8: No person shall hold meetings by night in the city.

Table 9: The penalty shall be capital for a judge or arbiter legally appointed who has been found guilty of receiving a bribe for giving a decision.

Table 10: No one is to bury or burn a corpse in the city.

Table 11: Marriages should not take place between plebeians and patricians.

Table 12: Whatever the People has last ordained shall be held as binding by law.

---

1. Which of the laws concern legal matters? What do they show about how Romans dealt with these matters?

2. Which laws relate to public health?

3. Which laws relate to the structure of Roman society? What can you conclude about Roman society from these laws?

4. Why do you suppose Table 8 banned nighttime meetings in Rome?

5. A capital crime is a crime that is punishable by death. What does Table 9 show about Roman attitudes toward bribery?

NAME _____ **DATE** _____

A. MULTIPLE CHOICE

Circle the letter of the best answer for each question.

1. Which was **not** a way the plebeians tried to gain equality with the patricians?
   a. walk out of the city
   b. go on a hunger strike
   c. have tribunes veto unfair laws
   d. have an assembly of their own

2. What was the point of Menenius's story about the body parts?
   a. All the groups in Rome had to work together.
   b. The plebeians should not expect any more food than they already had.
   c. The patricians could get along without the plebeians.
   d. The plebeians were not trained for war.

3. The tribunes' veto power was very important because it meant that
   a. the plebeians could block Senate decrees they thought were unfair.
   b. the patricians could not enter the Assembly.
   c. the tribunes were members of the Senate.
   d. no plebeian could be forced into slavery to pay debts.

4. The Senate agreed to write the Twelve Tables because
   a. the plebeians agreed to return to the _status quo._
   b. they were held hostage.
   c. patricians wanted written laws, too.
   d. they wanted to ease tension between rich and poor.

5. What is the best statement of why written laws are important?
   a. It gives work to engravers.
   b. It creates a class of lawyers.
   c. It gives rich and poor equal justice.
   d. It makes the courts more important.

B. SHORT ANSWER

Write one or two sentences to answer each question.

6. Why did the plebeians become free to complain about the lack of justice?

   _____

   _____

7. Why do written laws make justice more equal?

   _____

   _____

8. What could Roman citizens do if a court gave them a death sentence?

   _____

   _____

C. ESSAY

On a separate sheet of paper, write an essay describing the class conflict in Rome discussed in this chapter. Explain why the plebeians and patricians did what they did, and whether you think the conflict was ever truly resolved.

CHAPTER 5

FATHERS, GODS, AND GODDESSES: RELIGION IN ANCIENT ROME PAGES 36–40

FOR HOMEWORK

STUDENT STUDY GUIDE

pages 19–20

CAST OF CHARACTERS

Livy Roman historian (59 BCE–17 CE)

Vestal (ves-tul) **Virgins** unmarried priestesses who performed rituals honoring goddess Vesta

VOCABULARY

toga virilis (vuh-RIL-iss) man's garment

paterfamilias (PAH-tur-fuh-MIL-ee-us) head of a family

THEN and NOW

Juno was the patroness of marriage as well as the Queen of the Gods and Jupiter's wife. Today, the month of June, which is named for Juno, is one of the most popular months for weddings.

CHAPTER SUMMARY

Roman religion, government, and family were closely linked. Understanding Roman gods and beliefs helps us understand how the Romans thought and acted.

PERFORMANCE OBJECTIVES

▶ To explain the organization of Roman family life
▶ To understand the role of religion in Roman family and state life
▶ To identify various Roman gods and their roles
▶ To explain how and why Romans borrowed gods from other cultures

BUILDING BACKGROUND

Display a picture of a shrine or worship sanctuary. Talk about the purpose of this sacred place. Tell students that they will read about the shrines Romans had in homes and the temples they built in public places to stay in constant contact with their gods.

WORKING WITH PRIMARY SOURCES

Refer students to the statue of the Roman citizen on page 36. Make sure students understand how the author can make the inferences about the Roman in the accompanying text (observation of the artifact combined with other knowledge of the subject). Have students turn to the pictures on pages 29 and 45, and discuss what they can tell about these Romans from their statues.

GEOGRAPHY CONNECTION

As students read this chapter, refer them to the historical map of the expansion of Rome on page 60. Have them use the map to see how the Romans came into contact with other religions and absorbed foreign gods into their own religion.

READING COMPREHENSION QUESTIONS

1. What evidence does the author give that religion was an important part of Roman life? (*Every Roman household had its own shrine and gods. Each family had religious rituals connected to common activities. Families made daily sacrifices to the gods to keep them happy and receive their protection.*)
2. What early Roman religious beliefs fed into this emphasis on religion? (*Early Romans were farmers who saw the gods in all forces of nature.*)
3. What could happen if Romans failed to please their gods? (*Bad things could happen to the household or to the state. Vestal Virgins could be left to die if they did not carry out their duties.*)
4. Why did Romans borrow gods from other peoples? (*They thought if they prayed to their enemies' gods, those gods would help them in battle or in other aspects of life.*)
5. Distribute copies of the blackline master for Chapter 5 and have students complete the activity to learn more about the Romans' relationship to their gods.

CRITICAL THINKING QUESTIONS

1. Compare and contrast the Roman family and the Roman state. (*Compare: The oldest man was the paterfamilias, or head of the family, as the consul was the head of the state. Every Roman home had household gods, the Lares, as Rome had city gods. The paterfamilias was in charge of religious rites and sacrifices, as the consuls were for the state. Contrast: The paterfamilias had life-and-death power over members of the family. Consuls or the Senate could condemn someone to death, but the condemned could appeal to the Assembly in those cases.*)

2. What was a paterfamilias's relationship to his ancestors? How do you know? (*He felt a strong bond with ancestors and was very proud of them; ancestral masks were hung in his home and he carried them in important processions; he prayed and made sacrifices in their honor.*)

SOCIAL SCIENCES

Civics   Roman leaders of state and family took their authority from their model of religion. As Jupiter ruled over the gods as father and king, consuls ruled the country and the paterfamilias ruled the family. Have students discuss how this model for power contrasts with the model of modern democracy.

READING AND LANGUAGE ARTS

Reading Nonfiction   Have students reread the epitaphs of the Scipios on page 36, and elicit that an epitaph memorializes the deceased. It is a brief summary of what was most important about the person. Ask students to write an epitaph for someone they consider a great leader of our time.

Using Language   Tell students that the relationship between the structure of the Roman state and the Roman family is an example of an *analogy*: it shows a resemblance between two things that are otherwise unlike. Lead students in recognizing other examples of analogies, either from their studies or from their daily lives. Have them state each analogy in this form: *A is like B because . . .*

SUPPORTING LEARNING

English Language Learners   Use the Misnumbered Months feature on page 39 to improve students' understanding of Latin roots of common English words such as *acqua* (water) in "aquarium" and *liber* (book) in "library."

Struggling Readers   Have students make a main idea map (see the graphic organizer at the back of this guide) about the paterfamilias, described on page 37. They should write *paterfamilias* in the large central circle. The surrounding circles should each be labeled with supporting details, such as *children; family; slaves; punishment.*

EXTENDING LEARNING

Enrichment   Ancestral and religious masks are an important part of many cultures. Ask students to research one type of these masks, such as African or Native American masks, and to make a model of one to display in class.

Extension   Have volunteers stand and read aloud the epitaphs of the Scipios on page 36 as if they were orators at the funerals of these Romans. If students wrote their own epitaphs, they can read them as well.

WRITING

Explanation

A teenage Roman boy received a *toga virilis* as a symbol of reaching manhood. Discuss with students what objects or events symbolize adulthood in our society. Have them write a paragraph about one of these things, telling why it symbolizes maturity.

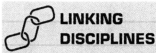

LINKING DISCIPLINES

Health When a baby was born in an ancient Roman family, certain religious rituals were performed in an effort to ensure the child's health and good fortune. Brainstorm with students how modern medicine is used to ensure children's health today (*vaccinations, check-ups, x-rays, medicines, and so on*).

CALLING ON THE GODS IN TIME OF WAR

Directions

With a partner, read this excerpt from "The Roman Way of Declaring War" written by the Roman historian Livy in his *History of Rome*. According to Livy, the first person who called on the gods in this way was Ancus Marcius, fourth king of Rome, around 650 BCE. His formula was followed for centuries. Then answer the questions.

> The [Roman] envoy when he comes to the frontier of the offending nation, covers his head . . . and says: *Hear, O Jupiter, and hear ye lands* _____ *[of such and such a nation], let Justice hear! I am a public messenger of the Roman people. Justly and religiously I come, and let my words bear credit!* Then he makes his demands, and follows with a solemn appeal to Jupiter. *If I demand unjustly and impiously that these men and goods [in question] be given to me, the herald of the Roman people, then suffer me never to enjoy again my native country!*
>
> These words he repeats when he crosses the frontiers; he says them also to the first man he meets [on the way]; again when he passes the gate; again on entering the [foreigners'] market-place, some few words . . . being changed. . . . He declares war, thus: *Hear, O Jupiter and you too, Juno—Romulus also, and all the celestial, terrestrial, and infernal gods! Give us ear! I call you to witness that this nation* [here he would name the nation] *is unjust, and has acted contrary to right. And as for us, we will consult thereon with our elders in our homeland, as to how we may obtain our rights.* . . . [This practice was followed in centuries that followed.]

1. Why do you think the Romans called on the gods when they declared war?

_____

_____

_____

_____

2. Livy notes that this ancient set of rules for declaring war became a practice used for centuries. Why do you think these rules continued to be followed for so long?

_____

_____

_____

_____

3. What conclusions can you draw about Roman beliefs about their gods and goddesses from this excerpt?

_____

_____

_____

_____

NAME   **DATE**

A. MULTIPLE CHOICE

Circle the letter of the best answer for each question.

1. Roman families were like miniature states because they
   a. traded with other families as states trade with each other.
   b. had their own laws, which were not affected by Roman laws.
   c. had their own religions and governments.
   d. were very large.

2. What was **not** a right of the paterfamilias?
   a. sell a disobedient slave   **c.** disobey the gods
   b. execute a son   **d.** abandon an unwanted baby

3. Why did the household god Janus have two faces?
   a. to lie to outsiders and tell the truth to family
   b. to let friends in and keep enemies out
   c. to open and shut the door
   d. to keep the fireplace spirit alive

4. If the flame guarded by the Vestal Virgins went out, the Romans believed
   a. nothing would happen.   **c.** the city was in grave danger.
   b. they would conquer new people.   **d.** the goddess Vesta was asleep.

5. Romans adopted new gods that they thought
   a. might be useful.   **c.** were warlike.
   b. were handsome.   **d.** would hurt them.

B. SHORT ANSWER

Write one or two sentences to answer each question.

6. What would a Roman father do when a baby was born in the family?

_____

_____

7. As Rome's society became more complicated, how did the job of keeping the gods happy change?

_____

_____

8. How did later Roman gods differ from the older Roman gods?

_____

_____

C. ESSAY

The chapter says "Roman religion, government, and family were all closely connected." Write an essay on a separate sheet of paper explaining how this statement is true.

HANNIBAL, ROME'S WORST ENEMY: THE BATTLE FOR THE MEDITERRANEAN PAGES 41–46

STUDENT STUDY GUIDE

pages 21–22

NAMES TO KNOW

Hamilcar (HAM-ul-kar) **Barca** (BAR-kuh) Carthaginian general in First Punic War; father of Hannibal

Hannibal Carthaginian general in Second Punic War; greatest enemy of Rome

Scipio (SIP-ee-o) **Africanus** (af-ri-KAH-nus) Roman general who defeated Hannibal

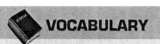 **VOCABULARY**

cavalry soldiers on horseback

THEN and NOW

Modern armies still have cavalry, although these soldiers no longer ride horses into battle. The term now applies to forces designed to move and attack quickly with light armored vehicles. These troops rely on surprise and speed to be successful.

CHAPTER SUMMARY

In the Punic Wars, Carthage and Rome battled for supremacy in the Mediterranean. Hannibal's stunning military strategies are legendary even today. The ultimate Roman triumph in this titanic struggle set the course of world dominance for centuries to come.

TEACHING OBJECTIVES

▶ To follow the sequence of events in the Punic Wars
▶ To identify Roman and Carthaginian leaders
▶ To describe the strategies of Hannibal and explain their effectiveness
▶ To explain the importance of Roman victory in the Punic Wars

SET THE STAGE

Ask students how modern soldiers ride into battle. (*on tanks, trucks, and other mechanized vehicles*) Refer students to the picture of the Battle of Zama on page 46. Have them imagine being a Roman foot soldier facing an attack by war elephants. What would their natural reaction be? Tell students they will read about just such battles between Romans and Carthaginians.

WORKING WITH PRIMARY SOURCES

Polybius was a Greek historian whose 40-book *Histories* series (written after 168 BCE) documents Rome's rise to supremacy in the Mediterranean world in the 3rd and 2nd centuries BCE. Only five of the *Histories* have survived in their entirety. Book III gives a detailed version of the Battle of Cannae, the events leading up to it, and the different troops on both sides. You may wish to read excerpts from the account to students. One source is *www.fordham.edu/halsall/ancient/polybius-annae.html*. Have students draw conclusions about the battle and those who fought in it.

GEOGRAPHY CONNECTION

Movement Refer students to the map of the Second Punic War on page 42. Have them identify the route Hannibal took on his invasion of Italy and estimate the distance from the start in Spain to the first battle at Trebia. (*approximately 1,000 miles*) Have them speculate on why it took the army five months to travel this distance. (*poor roads, supplying the army and elephants, rough terrain in Alps*) Students can use the blackline master for Chapter 6 to learn more about this journey.

READING COMPREHENSION QUESTIONS

1. Why did Hannibal become Rome's worst enemy? (*His father, Hamilcar Barca, was a Carthaginian general during the First Punic War. He hated the Romans for defeating his state, and passed on that hatred to his son, who became an even greater general.*)
2. Who founded Carthage? Where was it located? (*Traders from Phoenicia in Lebanon founded Carthage as a trading post in North Africa.*)
3. Why was the competition between Rome and Carthage so fierce? (*Both wanted to control the western Mediterranean. They were two expanding, powerful states that were near each other.*)

4. When were the Punic Wars fought? What was the final outcome? (*The Punic Wars were fought between 264 and 146 BCE. Although Rome suffered some shocking losses, it ultimately defeated and destroyed Carthage, and took control of the western Mediterranean world.*)

CRITICAL THINKING QUESTIONS

1. Compare and contrast Rome and Carthage. (*Both were strong, proud cities on the Mediterranean that wanted to control trade there. Rome had shown military might on land. Carthage had more wealth and naval superiority.*)

2. What does their invention of a grappling machine suggest about the Romans? (*Possible answer: They were resourceful, determined people who recognized their weaknesses and found ways to overcome them. They were eager to enter new arenas and willing to learn new skills.*)

3. What was Hannibal's greatest strength as a general? Give examples. (*Possible answer: He was a clever strategist and did the unexpected. He tricked the Romans into entering a narrow pass at Lake Trasimene and ambushed them.*)

4. Distribute copies of the blackline master for Chapter 6 so students can analyze the chronology of the Punic Wars.

SOCIAL SCIENCES

Economics   Ask students to find facts about elephants: how much they eat and drink in a day, what sort of care they need. Hannibal started his journey from Spain with 34 elephants. Have students figure out the amount of supplies needed each day, week, and month for the elephants.

READING AND LANGUAGE ARTS

Reading Nonfiction   Have students preview the chapter by looking at the title, pictures, graphic aids, and sidebars. Help them formulate questions that they expect will be answered by the chapter: *I can tell by the chapter title that Rome will be at war. Who will they fight? Where will it take place? What are the stakes?* Have students write their questions in one column of a two-column chart, and answer the questions with information from the text as they read.

Capitalization   Remind students that, in English, proper nouns such as names of people, countries, wars, battles, rivers, and places are capitalized. Assign small groups a section of the chapter, and have them list the proper nouns they find and sort them into categories.

SUPPORTING LEARNING

Reteaching   Have students create a cause and effect chart to show how Rome finally defeated Hannibal.

EXTENDING LEARNING

Enrichment   Have students draw a diagram of Hannibal's classic battlefield strategy based on Polybius's account of the Battle of Cannae. (See Working with Primary Sources.)

Extension   To help students understand the size of elephants, use a yardstick to measure the height of your classroom ceiling and compare it to the height of an elephant (12 feet at the shoulders). Then have students predict whether the entire class weighs less or more than an elephant. Have them write down their weights on slips of paper. Collect the slips and have students add the numbers.

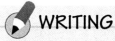

WRITING

Ask students to put themselves in Hannibal's place and write a journal entry describing the Battle of Lake Trebia and his plans and hopes for the future.

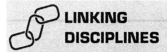

LINKING DISCIPLINES

Art Have students reread the description of the elephants in battle. Ask students to work in a group to make a mural depicting the Battle of Lake Trebia, showing soldiers on elephants and horses.

NAME   **DATE**

WORKING WITH TIMELINES: THE PUNIC WARS

Directions

Study the timeline of the Punic Wars. Then answer the questions.

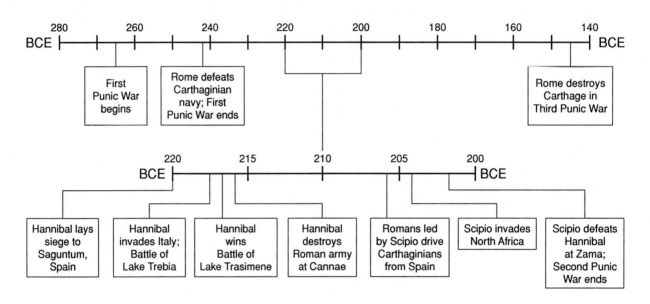

1. What time period does the main timeline show? How many years is that?

_____

2. What time period does the lower timeline show? How many years is that?

_____

3. Which occurred first, Rome defeating the Carthaginian navy or Hannibal destroying the Roman army at Cannae?

_____

4. In what year did Hannibal lay siege to Saguntum? How many years after that was Hannibal defeated at Zama?

_____

5. Why is it useful to have a separate timeline for 220–200 BCE?

_____

_____

NAME _____ **DATE** _____

A. MULTIPLE CHOICE

Circle the letter of the best answer for each question.

1. The Carthaginians were seafaring people whose origins were in
   a. Greece.   **c.** Lebanon.
   b. North Africa.   **d.** Spain.

2. Why were the Punic Wars fought?
   a. For control over the western Mediterranean
   b. For control over the eastern Mediterranean
   c. For control over Carthage's source of war elephants
   d. For control over Rome's armies

3. At the start of the Second Punic War, Hannibal was
   a. ruler of Carthage.   **c.** a Roman captive.
   b. admiral of Carthage's navy.   **d.** general of Carthage's army in Spain.

4. What was Hannibal's plan to defeat Rome?
   a. defeat Roman armies in Spain
   b. defeat Roman navies in the Mediterranean
   c. invade Italy and destroy the Romans there
   d. invade Italy and settle there

5. What plan did the Romans use to end Hannibal's threat?
   a. let Hannibal's army get worn out in small battles and cut off its supplies
   b. face Hannibal in two large battles and defeat him
   c. surround Hannibal's army with the Roman navy
   d. negotiate a truce in the war

B. SHORT ANSWER

Write one or two sentences to answer each question.

6. Why did Hannibal become involved in the Punic Wars?

_____

_____

7. What great battles did Hannibal win against Rome?

_____

_____

8. Why was the Battle of Cannae a turning point in the Second Punic War?

_____

_____

C. ESSAY

On a separate sheet of paper, write an essay describing the result of the Punic Wars for Rome and for Carthage.

DECLINE OF THE ROMAN REPUBLIC

PAGES 47–71

UNIT OBJECTIVES

Unit 3 covers events from the Second Punic War (about 217 BCE) until the death of Cicero and the end of the Republic in 43 BCE. In this unit, your students will learn

- the great expansion of the Roman empire under the Republic.
- the adoption of Greek culture by wealthy Romans after the subjugation of the Greek city-states.
- the life of the millions of enslaved foreigners in the empire.
- the rise of *populares* politicians and their effect on the institutions of the Republic.
- the corruption and violence that marked the final years of the Republic.

PRIMARY SOURCES

Unit 3 includes excerpts from the following primary sources:

- Plutarch, *Life of Cato*
- Plutarch, *Life of Crassus*
- Plutarch, *Life of Tiberius Gracchus*
- Plutarch, *Life of Cicero*
- Cicero, *About Constitutions*
- Cicero, *Letters to Atticus*
- Cicero, *An Essay About Duties*
- Cicero, *On the Orator*
- Cicero, *Letters to His Friends*
- Cicero, *Second Philippic*
- Diodorus, *The History of the World*
- Cato, *On Agriculture*
- Sallust, *Catiline*
- Appian, *Civil Wars*

Pictures of artifacts from Republican times can also be analyzed as primary sources. Students can use these pictures to learn more about the people of the time.

- Bust of Cato the Elder
- Museum copy of Roman room, 1st-century BCE
- Surgeons' instruments
- Coffin with domestic scenes and slavery
- Funeral altar of freed slaves
- Mosaic of slaves
- Statue of orator Aulus Metellus
- Bust of Cicero
- Relief sculpture of teacher and students

BIG IDEAS IN UNIT 3

Conflict, exchange, freedom, and **change** are the big ideas presented in Unit 3. The conflict in this unit is between Romans who were for and those who were against change. One group, the slaves, wanted freedom. Another group, the poor, wanted freedom to work and earn a living. Another group, the *populares,* wanted a share of the political power held by the wealthy senators. And the wealthy wanted to emulate Greek society.

You may want to introduce these ideas by discussing what people in various walks of life—poor, rich, powerful, powerless—want in life.

GEOGRAPHY CONNECTION

Rome's change from a western Mediterranean power to an empire that dominated the whole Mediterranean world is the most important development in this unit. Use the map on page 60 to trace this expansion. You may also wish to display historical maps showing the succession of empires in the Middle East—Persian to Greek to Roman—to show the influences that the Romans came under as they conquered territories to the east.

TIMELINE

336 BCE	Alexander the Great begins his conquests
196 BCE	Romans defeat Macedonians
146 BCE	Romans conquer Greece
135 BCE	Slave rebellion in Sicily
133 BCE	Tiberius Gracchus elected tribune
123 BCE	Gaius Gracchus elected tribune
90 BCE	Rome's Italian allies rebel (War of the Allies)
73 BCE	Slave rebellion led by Spartacus
60 BCE	Julius Caesar forms First Triumvirate
57 BCE	Cicero banished from Rome

UNIT PROJECTS

History of Slavery

Rome was not the only ancient civilization to have large numbers of slaves doing its menial work. Slavery was also common in Persia, Egypt, Greece, and other places in the ancient world. Have small groups research this topic for different civilizations, and draw up charts characterizing slavery in each society. Bring the class together to compare and contrast slavery around the ancient world.

Chronology

Students can make parallel timelines showing that different types of events were happening simultaneously. For example, this unit discusses three distinct activities that were roughly contemporaneous: the expansion of Rome, rebellions within Rome, and political changes in Rome. This will help students understand the interrelatedness of events from different spheres.

Gladiators

Have volunteers research more information about those who fought for the entertainment of the Romans. Most gladiators were condemned criminals, prisoners of war, or slaves. An owner of gladiators was known as a *lanista.* Criminals who had committed a capital crime had to enter the arena without weapons. Others were trained in combat specialties at a *ludi,* or gladiator school. Gladiators were only required to fight two or three times a year and could earn freedom if they survived three to five years. However, few survived this long.

"Greek" Envy

Wealthy Romans admired Greek elegance and wanted to live like the Greeks did. Envying someone else's life style is a common emotion, even today. Have students cut out pictures of people or groups whom they admire. Have them make a display showing what is admirable and not so admirable about these people's way of life.

Modern *Populares*

Populares were Roman politicians who claimed to speak for the mass of citizens who had little power in the Republic. Some of them, like the Gracchi, were sincerely interested in helping the powerless; others were only interested in helping themselves. Have students make up biographies of fictional modern *populares,* both sincere and insincere. They can also draw caricatures of both types of politician.

Valuing Human Life

The last years of the Roman Republic were a time when the worth of a human life was greatly devalued. Power seemed to be more important than morality. If you disagreed with a powerful person, you might be killed. Have students discuss the ramifications of this lust for power. Have them relate the discussion to the present day.

ADDITIONAL ASSESSMENT

For Unit 3, divide the class into groups and have them all undertake the Modern *Populares* project so you can assess their understanding of similarities between the Roman Republic and our own political system. Use the scoring rubric at the back of this guide to assess students' work, and have students rate their own work with the self-assessment rubric.

LITERATURE CONNECTION

Plutarch's *Lives* can be read like literature as much as history. His works are full of vivid descriptions, rounded characters, setting, and narrative. Copies of the *Lives* are available in libraries as well as on the Internet. Have students read more extensively in the *Lives* cited in this unit—Cato, Crassus, Tiberius Gracchus, and Cicero. Have small groups find examples of the narrative elements—setting, character, plot, climax, denouement—in each.

Students will enjoy reading the following books that will extend their understanding of Rome during this period.

- ▶ Matyszak, Philip. *Chronicle of the Roman Republic.* London: Thames & Hudson, 2003. Nonfiction. AVERAGE
- ▶ Ray, Mary. *The Ides of April.* Bathgate, ND: Bethlehem Books, 1999. Fiction. ADVANCED
- ▶ Simpson, Judith. *Ancient Rome.* New York: Time-Life Books, 1997. Nonfiction. EASY
- ▶ Time-Life Editors. *When Rome Ruled the World (What Life Was Like* series*).* New York: Time-Life Books, 1997. Nonfiction. ADVANCED

UNIVERSAL ACCESS

The following strategies are designed to cover a range of learning styles and reading, language, and skill levels.

Reading Strategies

- To facilitate reading, help students preview the artwork and the captions in each chapter to make predictions about the people involved in the events.

- There are more words defined in the margins in this unit than in previous units. Have students maintain a class word file. Ask one or two students to create word cards for each chapter. On each card, students should write the word, define it, and use it in a sentence. They may illustrate the word as well.

- Have partners read sections of the chapters to each other, and then ask each other questions about the content: What is the main idea of this passage? What details or examples support the main idea?

Writing Strategies

- Have partners make a four-column chart with headings for each of the unit's big ideas. Partners should get together after reading each chapter to jot down their observations in each category.

- Have students create character webs for the important personalities discussed in the unit: Cato, Spartacus, Crassus, the Gracchi, Cicero, Pompey, Mark Antony. Tell students to use the webs to evaluate and compare the characters of each person.

- Have students list reasons for the decay and destruction of the Roman Republic. Students should state what they think was the most important factor in the Republic's decline

Listening and Speaking Strategies

- Point out the still photograph from the movie *Spartacus* on page 53. Explain that dramatic stories like this one are often used to make great movies. Elicit from students other dramatic historical stories that have been used as the basis of movies, and discuss why these stories are so compelling.

- Model reading aloud a passage from Cicero from Chapter 10. Have volunteers read the same passage or other passages, giving their own interpretations of Cicero's speaking style.

UNIT VOCABULARY LIST

The following words that appear in Unit 3 are important for your students' understanding of the social studies content as well as for development of literacy. Use these words for vocabulary study or to reinforce language arts skills (e.g., synonyms, compound words, prefixes and suffixes, and related words). The words are listed below in the order in which they appear in the chapters.

Chapter 7	Chapter 8	Chapter 9	Chapter 10
passionate	sketchy	oration	pompous
frugal	fringe	mushroomed	conceited
ruthless	auction	aristocrat	disdained
scornfully		unruly	recruit
hindsight		eligible	cooperate
		corrupt	

A ROMAN THROUGH AND THROUGH: CATO AND GREEK CULTURE   PAGES 47–52

CAST OF CHARACTERS

Cato (KAY-to) Roman general and senator who supported Roman culture

Alexander the Great creator of Greek empire in 4th century BCE

Antiochus (an-TIE-uh-kus) **III** Greek king defeated by Rome, 2nd century BCE

VOCABULARY

oration persuasive speech

aqueduct structure that brings water from far-off sources to where it is needed

THEN and NOW

Discuss with students whether Cato's warnings can be applied to the United States today. Compare and contrast Rome and the United States, and try to reach a consensus on whether we should be worried or encouraged by change.

CHAPTER SUMMARY

The story of Cato illustrates the clash of traditional values and the impulse to change the culture by borrowing the best from other cultures. It shows the tensions that are part of any growing, vital society, and the inevitability of change.

PERFORMANCE OBJECTIVES

- ► To understand the traditional values of Cato and early Rome
- ► To analyze how international activities lead to cultural and social change
- ► To explain the role of Alexander the Great and Antiochus in bringing change to Rome

BUILDING BACKGROUND

Ask students to complete the statement "Society is changing for the (better *or* worse)." Invite volunteers to explain their choice and cite examples as proof. Explain to students that they will read about a time when Roman culture and society was changing and a leader who feared and hated that change.

WORKING WITH PRIMARY SOURCES

Most of the excerpts in this chapter are from Plutarch's *Lives,* his series of 50 biographies of famous Greeks and Romans. Plutarch used older sources to write about people who lived hundreds of years before his time. Plutarch showed the total person: faults as well as greatness, and small details as well as major events. You may want to have students compare Plutarch's style with the style of biographies they have read.

GEOGRAPHY CONNECTION

Interaction   Help students locate the area conquered by Alexander the Great on a world map. They should recognize that all of the civilizations in that region were much older and in many ways more advanced than the Roman civilization. Remind students of how the Romans were influenced by the Etruscans, and have them predict what effect the Greek and Asian cultures will have on them.

READING COMPREHENSION QUESTIONS

1. Describe who Cato was and what he was like. (*Cato was a successful and respected Roman general, senator, and censor. He was a devoted father and traditionalist who insisted on sticking with old-fashioned, simple Roman values. He was fiercely proud of Rome, and hated Carthage and foreigners who would change Roman ways.*)

2. How did Greek culture spread throughout the eastern Mediterranean world and the Near East? (*Alexander the Great conquered the entire area and established 70 Greek cities throughout.*)

3. How did Rome come into direct contact with Greek civilization? (*It helped Macedonian cities overthrow their Greek ruler, Philip V, and then declared itself protector of the Greek cities. Rome then defeated the Asian king Antiochus III and became ruler of the Greek world.*)

4. What did Romans borrow from Greek culture? *(home decoration and architecture, art, literature, language, oratory style, clothing)*

CRITICAL THINKING QUESTIONS

1. What characteristics of Cato do you think Romans admired? Why? *(his bravery, military skill, love of family, and willingness to live by his simple, traditional values; these attributes had helped make Rome strong and successful.)*

2. Why do you think Cato disliked the way wealthy Romans lived? *(Possible answer: He believed that wealth led to leisure and free spending and a loss of focus on moral values. Undisciplined Romans would be easy to conquer.)*

3. Why did wealthy Romans hate Cato, while the commoners loved him? *(Wealthy people could pay for the Greek commodities they admired, but poor people had to live simply, as Cato advocated. Cato confirmed that their lifestyle was worthy and admirable.)*

SOCIAL SCIENCES

Science, Technology, and Society   Distribute the blackline master for Chapter 7 and have students complete the activity to learn more about Roman attitudes toward doctors.

READING AND LANGUAGE ARTS

Reading Nonfiction   Read aloud the last paragraph on page 51 to students before they begin reading the chapter. As they read, have them draw conclusions about the character traits that Roman patricians and plebeians cherished.

Using Language   Tell students that an *adage* is a saying that uses figurative language to make an observation. Discuss Cato's adage "Greeks speak from the lips; Romans speak from the heart." Ask students what this means. Ask them to brainstorm and explain other adages.

SUPPORTING LEARNING

English Language Learners   Have students use a dictionary to learn the modern meaning of *censor*. Have them relate the definition to Cicero's explanation of a censor's duties in Roman times.

Struggling Readers   Have students use the main idea map found in the back of this guide to create a character web for Cato, placing his name in the middle and surrounding it with his important character traits.

EXTENDING LEARNING

Enrichment   Students will use maps to learn more about how the Romans gained control of the Greek world. Interactive maps showing the growth of Roman territory can be found at the Illustrated History of the Roman Empire website listed on the Websites page at the back of students' books: *www.roman-empire.net*.

Extension   Have students read aloud longer excerpts about Cato from Plutarch's *Lives*. Translations of Plutarch's works can be found at the Internet Classics Archive listed on the Websites page at the back of students' books: *http://classics.mit.edu*.

WRITING

Persuasion
Romans excelled in oratory—speeches persuading people to act or think a certain way. Have students imagine they are Cato and write a short speech to persuade Romans to take up a simple lifestyle.

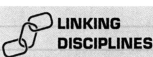
LINKING DISCIPLINES

Health Roman home remedies for such health problems as anemia, fever, and poisonous bites appear on page 50. Have students ask older family members how they would treat common illnesses such as colds, flu, fever, stomach ache, and muscle aches. Make a class list of modern remedies.

NAME _____   DATE _____

MEDICAL HUMOR, ROMAN STYLE

In ancient Rome, anyone could decide to be a doctor and start practicing. It was a profession without rules, formal training, or licensing. Successful doctors had apprentices, men who learned by observing. Unsuccessful doctors found other work.

Directions

In the left column of the chart are epigrams—short, satirical statements—about Roman doctors, mostly credited to the Roman writer Martial. With a partner, read each epigram aloud. Then, in the right column, write a statement interpreting the point of the epigram.

Medical Epigrams . . .	. . . and Their Meanings
1. "I didn't have a fever, doctor, when I called you, but now I do."	
2. "You are now a gladiator, although until recently you were an eye doctor. You did the same thing as a doctor that you do now as a gladiator."	
3. "Some doctors charge the most excessive prices for the most worthless medicines and drugs."	
4. "Until recently, Diaulus was a doctor; now he is an undertaker. He is still doing as an undertaker what he used to do as a doctor."	

NAME　　　　　　　　　　**DATE**

A. MULTIPLE CHOICE

Circle the letter of the best answer for each question.

1. Cato modeled his life on the traditional values of
   - **a.** ancient Greece.
   - **b.** ancient Rome.
   - **c.** modern Greece.
   - **d.** modern Rome.

2. Cato ended all of his orations with a plea to
   - **a.** go back to the old ways.
   - **b.** destroy Carthage.
   - **c.** live simply.
   - **d.** rebuild the Senate building.

3. After Rome conquered Greece, wealthy Romans started to
   - **a.** want more conquests.
   - **b.** go back to the old values.
   - **c.** move to Asia.
   - **d.** live in Greek elegance.

4. Cato fought against things that weren't "Roman" because he
   - **a.** wasn't Roman himself.
   - **b.** was afraid power and wealth would cause Rome to collapse.
   - **c.** was a bitter old man.
   - **d.** didn't like Africans.

5. In the end, Cato's fears proved to be unnecessary because
   - **a.** Rome was already lost.
   - **b.** Rome increased its power for hundreds of years.
   - **c.** the Greeks conquered Rome.
   - **d.** there were no more threats to Rome.

B. SHORT ANSWER

Write one or two sentences to answer each question.

6. Cato was supposed to have said, "Greeks speak from the lips; Romans speak from the heart." Explain what contrast Cato is making between Greeks and Romans.

   _____

   _____

7. How did Roman commanders deal with the Greek cities after the defeat of Antiochus?

   _____

   _____

8. What were Cato's duties as censor?

   _____

   _____

C. ESSAY

Write an essay on a separate sheet of paper explaining why Cato was hated by wealthy patricians but was a hero to ordinary Romans.

CHAPTER 8

SPARTACUS THE REBEL: SLAVERY IN ANCIENT ROME

PAGES 53–58

CAST OF CHARACTERS

Spartacus (SPAR-tuh-kus) leader of Roman slave revolt, 73 BCE

Crassus (KRASS-us) Roman general who finally defeated Spartacus

 LINKING DISCIPLINES

Math Review the numbers presented in the text about Spartacus's rebellion. Have students make up word problems using these numbers to show how remarkable Spartacus's victories were and how dramatically the slave rebellion grew. For example: 70 gladiators defeated 3,000 Roman soldiers. How many times more soldiers were there than gladiators? *(3,000 divided by 70 equals about 43 times as many soldiers)* Seventy gladiators grew to an army of 70,000. By what percent did Spartacus's army grow? *(100,000 percent)*

CHAPTER SUMMARY

As Rome conquered the Mediterranean world, foreign prisoners were made slaves to their Roman masters. Most of these millions of slaves were treated harshly and were denied freedom for life. They were forced to work on farms, in mines, in homes, and as gladiators. The cruel treatment led to periodic slave rebellions, all of which, including the one led by Spartacus in 73 BCE, were bloodily crushed.

PERFORMANCE OBJECTIVES

- ▶ To describe the life of Roman slaves
- ▶ To summarize the events of the slave rebellion led by Spartacus
- ▶ To compare and contrast treatment of different classes of slaves

BUILDING BACKGROUND

Invite students to share what they know about slavery in the United States from 1619 to 1865. Explain that they will be reading about slavery in ancient Rome. Have them be aware of common characteristics of ancient and more modern slavery.

WORKING WITH PRIMARY SOURCES

Two of the three sources in this chapter—Diodorus and Cato—were contemporaries of what they described. This lends their words an immediacy that writers who are looking back on a subject don't have. Ask students what types of sources are contemporary with events reported. *(diary, journal, newspaper, TV/radio/Internet reports, and so on)*

GEOGRAPHY CONNECTION

Location Have students turn to the Ancient Roman World map at the front of their books and locate Thrace. Then have them compare that map with the map on page 60 to understand what the author means by "the eastern fringe of Rome's huge empire."

READING COMPREHENSION QUESTIONS

1. Who made up the slaves in the Roman Republic? What work did they do? *(Most slaves were foreign prisoners captured as Rome conquered the Mediterranean world. Some were Italians who couldn't pay their debts and fell into slavery. They built roads and aqueducts, cleaned public toilets and baths, worked in mines, did farm labor, and worked at crafts and in the homes of their masters.)*

2. How did the Romans treat their slaves? *(Many slaves were treated brutally. The Romans thought of them as things that could be sold or killed as they wished. Slaves performed the back-breaking jobs such as silver mining and construction. They were used as gladiators. Other slaves had a better life—working in their master's house, doing skilled craftwork. Except for those who could buy their freedom, slaves were slaves for life.)*

3. What happened in the slave revolt of 73 BCE? What was the final outcome? *(Spartacus led a breakout by 70 gladiators, who defeated troops sent to capture them again and again. Eventually, 70,000 slaves joined the rebellion. Finally,*

Crassus put down the revolt with the harshest measures, killing most of the rebels and crucifying 6,000 of them.)

4. Distribute copies of the blackline master for Chapter 8. Have students complete the activity to compare and contrast the lives of slaves and freedmen.

CRITICAL THINKING QUESTIONS

1. What details show that Romans tried to humiliate and break the will of slaves? *(Slaves were often branded or forced to wear a metal collar, and were treated as things rather than as people. They were given the worst jobs. They were bought and sold as their masters desired. Their suffering in gladiator games was considered entertainment.)*

2. Why do you think so many slaves joined Spartacus's rebellion? *(Possible answer: They were desperate to escape from the torment and hardship of slavery. When they learned of Spartacus's seemingly miraculous victories, they began to believe they could win freedom.)*

3. Some slaves gained freedom legally. Compare and contrast the lives of freedmen and slaves. *(Slaves had no rights to marry or own property, but freedmen could do both. Freedmen could not be sold as slaves could. They could earn money and move about freely. However, because they had to earn a living, many freedmen remained with their masters; most were desperately poor.)*

SOCIAL SCIENCES

Economics   Being a slaveowner was as much an economic decision as anything else. Owners profited by owning slaves, but there were also costs involved. Have small groups of students brainstorm either profits or costs of owning slaves, and then come together to evaluate the economics of slavery.

READING AND LANGUAGE ARTS

Reading Nonfiction   The primary sources in this chapter indicate the Roman attitude toward slaves. Have volunteers read these aloud, along with the "Slaves and Masters" excerpt from Seneca in *The World in Ancient Times Primary Sources and Reference Volume*, and distinguish the words showing the Romans' point of view.

Using Language   This chapter uses vivid adjectives to reveal the Roman slaves' experience. Have students find examples of these adjectives and tell how these words affect them.

SUPPORTING LEARNING

English Language Learners   Have partners make a list of adjectives in the chapter, such as *sizzling-hot, backbreaking, dreadful,* and *brutal*. Partners should then define these words from context and use them in sentences.

Struggling Readers   To summarize Roman slavery, have students make a three-column chart with the headings *Becoming a Slave, Life as a Slave,* and *Becoming a Freedman*, and complete the chart with details from the chapter.

EXTENDING LEARNING

Enrichment   Have students do research to find out the history of slavery in various countries. Students can create a timeline showing advances and setbacks in freedom around the world.

Extension   Have students reread the description of the battles between the slaves and the Roman army. Ask them to draw a scene depicting one of these battles.

WRITING

News Article
Spartacus and his army of rebel slaves struck fear in the hearts of Roman citizens. Have students write a news article reporting on various aspects of the rebellion. Students may include opinions of Roman citizens, senators, and soldiers in their articles.

VOCABULARY

crucify execute by nailing victim to a cross

THEN and **NOW**

In early Rome, slaves were mostly people who got into debt they could not pay. Today, people can declare bankruptcy if they are unable to pay their debts. They gain protection from their creditors until they can get back on their feet financially.

NAME _____   DATE _____

SLAVES AND FREEDMEN

Directions

Use the Venn diagram below to compare and contrast the life of slaves and freedmen in ancient Rome.

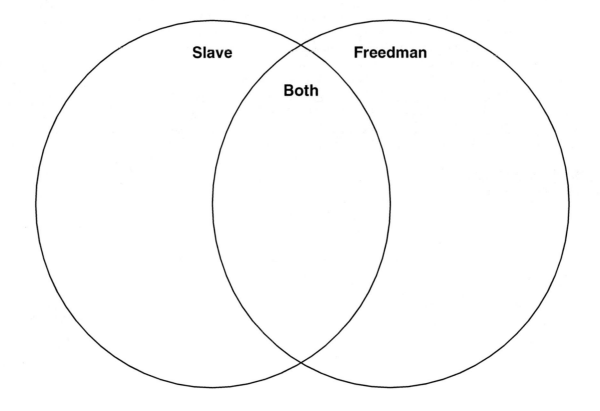

Slave   Freedman

Both

NAME   **DATE**

A. MULTIPLE CHOICE

Circle the letter of the best answer for each question.

1. How were most Roman slaves treated in Spartacus's time?
   a. They were treated well because they were expensive.
   b. They were treated kindly because there were so few of them.
   c. They were treated poorly because Rome was not yet wealthy.
   d. They were treated cruelly because Romans considered them to be not human.

2. The worst fate for slaves was to work
   a. in the houses of their masters.
   b. on the farms of their masters.
   c. in a craftsman's shop.
   d. in the silver mines of Spain.

3. Why was Spartacus so dangerous?
   a. He was a gladiator.
   b. He was a former senator.
   c. His force grew to 70,000 men.
   d. No Roman general would fight him.

4. How were the slaves who rebelled with Spartacus punished?
   a. They were returned to their masters.
   b. They were imprisoned.
   c. Their children were held hostage.
   d. They were crucified.

5. How could slaves gain their freedom legally?
   a. by outliving their masters
   b. by being bought by someone else
   c. by learning to read and write
   d. by buying their freedom

B. SHORT ANSWER

Read this passage from Plutarch about the end of Spartacus's rebellion. Then write complete sentences to answer each question.

> Spartacus . . . set all his army in array, and when his horse was brought him, he drew out his sword and killed him, saying, if he won the day, he should have a great many better horses of the enemies, and if he lost it, he should have no need of this one. And so making directly towards Crassus himself, through the midst of arms and wounds, he missed him, but killed two centurions that fell upon him together. At last being deserted by those that were about him, he himself stood his ground, and, surrounded by the enemy, bravely defending himself, was cut in pieces.

6. Why do you think Spartacus killed his horse? _____

_____

7. What can you tell about Spartacus's fighting skills from this passage?_____

_____

C. ESSAY

Using details from the chapter, write an essay on a separate sheet of paper describing the life of a Roman slave. Include how the person might have become a slave, what work the person did, and how the person's life might turn out.

TWO REVOLUTIONARY BROTHERS: THE GRACCHI AND THE DECLINE OF THE REPUBLIC PAGES 59–65

STUDENT STUDY GUIDE

pages 27–28

CAST OF CHARACTERS

Tiberius and **Gaius Gracchus** 2nd-century BCE tribunes; fought against power of nobles and to improve life of plebeians

THEN and NOW

The assassinations of the Gracchi marked the beginning of a violent time in Roman politics. Today, some say that American society is becoming increasingly violent. Discuss whether students believe this trend is an omen that American society will decline and America will lose power.

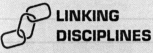

LINKING DISCIPLINES

Art Ask students to sketch a scene from the life of one of the Gracchi, and supply a caption explaining what is happening.

CHAPTER SUMMARY

During the Punic Wars (264–146 BCE) Rome had grown dramatically, but its rulers weren't keeping up with the times. Workers were losing jobs to slaves, poor farmers were losing their land, mobs were roaming the streets, and the army was unruly. The Gracchi brothers tried to redress the imbalance of power between poor and rich by working for land reform. But violence ended their careers as tribunes and became a part of Roman politics until the end of the Republic.

PERFORMANCE OBJECTIVES

▸ To compare and contrast Tiberius and Gaius Gracchus
▸ To explain why there was civil unrest in Rome, despite the empire's success
▸ To describe the sequence of events that led to the deaths of the Gracchi brothers
▸ To identify events that grew out of the Gracchi reforms

BUILDING BACKGROUND

Ask students to list ways in which American society and government needs to be reformed, or changed for the better. Discuss recent scandals that have affected sports, business, or government. List positive actions that people can take to make reforms.

WORKING WITH PRIMARY SOURCES

Sallust's *Catiline* is an account of Catiline's demagogic conspiracy to take over the government of Rome in 63 BCE. Although the work is not considered historically accurate, it gives graphic details about the crisis in the Roman empire at the time.

GEOGRAPHY CONNECTION

Movement   Using the map on page 60, have students compare the size of the Roman Empire in 241, 146, and 44 BCE. Ask them to predict what kind of stresses this kind of rapid growth would place on Rome, its leaders, and the people they conquered.

READING COMPREHENSION QUESTIONS

1. What problems did Rome experience because of its rapid growth? (*massive unemployment as workers' jobs were taken by slaves, poverty for poor farmers whose land was bought by the wealthy, angry mobs in Rome, unruly army, greed, bribery, corruption*)
2. What office did Tiberius Gracchus hold? What power did it give him? (*Tribune; he could protect the rights of the commoners and balance out the power of the wealthy.*)
3. What law did Tiberius get passed? (*Lands taken by Rome would be largely given to the poor; ownership of such lands would be limited to 300 acres.*)
4. What reforms did Gaius Gracchus fight for? (*a grain law that kept the price of grain low for the poor, jury reform so that men other than senators were included, rights of citizenship for Italian allies of Rome*)
5. Distribute copies of the blackline master for Chapter 9 and have students categorize the reforms of Tiberius and Gaius Gracchus.

CRITICAL THINKING QUESTIONS

1. How did the Gracchus brothers differ from most of Rome's elected officials of the time? (*They did not abuse power to enrich themselves; they tried to make life better for the poor while benefiting Rome.*)
2. Explain why Tiberius's land reform would be "a 'win' for everyone." (*Possible answer: It provided the poor with farmland so they could work and feed themselves. As landowners, they would be eligible for armed service, which would help Rome's armies and benefit the state. They would no longer have reason to rebel against the government.*)
3. Why did the Senate hate and fear Tiberius and Gaius? (*Both men ignored traditional legal and political methods, tried to eliminate corruption, and threatened the source of wealth for the upper class. Officials also feared that Tiberius wanted to become a tyrant king, and so take away their power.*)
4. Why was Rome willing to grant citizenship to its Italian allies? (*The allies became a threat because they set up their own capital and issued their own currency. Roman officials probably thought their allies might next attack them; making them citizens would avoid conflict and strengthen the empire.*)

SOCIAL SCIENCES

Civics   Citizens of the United States have rights guaranteed by the Constitution and the Bill of Rights. They also have responsibilities, such as obeying laws and voting. Ask students to compare the rights and responsibilities of Roman citizens in about 100 BCE. Have them give examples of ways in which Romans had neglected their responsibilities.

READING AND LANGUAGE ARTS

Reading Nonfiction   The chapter compares and contrasts the Gracchi brothers with the corrupt Roman officials of the time, and with each other. As students read, have them complete one comparison-contrast chart for the Gracchi and the officials and one for the two brothers. Then have students meet in small groups to collate their findings.

Using Language   Have students find similes in the chapter. Explain that similes use the words *like* or *as* to point out similarities between things. Ask students to write similes describing Gaius and Tiberius Gracchus.

SUPPORTING LEARNING

English Language Learners   Partners will pretend to be Tiberius and Gaius Gracchus. Have them talk to each other as the brothers might have about their dreams and hopes for Rome.

Struggling Readers   Students will use the cause and effect chart (see the T-chart at the back of this guide) to show the Gracchi reforms and their intended results. Tell students to evaluate whether the Gracchi reforms were successful.

EXTENDING LEARNING

Enrichment   Have students research in recent newspapers issues that they feel could use reform. Students may wish to give speeches to the class about the issue and what action they would take.

Extension   Pairs of students will write speeches the Gracchi might have made. One student will read the speech to the class while the other student acts it out in the style of either Tiberius or Gaius.

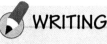

Persuasion List arguments for and against the passage of one of the Gracchi reforms. Have students imagine how either of the Gracchi would refute opposing arguments. Then ask them to write a Letter to the Editor this brother might have written to the *Roman Times* to win the support of fellow Romans.

 VOCABULARY

Mediterranean (MED-uh-tuh-RAY-nee-uhn) **Sea** sea "in the middle of the land" (surrounded by Roman Empire)

importance influence

infuriated made someone angry

revolutionary person who wants major changes in government

populares Roman politicians who spoke for the plebeians

NAME _____   **DATE** _____

THE REFORMS OF GAIUS AND TIBERIUS GRACCHUS

Directions

As you read the chapter, use the chart to write which reforms were sought by Tiberius Gracchus and which reforms were sought by Gaius Gracchus. Then answer the questions.

Tiberius Gracchus	Gaius Gracchus

1. Which of Tiberius's reforms do you think was best for Rome? Explain. _____

_____

_____

_____

_____

2. Which of Gaius's reforms do you think was best for Rome? Explain. _____

_____

_____

_____

_____

3. Explain why you think that the Gracchi reforms were not successful in the end. _____

_____

_____

_____

_____

A. MULTIPLE CHOICE

Circle the letter of the best answer for each question.

1. The Gracchi were the first of a type of Roman politicians called *populares,* who spoke for the
   a. senators.
   b. common people.
   c. tribunes.
   d. slaves.

2. When the Gracchi entered politics, the Republic was in trouble because
   a. its farmlands were no longer fertile.
   b. its people were dying out.
   c. its government had not kept up with changing conditions.
   d. there was a lack of corruption.

3. A major problem in Rome at the time was
   a. the large number of slaves.
   b. mobs of unemployed workers.
   c. untreated sewage.
   d. unpaved streets.

4. In order to change the way things were in Rome, the Gracchi had to
   a. fight against the power of the nobles.
   b. fight against each other.
   c. gain control of the army.
   d. rebuild the city anew.

5. Because they tried to revolutionize the Roman government, the Gracchi were
   a. honored with statues.
   b. killed by mobs.
   c. elected senators.
   d. elected tribunes.

B. SHORT ANSWER

Write one or two sentences to answer each question.

6. How did Tiberius Gracchus try to reform Roman land ownership?

 _____

 _____

7. How did Gaius Gracchus's grain law help poor Romans?

 _____

 _____

8. What did Roman senators think of Tiberius Gracchus when he began to walk through Rome accompanied by bodyguards?

 _____

 _____

C. ESSAY

On a separate sheet of paper, write an essay summarizing how the Gracchi tried to make Rome a better place to live for all Romans.

FOR HOMEWORK

STUDENT STUDY GUIDE

pages 29–30

CAST OF CHARACTERS

Cicero 1st-century BCE consul and orator; tried to save Republic

Pompey (PAHM-pee) general, First Triumvirate member; took part in civil wars that destroyed Republic

Julius Caesar (SEE-zer) statesman, general, First Triumvirate member

Mark Antony politician and soldier who ordered Cicero murdered

 **VOCABULARY**

innate born with, as a skill

civil having to do with citizens or the state

triumvirate group of three people who share power

CHAPTER SUMMARY

Cicero was an eloquent speaker and one of the great leaders of the Roman Republic. He also wrote many letters that tell us about the crisis in Rome at the end of the Republic. There was widespread chaos as generals fought for power. As consul, Cicero put down a *popularis* rebellion, but he soon lost influence to Pompey and Julius Caesar. In the end, Cicero was unable to halt the destruction of the Republic.

PERFORMANCE OBJECTIVES

▶ To understand the personal qualities and motivations of Cicero
▶ To follow the sequence of events at the end of the Roman Republic
▶ To describe the conflicts between aristocrats and *populares*

BUILDING BACKGROUND

Ask students which they think has the greater power to change society: words or weapons. Invite volunteers to explain their opinions. Explain that this chapter describes the life of a great leader who used words to try to save the Roman Republic.

WORKING WITH PRIMARY SOURCES

As the author says, Cicero's own words give the best picture of his life and life in the Rome of his time. Discuss with students the advantages and disadvantages of learning about a person through autobiographical material.

GEOGRAPHY CONNECTION

Place   Have students find Gaul on the map on page 60. Explain that Cisalpine Gaul is the area in dark green southwest of the Rhone River. Discuss the physical features of this location and why they are significant. Help students understand the threat that the Germans posed to the Romans, and how important it was for the Romans to defeat the Germans there.

READING COMPREHENSION QUESTIONS

1. Why do we know so much about Cicero? (*Many of his letters, speeches, and essays have survived. He wrote extensively about his life, opinions, and the Roman world of his day.*)

2. How did Cicero manage to rise to Rome's highest office? (*He was brave, brilliant, and determined. He worked hard and swayed large crowds with his oratory.*)

3. What was the First Triumvirate and who were its members? (*a council of three people who shared power, in effect controlling Rome; Julius Caesar, Pompey, and Crassus*)

4. Who killed Cicero and why? (*Mark Antony, because Cicero had spoken out against Antony's dictatorship of Rome*)

5. Distribute copies of the blackline master for Chapter 10 and have students complete the activity about the sequence of events leading to the end of the Republic.

CRITICAL THINKING QUESTIONS

1. What good and bad traits did Cicero possess? *(He was a master of oratory and the written word; he was honest and openly expressed his emotions. Cicero genuinely loved Rome and hoped to restore the Republic to health. However, he was also pompous and conceited and a snob.)*

2. How could Pompey start out being Cicero's friend, then become his enemy, and then be his friend again? *(Possible answer: Pompey was ambitious for power. He made alliances with people who could help him. Since Cicero opposed the First Triumvirate, Pompey could not be his friend. When Pompey once again needed Cicero's political skills, he helped recall Cicero from exile.)*

3. Was Cicero a success or a failure? Explain. *(Possible answer: Since he climbed to the top of the political ladder without being an "insider," and was recognized as a genius and master orator, he did succeed. However, he failed to accomplish his goal of saving the Republic.)*

SOCIAL SCIENCES

Civics   The Roman Republic fell when individual leaders tried to gain absolute political power for themselves. Have students use the chapter to write a paragraph discussing the disadvantages to citizens of living under an absolute ruler.

READING AND LANGUAGE ARTS

Reading Nonfiction   Have students evaluate the author's point of view about Cicero. Read this from page 71: "Perhaps he was in the right place at the wrong time. Generals, not orators, ruled Rome in the 1st century BCE." Ask students to find other evidence of the author's feelings toward Cicero.

Using Language   The chapter has many colloquialisms—expressions used in casual conversation: *looked down on, put across his ideas, join their club, against all odds, an old pro,* and others. Have partners find these expressions and use context clues to explain their meaning to each other.

SUPPORTING LEARNING

English Language Learners   Use Cicero's words on page 71 ("I defended the Republic . . .") to discuss figures of speech, or phrases that mean more than the definitions of the words. Elicit from students other figures of speech and their meanings.

Struggling Readers   Distribute the blackline master for Chapter 10 so students can review the sequence of events leading to the death of the Republic. Have them use this information to make their own cause and effect charts (see T-chart at the back of this guide).

EXTENDING LEARNING

Enrichment   Have students find copies of Cicero's works (or passionate American speeches) on the Internet or in books. (American speechmakers include Dr. Martin Luther King, Jr., John Kennedy, Franklin Roosevelt, and Sojourner Truth.) Students can practice excerpts from these speeches and present them to the class.

Extension   Read the excerpts from Cicero's speeches aloud expressively so that students can understand his passion.

WRITING

Letter Review the relationship between Pompey and Cicero. Ask students to summarize the feelings each man might have had toward the other in 57 BCE. Have students write a letter from the point of view of one of these men, addressed to the other, expressing how he feels.

LINKING DISCIPLINES

Art Have students sketch scenes from Cicero's life. Students can then tape the scenes together to make a storyboard.

THEN and NOW

Cicero rose through the political ranks after gaining renown as a lawyer. Today, many politicians begin their careers as attorneys. Discuss the reasons why this profession is a logical stepping stone to political office.

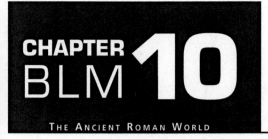

NAME _____   DATE _____

THE END OF THE ROMAN REPUBLIC

Directions

Read the list of events in the box. Then copy each event in the correct place on the flow chart below to show how they led to the end of the Roman Republic.

1. Triumvirate of Pompey, Julius Caesar, and Crassus rule Rome

2. Hunger and joblessness in Rome

3. Germans defeat Roman armies

4. Civil war among the generals

5. Poor people are recruited as soldiers

6. Soldiers become more loyal to their generals than to the Republic

7. German tribes move into Roman territory in Gaul

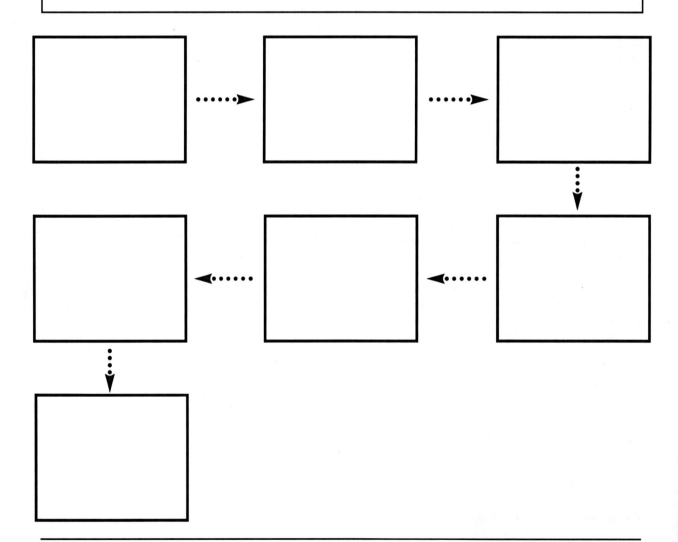

NAME   **DATE**

A. MULTIPLE CHOICE

Circle the letter of the best answer for each question.

1. When German tribes invaded Italy, the Romans defeated them by
   a. paying them tribute.
   b. recruiting poor men into the army.
   c. making patricians work harder.
   d. recruiting slaves into the army.

2. This strategy caused long-term problems for Rome because the new soldiers
   a. were loyal to a general, not Rome.
   b. were too untrained to be useful.
   c. would not fight for very long.
   d. did not know how to take orders.

3. Ruthless generals took advantage of this situation to try to gain power
   a. for the Republic.
   b. for the people.
   c. for themselves.
   d. for their soldiers.

4. By 60 BCE, a triumvirate of Romans had taken control of the government. These men were
   a. Cicero, Caesar, and Crassus.
   b. Cicero, Crassus, and Pompey.
   c. Caesar, Crassus, and Pompey.
   d. Pompey, Cicero, and Mark Antony.

5. What got Cicero in trouble with the powerful leaders?
   a. He wouldn't give them money.
   b. He tried to save the Republic by speaking out against them.
   c. He wanted to leave Rome.
   d. He wouldn't fight in the civil wars.

B. SHORT ANSWER

Write one or two sentences to answer each question.

6. What was Cicero best known for?

_____

_____

7. What were the important qualities of the leaders who formed the First Triumvirate?

_____

_____

8. Why did Cicero die a disappointed man?

_____

_____

C. ESSAY

About Cicero, the chapter says, "Perhaps he was in the right place at the wrong time." Use the information in the chapter to analyze this statement. Knowing what you do about Cicero, could he have done anything else? On a separate sheet of paper, write an essay telling your opinion of Cicero.

UNIT 4
CREATION OF THE ROMAN EMPIRE
PAGES 72-101

Chapter 11 "I Came, I Saw, I Conquered": Julius Caesar and the Roman Triumph

Chapter 12 Power-Mad or Madly in Love? Cleopatra, Queen of Egypt

Chapter 13 The Emperor's New Names: The Reign of Augustus

Chapter 14 Misery, Mistrust, Madness, and Murder: The Successors of Augustus

UNIT OBJECTIVES

Unit 4 covers events from the last years of the Roman Republic (about 60 BCE), through establishment of the Roman Empire and the Augustan dynasty, and up to the death of Domitian and the end of the second imperial dynasty in 96 CE. In this unit, your students will learn

► the change from republican to imperial style of government.
► the personalities and accomplishments of the first emperors of Rome.
► the life of the mysterious Cleopatra.
► the effects that individual emperors had on Rome.

PRIMARY SOURCES

Unit 4 includes excerpts from the following primary sources:

► Augustus, *My Achievements*
► Plutarch, *Life of Caesar*
► Plutarch, *Life of Antony*
► Suetonius, *Life of the Deified Julius*
► Suetonius, *Life of Augustus*
► Suetonius, *Life of Claudius*
► Suetonius, *Life of Tiberius*
► Suetonius, *Life of Caligula*
► Suetonius, *Life of Nero*
► Suetonius, *Life of Vespasian*
► Tacitus, *Life of Agricola*

Pictures of artifacts from the early Roman Empire can also be analyzed as primary sources. Students can use these pictures to draw conclusions about the personalities discussed in the book.

► Coin of Caesar
► Bust of Julius Caesar
► Bust of Cleopatra
► Statue of Egyptian goddess Isis
► Bust of Mark Antony
► Statue of Augustus
► Carving from Altar of Augustan Peace
► Coin of Altar of Peace
► Cameo of scenes from Tiberius's rule
► Bust of Caligula
► Coin of Nero

BIG IDEAS IN UNIT 4

Conflict, change, and **government** are the big ideas presented in Unit 4. The conflict in this unit is between Romans who supported the Republic and those who supported the Empire. The imperial form of government won out in this conflict, changing the power structure of Rome forever. Power, once in the hands of the citizens, was now controlled by one person—the emperor. This form of government maintained the Roman Empire throughout the rest of its existence. You may want to introduce these ideas by eliciting what your students know about our own national government—who has the ultimate power, who controls the day-to-day activities, who makes the laws, and so on.

GEOGRAPHY CONNECTION

In this time period, Roman power stretched from Spain in the west to Egypt and Syria in the east. Have students look at the map on page 95 to get an overview of the size of the empire. (Claudius's invasion of Britain is not shown.) Have students use the mileage scale to estimate the extent of the empire from east to west and north to south, and predict the challenges of ruling such a large area from a central location.

TIMELINE

60 BCE	First Triumvirate formed: Julius Caesar, Pompey, Crassus
58 BCE	Caesar begins conquest of Gaul
49 BCE	Caesar returns to Rome against wishes of the Senate
48 BCE	Caesar defeats Pompey; gains absolute power in Rome
44 BCE	Julius Caesar is murdered
43 BCE	Second Triumvirate formed: Octavian, Antony, Lepidus
42 BCE	Brutus and other conspirators defeated at Philippi
31 BCE	Mark Antony and Cleopatra defeated at Actium
27 BCE	Octavian becomes "Augustus"
2 BCE	Augustus named "Father of the Country"
14 CE	Death of Augustus; Tiberius becomes emperor
37 CE	Caligula becomes emperor
41 CE	Claudius becomes emperor
54 CE	Nero becomes emperor
69 CE	Augustan dynasty ends; Vespasian becomes emperor
79 CE	Titus becomes emperor
81 CE	Domitian becomes emperor

UNIT PROJECTS

Military History

Small groups of students can use print or online sources to investigate the military campaigns of Julius Caesar. Have them make a map of the Gallic campaigns indicating the years of the actions and the territories conquered.

Chronology

The events and relationships between people in this unit are very complex and are compressed into a relatively short span. Students can use the Cast of Characters in the front of their book to create a timeline showing which characters' lives overlapped each other. Have students draw a timeline in their books from 100 BCE to 100 CE. Below the timeline, they should draw the lifespans of the important people in the text.

Pharaohs

Small groups can report on the rule of the pharaohs in Egypt. Have them find out more about the role of the pharaoh, how the Egyptian government operated, and important rulers in the Ptolemaic line. Students can make a genealogical tree to show Cleopatra's ancestry.

Youthful Rulers

Cleopatra became pharaoh when she was 18; Augustus became a senator and was part of the Second Triumvirate at about the same age. Small groups can investigate other rulers who came to power at a young age throughout history. Examples include Queen Victoria of England, Catherine the Great of Russia, Louis XIV of France, and Tutankhamen of Egypt. Students should find out at what age they became rulers, whether someone else ruled the country for a time (regent), and how they ruled their countries. Groups can make bulletin board displays to show their work.

ADDITIONAL ASSESSMENT

For Unit 4, divide the class into groups and have them all undertake the Pharaohs project so you can assess their understanding of the influence of the Egyptian civilization on Rome. Use the scoring rubric at the back of this guide to assess students' work, and have students rate their own work with the self-assessment rubric.

LITERATURE CONNECTION

Two of the personalities in this unit—Caesar and Augustus—wrote autobiographical works that still survive. It will be interesting for your students to compare these personal accounts of events with the accounts given by Roman historians.

Students will also enjoy reading the following books that will extend their understanding of Rome during this period.

▶ Adkins, Lesley and Roy. *Handbook to Life in Ancient Rome.* New York: Oxford University Press, 1998. Nonfiction. ADVANCED
▶ Connolly, Peter. *Ancient Rome.* New York: Oxford Unversity Press, 2001. Nonfiction. EASY
▶ Coolidge, Olivia. *Caesar's Gallic War.* North Haven, CT: Linnet Books, 1991. Fiction. AVERAGE
▶ Nardo, Don. *Rulers of Ancient Rome (History Makers).* San Diego, CA: Lucent Books, 1999. Nonfiction. AVERAGE

UNIVERSAL ACCESS

The following activities are designed to cover a range of learning styles and reading, language, and skill levels.

Reading Strategies

▶ Have students use a K-W-L chart to assist them in their reading. Preview each chapter, and have students fill in the first column of the chart with what they *know* about the subject. Have them write what they *want to know* about the subject in the second column. When they are finished with the chapter, have them complete the third column by writing what they *learned*.

▶ There is a strong chronological component to this unit that you can use to help students organize their understanding of the material. As students read, have them outline their notes using the names of rulers as headings.

▸ Small groups can read the chapters together, with each member reading and taking notes about a different ruler. Groups should then come together, with each member orally summarizing his or her notes for the rest of the group.

Writing Strategies

▸ Have partners make a three-column chart with headings for each of the unit's big ideas. Partners should get together after reading each chapter to jot down their observations in each category.

▸ The lives of the personalities in this unit intertwine. Students can use a flowchart to show the relationship between them.

▸ The system of government established by Augustus served Rome for hundreds of years, but it had negative as well as positive aspects. Have students keep a two-column chart detailing these aspects of the empire as they read.

Listening and Speaking Strategies

▸ Point out the still photograph from the movie *Cleopatra* on page 83. Students may benefit from watching the movie at home—either with student partners or with their family members.

▸ Have students make masks of the personalities in this unit, using paper plates and craft sticks. Call on volunteers to come to the front of the class and tell facts about their chosen personalities while holding their masks in front of their faces.

UNIT VOCABULARY LIST

The following words that appear in Unit 4 are important for your students' understanding of the social studies content as well as for development of literacy. Use these words for vocabulary study or to reinforce language arts skills (e.g., synonyms, compound words, prefixes and suffixes, and related words). The words are listed below in the order in which they appear in the chapters.

Chapter 11	Chapter 12	Chapter 13	Chapter 14
bizarre	fluent	resolution	polio
omen	sibling	triumphal	sullen
soothsayer	smuggled	cutthroat	grudgingly
boundary	pacify	*triumvir*	malicious
legion	extravagant	decapitated	traitor
lieutenant	oblivious	landgrab	lenient
brine	undisputed	turmoil	grandeur
placard	Ptolemaic	network	thrifty
embankment	fatal	voluntarily	bankrupt
		proclaim	conspiracy

"I CAME, I SAW, I CONQUERED": JULIUS CAESAR AND THE ROMAN TRIUMPH   PAGES 72–78

CAST OF CHARACTERS

Julius Caesar (SEE-zer) brilliant general, consul, First Triumvirate member, dictator

Pompey (PAHM-pee) political rival of Caesar's

Brutus leader of senators who killed Caesar

Suetonius (swee-TOE-nee-us) 2nd-century CE biographer

 **VOCABULARY**

military having to do with armed forces and war

THEN and NOW

Caesar's achievements were so impressive that today his name represents the influence of Rome. All rulers of Rome after him took the name Caesar, and the name itself has become a synonym for *emperor* or *dictator*.

CHAPTER SUMMARY

Julius Caesar gained power through the political deal of the First Triumvirate. When the Triumvirate broke up, Caesar defeated Pompey in battle and took complete control of Rome's empire. As dictator, he passed many laws to improve life in Rome, but he made powerful enemies among the aristocrats. In 44 BCE, he was assassinated by these enemies, and Rome was plunged into a 13-year civil war that ended the Republic.

PERFORMANCE OBJECTIVES

▶ To chart Caesar's rise to power
▶ To describe the chaotic state of the Roman state in 44 BCE
▶ To explain what Caesar did for Rome as consul and dictator
▶ To understand why Caesar had enemies and why they killed him

BUILDING BACKGROUND

Have students tell what they think of when they hear the word *caesar*. Ask them to define *dictatorship* and name a country that is (or was recently) ruled by a dictator. Explain that they are going to read about one of the greatest rulers of Rome and the time of upheaval when he lived.

WORKING WITH PRIMARY SOURCES

Suetonius's most famous work is *The Lives of the Caesars*, biographies of Julius Caesar and the first eleven Roman emperors. Suetonius was a careful, accurate historian who was roughly contemporaneous with his subjects. His work is available in English translation and can be used by students.

GEOGRAPHY CONNECTION

Regions   Distribute the blackline master for Chapter 11, and have students study the map of Gaul. Ask them to describe the size of Gaul, and the large number of tribes that lived there. Explain that this is the region that Julius Caesar spent almost a decade conquering.

READING COMPREHENSION QUESTIONS

1. What benefits did Julius Caesar gain from the First Triumvirate? (*Caesar became consul, and then governor of Gaul, which made him rich and popular.*)
2. Why did the Senate declare Caesar an enemy of the state in 49 BCE? (*The senators and aristocrats were worried by Caesar's wealth, power, popularity, and intentions to take land from the rich and give it to the poor.*)
3. How did Caesar respond to this declaration? (*He marched on Rome with his army, defeated his enemy Pompey, and took control of the Roman government.*)
4. While he was dictator, what did Caesar accomplish? (*controlled the state's debt, reduced unemployment, boosted the economy, employed people in building projects, revised the calendar, built embankments to protect the city against floods*)
5. Distribute copies of the blackline master for Chapter 11 so students can learn more about Caesar's exploits in Gaul.

CRITICAL THINKING QUESTIONS

1. Were Caesar's enemies right to be suspicious of him? (*Possible answer: Caesar's ambition made him a danger to his enemies, as did his support of the Gracchi reforms. However, he made Rome a better, more powerful state during his reign as dictator.*)

2. Why do you suppose Caesar reached out to the Senate and pardoned his enemies after he returned to Rome? (*He saw that the government was in chaos and knew that civil war damages a nation. It was most important to restore order to Rome and heal the wounds of war.*)

3. The author calls Julius Caesar "perhaps the most extraordinary of all ancient Romans." Why, then, was he assassinated by those who were close to him? (*Caesar was changing the government of Rome. His assassins thought that they could save the Republic by killing him.*)

SOCIAL SCIENCES

Civics   Have students compare and contrast the Roman government in the time of Caesar and the government in the United States. Students should contrast how the head of the government was changed in Caesar's time with how it is changed in the United States now.

READING AND LANGUAGE ARTS

Reading Nonfiction   Have students draw a timeline of Caesar's life as recounted in the chapter. Then have them summarize the events in their own words using time-order clues such as *next, then, the next year,* and so on.

Using Language   The following phrases became part of our language because of Caesar: "I came, I saw, I conquered"; "You, too, Brutus?"; "crossing the Rubicon"; "The die is cast"; "Beware the Ides of March!" Have students write short scenes that illustrate the meaning of these phrases.

SUPPORTING LEARNING

English Language Learners   Review the common English expressions that stem from Caesar and the events of his life. Have students list common expressions from their first languages and explain their meaning in English.

Struggling Readers   Have students complete a two-column chart about the reign of Julius Caesar with the column headings *Positive for the Republic* and *Negative for the Republic.*

EXTENDING LEARNING

Enrichment   Point students to Shakespeare's play *Julius Caesar,* especially Brutus's speech after killing Caesar (Act III, Scene 2), and Mark Antony's response. Have students respond to both speeches.

Extension   Have small groups of students write skits involving Caesar and other Romans, such as Pompey, Crassus, and Brutus. The skits should explain why the other Romans supported or opposed Caesar, what they tried to do, how Caesar responded, and how the outcome affected Rome.

WRITING

Analysis
How would Caesar have fared as a politician in the modern United States? Have students write a paragraph evaluating Caesar's appeal to the masses and his chances for election to high office.

LINKING DISCIPLINES

Math Review the sidebar on page 75. Have students write and count through 20 using Roman numerals. Then ask them to write five problems, including simple addition, subtraction, multiplication, and division, using Roman numerals instead of Arabic numerals. Students can exchange papers and solve the problems.

JULIUS CAESAR IN GAUL

Directions

With a partner, read the following excerpts from Julius Caesar's *The Conquest of Gaul* (52 BCE). Then answer the questions 2–5 on a separate sheet of paper.

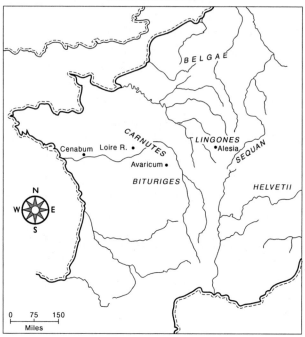

Caesar in Gaul 52 BCE

Caesar reached Cenabum in the territory of the Carnutes in two days, but by the time he had set up camp in front of the town, it was too late to attack that day. But there was a bridge over the Loire River right under the town walls, and he was afraid that the people who lived in Cenabum might escape under cover of night. So he ordered two legions to remain under arms all night.

Shortly before midnight the people of Cenabum moved silently out of the town and began to cross the river. Informed of this by his scouts, Caesar set the gates [in the wall] on fire and sent the legions he had kept ready for action into the town. The town was captured, all but a very few of the enemy were taken prisoner—for the narrow streets and bridge were blocked by the crowd of fugitives. After plundering and burning Cenabum, and distributing among his soldiers the prizes and prisoners, Caesar marched across the Loire into the territories of the Bituriges. . . .

[When Caesar was attacking Avericum, a fortified town in the territory of the Bituriges, his army ran short of food.] For several days the troops had no grain and saved themselves from starvation only by bringing in cattle from distant villages. Yet they did not say a word that was unworthy of Roman soldiers. . . . Indeed when Caesar addressed the men of each legion, at their work, and told them that if they found the lack of food unbearable he would abandon the siege, they begged him not to do so, saying they had served under him for many years without suffering any humiliation. . . . They would feel it a humiliation to abandon the siege now. . . .

When Caesar saw that his men were weakening and running short of weapons, he sent Labienus to their relief. . . . [Then] Caesar himself visited other parts of the lines, urging the men to hold out. . . . Finally as the struggle grew fiercer, he personally led a fresh detachment of men into battle. . . .

The enemy knew Caesar was coming by the scarlet cloak which he always wore in action to mark his identity; and when they saw the cavalry . . . and the cohorts following him . . . they joined battle. . . . The Romans dropped their spears and fought with their swords. . . . Suddenly the Gauls . . . broke and fled, but found their retreat cut off by the cavalry and were cut down. . . . If the Romans had not been tired after a long day's work . . . the enemy's army might have been annihilated. As it was, a large number were taken or killed by the cavalry.

1. On the map, trace the movements of Caesar and his army. Draw a symbol (swords, helmet, etc.) to show where fighting took place.

2. Caesar wrote about himself in the third person. How did that make it easier for him to praise himself? Give an example of such praise.

3. How did Caesar treat civilians in the cities and towns he attacked?

4. What example does Caesar give to show how loyal and dedicated his soldiers were?

5. Was Caesar an effective leader? Give details to support your opinion.

NAME   **DATE**

A. MULTIPLE CHOICE

Circle the letter of the best answer to each question.

1. Who were Julius Caesar's greatest supporters?
   a. senators   c. the Triumvirate
   b. plebeians   d. patricians

2. Which of the following is **not** a reason why the Senate declared Caesar an enemy of the state?
   a. Caesar's enemies were jealous of his wealth and fame.
   b. Caesar favored the Gracchi's plan to give land to the poor.
   c. Caesar had invaded Italy with his army.
   d. The bond between Pompey and Caesar had been broken.

3. What was the result of the civil war that Caesar started by returning to Rome?
   a. death of Caesar   c. destruction of Rome
   b. destruction of the Republic   d. death of all the senators

4. During the four years after he defeated his rivals, Caesar
   a. ruled as a tyrant.   c. was constantly at war.
   b. made improvements to Rome's   d. lived in Gaul.
   government and economy.

5. Caesar was assassinated by
   a. senators who believed they were   c. his own troops.
   saving the Republic.
   b. a soothsayer.   d. his own brother.

B. SHORT ANSWER

Write one or two sentences to answer each question.

6. Why was Julius Caesar the plebeians' favorite politician?

_____

_____

7. What benefit did Julius Caesar get from joining the First Triumvirate?

_____

_____

8. Why did Julius Caesar support Cleopatra instead of Ptolemy XIII in Egypt?

_____

_____

C. ESSAY

Write an essay on a separate sheet of paper answering this question: Was Julius Caesar a great Roman leader or a terrible Roman tyrant? Use details from the chapter to support your opinion.

CAST OF CHARACTERS

Cleopatra mysterious 1st-century BCE pharaoh of Egypt; made alliances with Caesar and Mark Antony

Caesarion (see-ZAIR-ee-un) Cleopatra's son by Julius Caesar.

Mark Antony partner, then enemy, of Octavian after Caesar's death

Octavia sister of Octavian; married to Mark Antony

Octavian Caesar's heir; avenged his death, then gained control of Rome

Ptolemy I (TALL-uh-me) first Macedonian king of Egypt

Ptolemy XIII (TALL-uh-me) Cleopatra's brother and consort

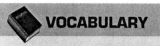

VOCABULARY

consort ruler's husband or wife

CHAPTER SUMMARY

The story of Cleopatra still fascinates. She was charming, intelligent, and wily. She brought under her influence some of the most powerful people of her time, including Julius Caesar and Mark Antony, and used her skills to keep control of Egypt despite facing dangerous foes. When she died, it marked the end of the 250-year reign of the Ptolemies in Egypt.

PERFORMANCE OBJECTIVES

▶ To understand the traditions of the pharaohs
▶ To relate people and events in the civil wars that followed Caesar's assassination
▶ To describe Cleopatra's appeal and power

BUILDING BACKGROUND

Ask students to list qualities for which Cleopatra is remembered today. Read Plutarch's quote about her on page 80: "The charm of her presence was irresistible. . . . Everyone who met her fell under her spell." Discuss that although Cleopatra may not have been physically beautiful, her character must have made her seem beautiful.

WORKING WITH PRIMARY SOURCES

Plutarch's *Life of Antony* is the main primary source used in this chapter. Have students use the Internet or the library to read longer sections of this source about Cleopatra. Have them compare Plutarch's words with the images of Cleopatra shown in the chapter.

GEOGRAPHY CONNECTION

Have students turn to the map of the Ancient Roman World at the front of their books. As they read the chapter, have them identify journeys Cleopatra made across the Mediterranean world (Egypt to Syria, Egypt to Rome, Egypt to Actium). Have them use the map scale to find out how far those journeys would have been by sea and by land.

READING COMPREHENSION QUESTIONS

1. When and why did Cleopatra inherit the kingdom of Egypt? (*In 51 BCE, when her father died; she had long been his favorite, and he had proclaimed her a goddess when she was four.*)
2. Why did Caesar support Cleopatra rather than Ptolemy XIII? (*She had become his lover, while Ptolemy had outraged him by murdering Pompey.*)
3. Where and how did Cleopatra and Antony meet? (*In Tarsus; Cleopatra sailed upriver to meet him in a grand procession, flaunting wealth and her power in order to seduce Antony.*)

4. In what ways was Cleopatra a typical ruler of Egypt? In what ways was she unusual? *(She married two brothers to co-rule, and she was ruthless in her quest for control of the throne; unlike her ancestors, she learned Egyptian, and she used her personal powers of charm and intelligence to manipulate others.)*

5. Distribute copies of the blackline master for Chapter 12 so students can trace the major events of Cleopatra's life.

CRITICAL THINKING QUESTIONS

1. What do Cleopatra's actions when Caesar first arrived in Alexandria tell about her character? *(She intelligently and decisively put together a plan of action that required bravery and secrecy. She artfully got Caesar to support her against her brother.)*

2. Do you think love or politics governed Mark Antony and Cleopatra's relationship? Why? *(Possible answer: Cleopatra seems always to have had power uppermost in mind, and Antony was sometimes guided by his heart and sometimes by his head. However, in their first years together, both seemed to be in love.)*

SOCIAL SCIENCES

Economy   The text says that when Cleopatra returned to Egypt after Julius Caesar died, the country was weakened by drought and poor harvests. Have students investigate what the economy of ancient Egypt was based on.

READING AND LANGUAGE ARTS

Reading Nonfiction

Using Language   Review the passages on page 82 that describe Cleopatra's dramatic style. Have students analyze the descriptions to discover what kinds of words create vivid images.

SUPPORTING LEARNING

English Language Learners   Since this chapter has a strong chronological component, you can use it to help students recognize time-order words. Have students identify the words and tell whether they indicate that something happened before, at the same time as, or after something else.

Struggling Readers   Have students use a two-column chart with the headings *Allies* and *Opponents* to document the important people in Cleopatra's life. Students should give a brief description of each person's relationship to Cleopatra.

EXTENDING LEARNING

Enrichment   Have partners create a "family tree" showing Cleopatra's family and friends. Students should use symbols to indicate each person's relationship to Cleopatra and if the relationship was broken, and a key explaining the symbols.

Extension   Have small groups dramatize one of the episodes of Cleopatra's life detailed in the chapter. One student should narrate the scene, while the others act it out with appropriate dialogue.

WRITING

Description Have students write a paragraph describing a colorful, dramatic event they have seen, such as the opening of the Olympic Games or a parade. Remind them that exact, concrete language and strong action verbs can strengthen their descriptions.

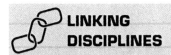

LINKING DISCIPLINES

Science Students can investigate the asp, or Egyptian cobra. They can draw pictures of the snake, explain how its neurotoxic venom works, show the snake's range in the wild, and explain its connections with ancient Egyptian rulers.

THEN and NOW

Royal marriage in ancient Egypt was inspired by business and politics, not love. Today, few nations are ruled by monarchs. However, their marriages are still of great public interest.

THE LIFE OF CLEOPATRA

Directions

Place the following details from Cleopatra's life in the correct order on the timeline.

Octavian declares war on Mark Antony and Cleopatra.

Cleopatra meets Mark Antony at Tarsus.

Mark Antony returns to Cleopatra in Egypt.

Octavian defeats Mark Antony at Actium.

Cleopatra becomes co-ruler of Egypt at age 18.

Julius Caesar comes to Egypt; puts Cleopatra back on throne.

Cleopatra gives birth to Mark Antony's children.

Plot to overthrow Cleopatra; she escapes to Syria.

Julius Caesar is assassinated; Cleopatra returns to Egypt.

Mark Antony's troops desert at Alexandria.

Cleopatra returns to Rome with Julius Caesar; son Caesarion is born.

Mark Antony dies in Cleopatra's arms; Cleopatra commits suicide.

A. MULTIPLE CHOICE

Circle the letter of the best answer to each question.

1. Which of the following does **not** describe Cleopatra?
   a. She could speak nine languages.
   b. She was proclaimed a goddess.
   c. She was irresistibly charming.
   d. She could not speak Egyptian.

2. Which of these people was Cleopatra's consort?
   a. Mark Antony
   b. Julius Caesar
   c. Ptolemy XIII
   d. Octavian

3. What strategy did Cleopatra seem to depend on to help improve Egypt?
   a. use prisoners to rebuild the country
   b. tax the people heavily to fund improvements
   c. make alliances with whoever was in power in Rome
   d. conquer new lands in Asia

4. Which event best shows Cleopatra's ability to scheme politically?
   a. coming back to Egypt from Syria and forming an alliance with Caesar
   b. marrying her brother, Ptolemy XIV, who became her second consort
   c. going back to Rome with Caesar
   d. sailing away from the decisive battle of Actium

5. Why did Cleopatra decide to end her own life?
   a. She could not make Octavian fall in love with her; he was going to make her a slave.
   b. Her greatest love, Mark Antony, had killed himself.
   c. She thought that by taking her life, she would save the life of her son, Caesarion.
   d. It was the only way for a pharaoh to die without being disgraced.

B. SHORT ANSWER

Write one or two sentences to answer each question.

6. What character traits set Cleopatra apart from the other Egyptian rulers in her dynasty?

   _____

   _____

7. Why did Cleopatra have to flee from Rome when Julius Caesar was assassinated?

   _____

   _____

8. Why did Cleopatra try to influence the rulers of Rome?

   _____

   _____

C. ESSAY

On a separate sheet of paper, write an essay telling your opinion of Cleopatra's skill as a diplomat. Support your opinion with details from the chapter.

THE EMPEROR'S NEW NAMES: THE REIGN OF AUGUSTUS

PAGES 87–93

CAST OF CHARACTERS

Augustus Caesar Octavian, first emperor of Rome; reigned 41 years; established *Pax Romana*

Horace 1st-century BCE lyric poet

Lepidus member of Second Triumvirate with Antony and Octavian

Tiberius Augustus's stepson and heir

Virgil 1st-century BCE poet who wrote the *Aeneid*

 VOCABULARY

legitimate legal; said of a child born to a married father and mother

conspirator secret plotter

confiscate seize by authority of the government

CHAPTER SUMMARY

Augustus was 18 years old when Julius Caesar, his adoptive father, was assassinated. Already a general, he formed the Second Triumvirate with Mark Antony and Lepidus in order to defeat Caesar's assassins. Augustus then defeated Antony, becoming master of the Roman world when he was 33. He reigned as emperor for 41 years, brought peace after years of civil war, reorganized the empire, built roads, and sponsored the arts.

PERFORMANCE OBJECTIVES

▶ To list the ways in which Augustus improved Rome and life for Romans
▶ To follow the sequence of events through which Augustus rose to rule
▶ To analyze Augustus's style of ruling

BUILDING BACKGROUND

Invite students to name teenagers who have been thrust into the public spotlight. Discuss the pros and cons of gaining fame or responsibility at an early age. Tell students this chapter tells about someone who assumed a critical political role while still a teenager.

WORKING WITH PRIMARY SOURCES

Distribute the blackline master for Chapter 13 so that students can read more of what Augustus wrote about himself. Have students complete the master.

GEOGRAPHY CONNECTION

Regions   Have students look at the map on page 95. Ask: What natural boundary did the empire have on the north? (*Danube River*) Elicit that in Africa and Syria, the natural boundaries of the empire were deserts.

READING COMPREHENSION QUESTIONS

1. What was the relationship between Julius Caesar and Octavius? How did it change on Caesar's death? (*Octavius was a grand-nephew and the favorite of Caesar, who believed the young man would accomplish much. In his will, Caesar adopted Octavius and left him a fortune.*)

2. What problems did Octavian have to overcome at the beginning of the *Pax Romana*? (*The government was a mess. Enemies on the frontiers were rebelling. He had to root out corruption in the Senate. Hundreds of senators had died in the civil wars.*)

3. How did Augustus make Rome a better place? (*created the empire; started first fire and police brigade; improved finances; gave free food to the poor; built the Forum; beautified the city; sponsored artists and poets*)

4. How did Augustus hold on to his authority and safeguard his life? (*He allowed freedom of speech and encouraged advice, and shared power with the magistrates. However, the magistrates were loyal to him alone. He also kept members of the Praetorian Guard on hand at all times and had them search any senator who came to see him.*)

CRITICAL THINKING QUESTIONS

1. Was Julius Caesar's opinion of Octavius justified? Explain. (*Possible answer: Yes: Caesar believed Octavius would do great things for Rome, and he did. Octavius brought peace, reorganized the government, and improved public safety, roads, finances, and the lives of the people.*)

2. How did Octavius manage to control the Senate and reform it while keeping it on his side? (*He replaced senators who had died with loyal, able men from Rome and other Italian cities; he avoided taking the title of king.*)

3. Why do you suppose Augustus reigned for 41 years whereas his great-uncle Caesar reigned only 4 years? (*Augustus defeated all his major enemies, while Caesar's enemies were all around him. Augustus learned that politicians are jealous of power and popularity, and so created the impression that he was not ruling Rome alone. As consul, Caesar did not listen to others' advice. Augustus kept the Praetorian Guard to protect him, whereas Caesar did not use bodyguards.*)

SOCIAL SCIENCES

Economics   Have students trace the map of the Roman Empire on page 95, and then draw roads connecting Rome with the other major cities. Have students infer how the roads Augustus built helped the economy of the empire. (*Building the roads gave people jobs. Farmers could move their goods to market easier. Traders could travel throughout the empire. The army could travel to distant places and enforce Roman laws and tax collecting.*)

READING AND LANGUAGE ARTS

Reading Nonfiction   Give students examples of cause-and-effect statements: *Because Octavian confiscated land to give to retired soldiers, Antony's wife and brother led a rebellion against Octavian.* Have partners review the chapter. One partner should write down the cause part of a sentence; the other partner should complete the sentence with the effect.

Using Language   Horace wrote odes, a form of lyric poem on a single subject that was both dignified and imaginative. Read an ode to students (John Keats's "Ode to a Nightingale" or "Ode on a Grecian Urn"). Have students write their own odes. Refer students to the excerpt from Horace's *Satires* in *The World in Ancient Times Primary Sources and Reference Volume*.

SUPPORTING LEARNING

English Language Learners   In a small group, talk about the different names of Augustus through his life. Then have students tell about their own names: their meanings, their family significance, or other interesting anecdotes.

Struggling Readers   Have students create a timeline of Augustus's life. They should show his disappointments as well as his accomplishments.

EXTENDING LEARNING

Enrichment   Have students investigate the Roman roads built by Augustus, and draw a labeled diagram showing how they were constructed. One useful website is *www.unrv.com/culture/roman-roads.php*.

Extension   Have partners read passages of the text to each other so they understand the details. Have partners ask each other questions about the reading.

WRITING

Evaluating Primary Sources Distribute copies of the blackline master for Chapter 13. Have students read the selections about Augustus's reign and write a paragraph evaluating the emperor's opinion of his actions and ruling style.

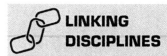

LINKING DISCIPLINES

Art Discuss what symbols would be appropriate for a modern altar of peace. Have students draw a design for such an altar.

THEN and NOW

The leaders of countries still face danger from enemies. Augustus used his Praetorian Guard to safeguard his life. Elicit from students who protects the President of the United States. *[the Secret Service]*

EVALUATING THE REIGN OF AUGUSTUS

Directions

In a small group, read the selection from Augustus's autobiography, *The Achievements of the Divine Augustus (Res Gestae)*, and the comments of the Roman historians Tacitus and Suetonius. Then on a separate sheet of paper, write a paragraph summarizing Augustus's achievements. State whether you agree with Augustus's evaluation of himself, and explain why.

Augustus

I undertook many civil and foreign wars by land and sea throughout the world, and as victor I spared the lives of all citizens who asked for mercy. When foreign peoples could safely be pardoned I preferred to preserve rather than to exterminate them. . . . I paid monetary rewards to soldiers whom I settled in their home towns after completion of their service. . . . I extended the territory of all those provinces of the Roman people on whose borders lay peoples not subject to our government. . . . I added Egypt to the rule of the Roman people. . . . In my sixth and seventh consulships, after I had extinguished civil wars, and at a time when with universal consent I was in complete control of affairs, I transferred the republic from my power to the dominion of the Senate and people of Rome. For this service of mine I was named Augustus by decree of the Senate . . . .

Tacitus

Octavian [Augustus] . . . took off the name of *triumvir* and put on that of consul, and . . . seduced the army with gifts, the general populace with free grain, and everyone with the lure of relaxation after the toils of civil war. Gradually he began to increase his power, taking to himself the functions of the Senate, of the magistrates, and of the laws. No one opposed him: his fiercest enemies had died, . . . while the rest of the *nobiles* were rewarded with riches and offices in direct proportion to their readiness to display a fawning servility. . . . Nor did the provinces object to this new state of affairs, since they had grown suspicious of the authority of the Senate and the people, due to the fierce rivalries of Rome's generals and the greed of her magistrates; furthermore, they felt that no aid was to obtained by recourse to the laws, which had been thrown into confusion by violence, political ambition, and (finally) money.

Suetonius

Nor was he moderate in victory [after the battle at Philippi], but, having sent the head of Brutus to Rome to be thrown at the foot of Caesar's statue, he vented his rage savagely against all the most distinguished of his captives, not omitting verbal abuse. When Perusia had been captured he punished many, answering those who tried to beg for mercy or who sought to make excuses for their actions with one phrase: "It is time to die." . . . He displayed his munificence to all ranks of the people on various occasions. Moreover, upon his bringing the treasure belonging to the kings of Egypt into the city, in his Alexandrian triumph, he made money so plentiful, that interest fell, and the price of land rose considerably. . . . He often made donations to the people . . . In a scarcity of grain, he would frequently let them have it at a very low price, or none at all. . . .

NAME   **DATE**

A. MULTIPLE CHOICE

Circle the letter of the best answer for each question.

1. When Augustus was 18 years old, he had to
  a. finish college.
  b. fight for control of the empire.
  c. live with his mother.
  d. learn military skills.

2. After Octavian and Antony became allies, their mission was to
  a. hunt down the conspirators who had killed Caesar.
  b. drive Lepidus out of Rome.
  c. restore republican government.
  d. find a successor to Caesar.

3. Although Rome was at peace, what major task faced Augustus?
  a. Rome's government and economy needed to be rebuilt.
  b. He needed to have a son so he could start a dynasty.
  c. He had to persuade the Senate to declare Julius Caesar a god.
  d. Rome needed to find new enemies to conquer.

4. What was the key to Augustus's long grip on power?
  a. He was not afraid to use the army against conspirators.
  b. He had many spies among all groups of people.
  c. He knew how to use power without seeming to seek it.
  d. He was too wealthy for anyone to attempt to bribe him.

5. Augustus participated in the destruction of the Republic, but he saved Rome. How did he do this?
  a. He became known as the father of his country.
  b. He strengthened the armies.
  c. He named Tiberius to be his successor.
  d. He turned the government into a system ruled by emperors.

B. SHORT ANSWER

Write one or two sentences to answer each question.

6. How did Augustus ensure that his troops remained loyal to him?

_____

_____

7. How did Augustus celebrate the beginning of the *Pax Romana*?

_____

_____

8. What seems to have been the only issue Augustus could not solve during his long reign?

_____

_____

C. ESSAY

Augustus can be described using three adjectives: *sharing*, *careful*, and *hard-working*. Write an essay on a separate sheet of paper explaining why each of these character traits applies to Augustus.

CHAPTER 14

MISERY, MISTRUST, MADNESS, AND MURDER: THE SUCCESSORS OF AUGUSTUS

PAGES 94–102

CAST OF CHARACTERS

Tiberius, Caligula, Claudius, Nero tyrannical emperors who followed Augustus

Agrippina (AG-ri-PEE-nuh) wife of Claudius, whom she poisoned

Vespasian (vuh-SPAY-zhun) ended civil wars in 69 CE; restored good government to empire (69–79 CE)

Titus emperor who continued Vespasian's reforms (79–81 CE)

Domitian (duh-MISH-un) tyrant who brought reign of fear to Rome (81–96 CE)

THEN and NOW

In ancient cultures, being left-handed was a curse: at the least it was unlucky; at the worst, it suggested evil. Today, scientists theorize that left-handedness results from a genetic factor.

CHAPTER SUMMARY

Just as Augustus illustrates the best result of a strong emperor, the rulers in this chapter illustrate the worst result of allowing absolute rule by one person. Have students read to learn of the problems Rome had under the successors of Augustus.

PERFORMANCE OBJECTIVES

► To identify the six emperors who followed Augustus
► To describe abuses of power and failures of government in these reigns
► To compare and contrast the characteristics of these emperors

BUILDING BACKGROUND

Introduce and have students discuss the meaning of the saying "Power corrupts; absolute power corrupts absolutely."

WORKING WITH PRIMARY SOURCES

Distribute the blackline master for Chapter 14. Have students read Tacitus's report of a speech by Claudius, and then answer the questions.

When discussing the reign of Claudius, refer students to what the primary sources say about him. Elicit that physical impairment does not have to hold a person back from great achievements.

GEOGRAPHY CONNECTION

Have students look at the map on page 95. Have them compare how much larger the Roman Empire was at Augustus's death than it was at Caesar's death (map, page 60). Talk about the reasons behind the expansion.

READING COMPREHENSION QUESTIONS

1. Why was Augustus reluctant to put Tiberius on the throne? (*Tiberius had some personal oddities and was left-handed. He was also sullen and quiet—not a good combination for a ruler.*)
2. How did Caligula change during his reign? (*He went mad and murdered indiscriminately. He married three of his sisters and tried to name his horse as consul.*)
3. How did Claudius come to be emperor? (*Caligula had not murdered him because no one thought Claudius was capable of ruling. He was the one imperial family member left alive when Caligula was killed.*)
4. What traits characterized the emperor Vespasian? (*goodness, practicality, thrift*)

CRITICAL THINKING QUESTIONS

1. Considering the dynasty started by Augustus, what conclusions can you draw about hereditary rule when the ruler has absolute power? (*Possible answers: It takes an extraordinary person to rule fairly and well and not be corrupted by the position's power. Hereditary rule is not the best way to fill the position of emperor. Other people around the emperor are always scheming to advance themselves or their relatives.*)

2. How was Vespasian able to end the abuse of the emperor's position? Did he solve all the ills of power? (*Vespasian was not of Augustus's family, and so was not part of the corruption of that group. He was a good, able ruler. Having the support of the army and not being connected to Augustus allowed him to reform the empire. However, because the position was still hereditary, the brutal Domitian came to the throne because he was a son of Vespasian.*)

SOCIAL SCIENCES

Economics   Review the reigns of Nero and Vespasian. Ask students to explain why the economy of Rome suffered under the former and thrived under the latter.

READING AND LANGUAGE ARTS

Reading Nonfiction   Have students look at the map on page 95. Then explain that natural borders are based on natural features: rivers, oceans, mountain ranges. Have students identify the natural borders that the Roman Empire had at this point.

Using Language   Refer students to the sidebars to understand the histories of the words *successor, sinister, dexterous,* and *palace.* Have them use a dictionary to learn the etymologies of *theory, acclaim,* and *emperor.*

SUPPORTING LEARNING

English Language Learners   In small groups, have students read sections of the text to each other and take notes.

Struggling Readers   As students read the chapter, have them make a two-column chart of each emperor's achievements and shortcomings.

EXTENDING LEARNING

Enrichment   Have students investigate Claudius's reign to see how he expanded the empire into Britain and other areas. Students can start their research at the Illustrated History of the Roman Empire website listed on the Websites page of their book: *www.roman-empire.net.*

Extension   Have volunteers act out the characteristics of the emperors who followed Augustus.

WRITING

Persuasion Ask students to write an essay to convince others which Roman emperor after Augustus was the best. Inform students that they will need to state their opinion clearly, provide evidence, and explain how it supports the opinion.

VOCABULARY

successor person who follows another person in an official post

palace emperor's mansion

LINKING DISCIPLINES

Science Caligula's madness was probably the result of brain disease. Ask students to find articles or books that explain some of the organic causes for mental illness. Have them suggest how Caligula might be treated today.

NAME DATE

THE SUCCESSORS OF AUGUSTUS

Directions

Use the following chart to summarize the positive and negative accomplishments of the emperors who followed Augustus.

Emperor	Positive Accomplishments	Negative Accomplishments
Tiberius		
Caligula		
Claudius		
Nero		
Vespasian		
Titus		
Domitian		

NAME   **DATE**

A. MULTIPLE CHOICE

Circle the letter of the best answer for each question.

1. Tiberius allowed Romans free speech and increased the treasury, but at the end of his reign no one felt safe because of his
   a. guards.   **c.** tax collectors.
   b. suspicions.   **d.** wife.

2. Scholars believe that Caligula turned into a monster because of
   a. a brain disease.   **c.** poison.
   b. jealousy of other people's power.   **d.** the pressure of being emperor.

3. Claudius's accomplishments included all of the following **except**
   a. a history of the Etruscans.   **c.** giving citizenship to citizens of the provinces.
   b. establishing a strong system of government.   **d.** making a wise choice in wives.

4. Nero is remembered mostly for
   a. attacking government corruption.   **c.** making careful legal decisions.
   b. returning power to the Senate.   **d.** playing the lyre while Rome burned.

5. Vespasian was different from the emperors who preceded him because
   a. he was not a member of the Augustan family, and could establish his own ruling style.
   b. he didn't care about expanding the empire.
   c. he never played an instrument.
   d. he treated the people unfairly.

B. SHORT ANSWER

Write one or two sentences to answer each question.

6. What were the good and bad qualities of the reign of Tiberius?

   _____

   _____

7. How was Nero replaced as emperor?

   _____

   _____

8. Why did Vespasian's dynasty end with his sons?

   _____

   _____

C. ESSAY

On a separate sheet of paper, write an essay telling which of the emperors who followed Augustus was the best, and which was the worst. Support your opinion with details from the chapter.

LIFE IN THE ROMAN EMPIRE

PAGES 102-120

Chapter 15 Childhood and Marriage, Mothers and Matriarchs: Women and Children

Chapter 16 A City Tells Its Tale: Pompeii and the Roman House

Chapter 17 All the Emperor's Men: Trajan and the Army

UNIT OBJECTIVES

Unit 5 explores life in the Roman Empire in the 1st century CE. It details family life, activities in Roman towns, and the military life. In this unit, your students will learn

- ▶ what childhood was like in Rome.
- ▶ the roles of common and aristocratic women.
- ▶ what the archaeological record of Pompeii tells us about Roman life.
- ▶ how the efficient Roman army conquered and protected such a large territory with such a small number of troops.

PRIMARY SOURCES

Unit 5 includes excerpts from the following primary sources:

- ▶ Pliny the Younger, *Letters*
- ▶ Pliny the Younger, *Panegyricus*
- ▶ Valerius Maximus, *Memorable Deeds and Words*
- ▶ Catullus, *Poems*
- ▶ Horace, *Epistles*
- ▶ Suetonius, *A Book About Schoolteachers*
- ▶ Juvenal, *Satires*
- ▶ Josephus, *The Jewish War*
- ▶ Cassius Dio, *Roman History*

Pictures of artifacts from this period can also be analyzed as primary sources. Students can use these pictures to draw conclusions about Roman life.

- ▶ Mosaic of young girl, Pompeii
- ▶ Roman toys
- ▶ Portable stove
- ▶ Relief sculpture of butcher shop
- ▶ Remains of Pompeiian man
- ▶ Mosaic of dog, Pompeii
- ▶ Statue of legionary soldier
- ▶ Trajan's Column
- ▶ Mosaic of legionary soldier

BIG IDEAS IN UNIT 5

Lifestyle is the big idea of Unit 5. These chapters concentrate on the lives of three groups of people who are not often featured in histories of the ancient world: women (including girls), the common people, and soldiers.

You may want to introduce this idea by first commenting that information about the lives of certain people in Rome has so far been missing from your study. Ask students who these people might be. Elicit that the lives of common people are often overlooked in histories of the ancient world because much of the work of ancient historians concentrated on rulers and other famous people. What we know about common people often comes from other sources—archaeological evidence, poetry, letters, inscriptions on tombstones.

GEOGRAPHY CONNECTION

In this time period, the Roman Empire reached about its greatest extent. Have students compare the map on page 115 with previous maps of the empire (pages 60 and 95). Help students understand that another way to look at the growth of the empire is how many large cities were under its rule at each time. Show the locations of these cities and why they are located in these areas.

TIMELINE

29 CE	Death of Livia, Augustus's wife
66 CE	Roman war against the Jews
79 CE	Mt. Vesuvius erupts, burying Pompeii and Herculaneum
96 CE	Nerva becomes emperor
98 CE	Trajan becomes emperor
212 CE	Julia Domna, mother of the emperor Caracalla, runs Roman government
222 CE	Julia Mammaea, mother of the emperor Alexander, rules Rome

UNIT PROJECTS

Chronology

The chapters of this unit are less concerned with events than with conditions of life in Rome. Express to students that reading these chapters is like looking at the history of Rome with a magnifying glass and seeing the details of life in a particular year. You might choose 79 CE as the year for Chapters 15 and 16, and 98 CE as the year for Chapter 17. You can also relate these chapters to Chapters 7 and 8, which also concentrated on life in Rome.

Roman Water Supply

Rome had public baths because the Romans had engineered aqueducts to bring a continuous supply of fresh water from the mountains to the city. Have students explore the science behind aqueducts. What principles of physics made it possible to transport water this way? Students can draw diagrams explaining the workings of the aqueducts and display them on the bulletin board.

Roman Schools

Have small groups investigate the way that teachers ran their schools. Students may wish to draw pictures of the classes or to act out the interaction between teacher and students. Refer students to the "School Is Hard Work" excerpt in *The World in Ancient Times Primary Sources and Reference Volume.*

Volcanic Eruptions

Students compare the eruption of Mount Vesuvius in 79 CE with other famous historical eruptions, such as Krakatoa in 1883 and Mount St. Helens in 1980. Students compare the eruptions in their effects on the environment as well as on humans.

ADDITIONAL ASSESSMENT

For Unit 5, divide the class into groups and have them all undertake the Roman Water Supply and Roman Schools projects so you can assess their understanding of the workings of everyday life in Rome. Use the scoring rubric at the back of this guide to assess students' work, and have students rate their own work with the self-assessment rubric. Be sure to distribute the library/media center research log (see rubric at the back of this guide) to help students evaluate their sources as they conduct their research.

LITERATURE CONNECTION

You may want to read the poems of Catullus or the works of Horace aloud to your students. Students will be able to understand the content with minimal assistance, although they may have difficulty with word meaning and sentence construction. Have students write their own poems in the form of the Roman authors that they read.

Students may also enjoy reading the following books that will extend their understanding of life in Rome during this period.

▶ Burrell, Roy, and Peter Connolly. *The Romans*. New York: Oxford University Press, 1998. Nonfiction. AVERAGE
▶ Corbishley, Mike. *Growing Up in Ancient Rome*. Mahwah, NJ: Troll, 1993. Nonfiction. EASY
▶ Harris, Robert. *Pompeii*. New York: Random House, 2003. Fiction. A young engineer has the task of repairing an aqueduct near Pompeii just days before the eruption of Mount Vesuvius in 79 AD.
▶ Time-Life Editors. *When Rome Ruled the World: The Roman Empire 100 BC to 200 AD (What Life Was Like series)*. New York: Time-Life Books, 1997. Nonfiction. ADVANCED
▶ Winterfeld, Henry. *Detectives in Togas*. Odyssey Classics, 2002. Fiction. AVERAGE

UNIVERSAL ACCESS

The following strategies are designed to cover a range of learning styles and reading, language, and skill levels.

Reading Strategies

▶ When discussing Pompeii (Chapter 16), review with students that artifacts are sources that historians use to draw conclusions about ancient civilizations. Have students infer how historians know what they know about the Pompeians from what has been excavated: How do they suppose they know that people had just sat down to a meal when they died? How do they know that priests were trying to protect sacred statues?

▶ Instead of having a chronological organization, these chapters deal with two or three subjects apiece. Assist students in defining those subjects, and have them create main idea statements for each. Then have them point out details or examples that support the main ideas.

▶ Have groups of three students read this unit, one chapter per student. Each group member should take notes on the reading. Group members should come together to tell each other what they learned about life in Rome during this period.

Writing Strategies

► Have students make an idea web, using the big idea *lifestyle* as the central circle. They can fill in the outer circles with details about the different groups of people discussed in this unit: women, children, Pompeians, soldiers.

► Model how to create an outline for a chapter, section by section. Have partners break the chapter into sections and then read the chapter together and write an outline of the information.

Listening and Speaking Strategies

► Small groups can create a monologue for Pliny the Elder or Pliny the Younger telling about the events after the eruption of Mt. Vesuvius. Students should present their monologues to the class, either live or through a recording.

► Encourage a group of students to prepare and present a "Person on the Street" interview involving a reporter for a Roman newspaper and a number of Roman legionaries. The question could be "What do you like (dislike) most about being in the Roman army?" Responders can be legionaries or auxiliaries, and should present details from the textbook.

UNIT VOCABULARY LIST

The following words that appear in Unit 5 are important for your students' understanding of the social studies content as well as for development of literacy. Use these words for vocabulary study or to reinforce language arts skills (e.g., synonyms, compound words, prefixes and suffixes, and related words). The words are listed below in the order in which they appear in the chapters.

Chapter 15	Chapter 16	Chapter 17
orator	gymnasium	cavalryman
epitaph	lavatory	legionary
exasperating	disintegrate	century
fugitive	graffiti	centurion
relief sculpture	denarii	discipline
		wield
		tactics
		makeshift
		predecessor
		auxiliary
		chain mail
		citizenship

FOR HOMEWORK

STUDENT STUDY GUIDE
pages 39–40

CAST OF CHARACTERS

Caracalla 3rd-century CE emperor

Livia influential wife and advisor of Augustus

Julia Domna wife of Septimius Severus who ran government when husband was away

Septimius Severus (sep-TIM-ee-us suh-VEER-us) 3rd-century CE emperor

 VOCABULARY

education training to develop skills needed for life

erase wipe clean to use again

matriarch woman who leads a family

CHAPTER SUMMARY

This chapter details the everyday lives of women and children in Rome. A woman's greatest purpose was to have children, and from the age of eleven, girls were prepared for marriage and child-rearing. Nonetheless, some women stepped beyond this role and became active in politics and business.

PERFORMANCE OBJECTIVES

▶ To describe the life events of a typical woman or child in ancient Rome
▶ To contrast the lives of wealthy and poor children
▶ To explain when and how some women began to have more influence

BUILDING BACKGROUND

Ask students to summarize events in a typical child's life in America today; for example, preschool, playing with friends, kindergarten and grade school, joining teams and organizations, and so on. Have them predict some ways the life of a child in ancient Rome would be different.

WORKING WITH PRIMARY SOURCES

Writings about common people from ancient times are much less frequent than writings about famous people, and so historians often need to use such things as inscriptions on tombstones to gain information about the life of common people. Help students understand that even a short tombstone inscription can yield important data: how long people lived, how many children they had, whom they were married to, their occupations, and so on.

GEOGRAPHY CONNECTION

Movement Have students locate Sicily and Greece on a map of the Roman Empire. Ask a volunteer to trace the movements of Livia and Tiberius from the time they fled Rome until they came out of hiding.

READING COMPREHENSION QUESTIONS

1. What rights did women have? What rights did they lack? (*They could own property and attend public events with men. Their lives were completely controlled, first by their fathers, then by their husbands and perhaps their fathers-in-law.*)
2. What did poor children do from an early age? What did wealthy children do? (*Poor children worked in the fields or shops to help the family and learn a trade. Rich children played and went to school until ready for marriage, politics, or the military.*)
3. What did Livia do that was unusual in her day? (*She advised Augustus on political matters and took action to influence politics.*)
4. Why was Julia Mammaea important? (*While her son was emperor from 222–235 CE, she ruled the empire, led troops into battle, and prevented the collapse of the government.*
5. Distribute copies of the blackline master for Chapter 15 so students can better understand Roman numerals.

CRITICAL THINKING QUESTIONS

1. What do the stories of Calpurnia and Blandinia illustrate about Roman women? *(They show that women married young, often to older men, and often died young; they also suggest intelligence and devotion on the part of these young wives.)*

2. Why was education important to the wealthy but not to the poor? *(The wealthy could afford to pay for schooling for their children. They also knew that in order to succeed in the aristocracy, their children would have to know Roman law, literature, and history as well as math. The poor, on the other hand, lived hand to mouth. Their children were needed for labor.)*

3. Why do you think Livia's advice was important to Augustus but merely a nuisance to Tiberius? *(Possible answer: Augustus had chosen Livia because he recognized her intelligence and he trusted and respected her. Tiberius, on the other hand, may have considered his mother a meddler, still trying to manage him as if he were a child.)*

SOCIAL SCIENCES

Civics   In ancient Rome, women could work, own property, and attend public events with men. Yet they had no control over their own lives, and their primary function was to have children. Have students compare the lives of Roman women with the lives of slaves.

READING AND LANGUAGE ARTS

Reading Nonfiction   Have students draw conclusions about the life Roman women and children from the primary sources in the chapter. For instance, students should conclude from Viccentia's tombstone (page 104) that children went to work very young.

Using Language   Have students pick out figurative expressions in the text; for example, *Livia wielded her power behind closed doors* (page 106) and *the empire tumbled into chaos* (page 107). Ask students to explain these expressions from context.

SUPPORTING LEARNING

English Language Learners   There are numerous words in the text that have multiple meanings. Help students use context to understand the meanings of words such as *simple* (page 103), "plain"; *built* (page 104), "paid for the construction of"; and *exercised* (page 105), "made use of."

Struggling Readers   Have students create sequence diagrams showing the life stages for poor and wealthy women in ancient Rome.

EXTENDING LEARNING

Enrichment   Have students investigate the life of Livia, with particular emphasis on how she influenced the early empire.

Extension   Have students create mock headstones for individuals based on the information in the text.

WRITING

Journal Have students imagine themselves as a Roman boy or girl and write a journal entry to tell about their day.

LINKING DISCIPLINES

Health Roman girls married young and began having children right away. How might these facts be related to the early deaths of so many young women? Ask students to explore the facts about pregnancy at an early age.

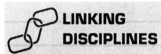

THEN and NOW

Just as today, dogs were a favorite pet in Roman times. Romans kept many kinds of birds as pets: pigeons, ducks, quail, geese. Cats started to gain status as pets around 1 CE.

EVERYDAY LIFE—ROMAN NUMERALS

Directions

Read about Roman numerals. Today they are used in royal titles, Super Bowls, Olympic Games, and names of popes. Then make up addition problems using Roman numerals. Exchange your problems with a partner and solve.

The Romans used only seven letters and a line to express all their numbers. A combination of letters could represent any number. A line over a number meant "multiply by 1,000." Here are the Roman numerals from 1 to 1,000. Letters were combined to make numbers not shown here.

1	I	11	XI	30	XXX		
2	II	12	XII	40	XL		
3	III	13	XIII	50	L		
4	IV	14	XIV	60	LX		
5	V	15	XV	70	LXX		
6	VI	16	XVI	80	LXXX		
7	VII	17	XVII	90	XC		
8	VIII	18	XVIII	100	C		
9	IX	19	XIX	500	D		
10	X	20	XX	1,000	M		

- ▶ If a smaller numeral occurs after a larger numeral, add: LXX = 50 + 10 + 10 = 70.
- ▶ If a smaller numeral appears before a larger one, subtract: IX = 10 - 1 = 9.
- ▶ Only I, X, or C can be used in front of another letter to indicate subtraction.
- ▶ Only a single numeral can be subtracted.
- ▶ I can be subtracted from V or X; X can be subtracted from L or C; and C can be subtracted from D or M.

Convert an Arabic number to Roman numerals. Example: 674

> 600 = D + C (500 + 100)
>
> 74 = L + XX + IV (50 + 20 + 4)
>
> 674 = DCLXXIV

Add Roman numerals.

Example: 68 + 13 or LXVIII + XIII

1. Write the two numbers next to each other: LXVIII + XIII.

2. Rearrange the numerals from greatest to least: LXXVIIIIIII.

3. There are six Is—simplify and rewrite as VI: LXXVVI.

4. The two Vs are the same as an X, so simplify to get LXXXI, or 81.

Example: 14 + 17 or XIV + XVII

1. Write the two numbers next to each other: XIV + XVII.

2. Notice that the I in XIV is being subtracted. That I cancels out one I in XVII, so cross them both out, leaving XV + XVI.

3. Rearrange the remaining numerals from greatest to least: XXVVI.

4. Simplify by combining the two Vs into an X: XXXI, or 31.

NAME   **DATE**

A. MULTIPLE CHOICE

Circle the letter of the best answer for each question.

1. When a Roman girl married, she
   a. left her father's control and could live her own life.
   b. left her father's control and came under the control of her husband.
   c. stayed under the control of her father for five more years.
   d. stayed under the control of her mother.

2. Although women were less valued than men in Rome, women had the right to
   a. divorce their husbands.
   b. marry whomever they chose.
   c. own property.
   d. build their own homes.

3. Childhood for poor Roman children was short because
   a. they had to work.
   b. they died young.
   c. Roman tradition required it.
   d. schools only taught up to age 11.

4. Roman boys learned the work they would do as adults by
   a. getting as much education as possible.
   b. following their fathers to work.
   c. learning from tutors.
   d. learning from their mothers.

5. Roman girls learned the work they would do as adults by
   a. getting as much education as possible.
   b. preparing for marriage at home.
   c. learning from tutors.
   d. learning from their fathers.

B. SHORT ANSWER

Write one or two sentences to answer each question.

6. How does a *matriarch* differ from a *patriarch?* How are they similar?

_____

_____

7. Why were some Roman teachers always teaching outdoors?

_____

_____

8. How did Livia exercise power during the reign of Augustus?

_____

_____

C. ESSAY

Three extraordinary women—Livia, Julia Domna, and Julia Mammaea—played important roles in ruling the Roman Empire. Using these three women as your examples, write an essay on a separate sheet of paper about how the influence of women in the empire changed over the years.

CAST OF CHARACTERS

Pliny (PLIH-nee) **the Elder** Roman fleet commander, writer, scientist, wrote about eruption of Mt. Vesuvius

Pliny (PLIH-nee) **the Younger** Roman writer and historian; witnessed eruption of Mt. Vesuvius with his uncle, Pliny the Elder

 VOCABULARY

plumbing pipes and taps that bring water into and out of a building

volcano mountain that erupts, sending molten rock, fire, and deadly gases into the environment

CHAPTER SUMMARY

In 79 CE, the volcano Vesuvius exploded, raining death and destruction on the Roman town of Pompeii at its base. The town and many of its people were completely covered with ash and lava. This happened so fast that the minute details of everyday life were preserved, giving modern archaeologists an extraordinary window into life in the Roman Empire.

PERFORMANCE OBJECTIVES

▶ To understand the cataclysm that destroyed Pompeii
▶ To learn about the lifestyle of people in a typical Roman town
▶ To understand how archaeologists learn about ancient civilizations

BUILDING BACKGROUND

Ask students to describe a volcano. Then brainstorm what happens to the surrounding area when a volcano erupts. Elicit that the countryside is covered with ash, rocks, and lava. Have them predict what would happen to any human habitations that were near such a volcano.

WORKING WITH PRIMARY SOURCES

The buried city of Pompeii is one of the finest examples of artifacts as primary sources. After reviewing the pictures of artifacts in the chapter and their captions, have students brainstorm the kinds of artifacts of our civilization that might be uncovered 2,000 years from now. How would future archaeologists be able to tell what the objects used for? What conclusions would they be able to draw about our civilization?

GEOGRAPHY CONNECTION

Location Have students use the mileage scale on the map on page 108 to determine the distance from Pompeii to Misenum, where Pliny the Elder and his nephew were when Mt. Vesuvius erupted.

READING COMPREHENSION QUESTIONS

1. Describe the economy of Pompeii. (*The people raised sheep, fruit, and grapes. They sold wool, cloth, and wine. The town had hotels, taverns, and wine bars.*)
2. Poisonous gases killed many of the people of Pompeii. What were some of the things they were doing when they died? (*hiding their treasures, eating meals, rescuing statues, baking bread*)
3. How did 19th-century archaeologists recreate the people and animals who died at Pompeii? (*They injected plaster into the spaces they found, and the casts showed children crouching, dogs running, and a woman with servants, among other things.*)
4. What other artifacts have archaeologists uncovered at Pompeii? (*graffiti scratched on the walls, mosaics*)
5. Distribute copies of the blackline master for Chapter 16 so that students may read more of the account of the eruption of Mt. Vesuvius by Pliny the Younger.

CRITICAL THINKING QUESTIONS

1. The text presents a seemingly complete picture of life in Pompeii in 79 CE. How do you suppose historians create this picture from the ruins of the town? *(Historians take the artifacts that were found and combine them with what they already know about Roman civilization from other writings to come up with an almost complete picture of life in Pompeii.)*

2. Compare and contrast life in Pompeii in 79 CE with life in your town today. *(Students should point out obvious differences, such as in diet, occupations, home design, public baths, and gladiator shows. They should also recognize overall similarities—many of the foods are the same as today, indoor plumbing, adults going to work, priests doing religious activities, people with valuables that they wanted to preserve, people trying to save their lives in the face of disaster.)*

SOCIAL SCIENCES

Science, Technology, and Society   Use an online or print encyclopedia to get information about tools and techniques used by archaeologists. Have students relate these to the work done by archaeologists at Pompeii.

READING AND LANGUAGE ARTS

Reading Nonfiction   Have students read the graffiti presented in *The World in Ancient Times Primary Sources and Reference Volume* to see other day-to-day concerns of Pompeians.

Using Language   Point out to students that this chapter is written in time order. Have students summarize the events in the chapter, using time-order words such as *first, next, then, later,* and so on.

SUPPORTING LEARNING

English Language Learners   Point out the use of strong adjectives and vivid verbs in the text. Have students write down five examples of each, and use them in sentences of their own.

Struggling Readers   Have students write in their own words the descriptions of the day given by Pliny the Younger.

EXTENDING LEARNING

Enrichment   Have students read extracts from the works of Pliny the Elder to experience his wide-ranging intellect.

Extension   Use online resources to find more pictures of artifacts from Pompeii. Ask students to discuss what they can learn from these artifacts. One source of pictures is *http://wings.buffalo.edu/AandL/Maecenas/italy_except_rome_and_sicily/pompeii/thumbnails_contents.html*.

WRITING

Journal Have students imagine they are Pliny the Younger. Ask them to write a journal entry describing their feelings about their uncle's actions on the day of the eruption.

LINKING DISCIPLINES

Science Have students investigate volcanic eruptions: warning signs, why they occur, types of eruptions, products of eruptions, how eruptions change the landscape. Students can create bulletin-board displays of the information they find. Students might use the USGS website about Hawaiian volcanoes: *http://hvo.wr.usgs.gov.*

NAME _____ **DATE** _____

THE ERUPTION OF MT. VESUVIUS

Directions

With a partner, read the excerpt from Pliny the Younger's letter to Tacitus about his own experience at Misenum during the eruption of Mt. Vesuvius. Then answer the questions on a separate sheet of paper.

Now the day begins, with a still hesitant and almost lazy dawn. All around us buildings are shaken. We are in the open, but it is only a small area and we are afraid, nay certain, that there will be a collapse. We decided to leave the town finally; a dazed crowd follows us, preferring our plan to their own (this is what passes for wisdom in a panic). Their numbers are so large that they slow our departure, and then sweep us along. . . .

The carts that we had ordered brought were moving in opposite directions, though the ground was perfectly flat, and they wouldn't stay in place even with their wheels blocked by stones. In addition, it seemed as though the sea was being sucked backwards, as if it were being pushed back by the shaking of the land. Certainly the shoreline moved outwards, and many sea creatures were left on dry sand. Behind us were frightening dark clouds, rent by lightning twisted and hurled, opening to reveal huge figures of flame. These were like lightning, but bigger. At that point the Spanish friend urged us strongly: "If your brother and uncle is alive, he wants you to be safe. If he has perished, he wanted you to survive him. So why are you reluctant to escape?" We responded that we would not look to our own safety as long as we were uncertain about his. Waiting no longer, he took himself off from the danger at a mad pace. It wasn't long thereafter that the cloud stretched down to the ground and covered the sea. It girdled Capri and made it vanish, it hid Misenum's promontory. Then my mother began to beg and urge and order me to flee however I might, saying that a young man could make it, that she, weighed down in years and body, would die happy if she escaped being the cause of my death. I replied that I wouldn't save myself without her, and then I took her hand and made her walk a little faster. She obeyed with difficulty, and blamed herself for delaying me.

Now came the dust, though still thinly. I look back: a dense cloud looms behind us, following us like a flood poured across the land. "Let us turn aside while we can still see, lest we be knocked over in the street and crushed by the crowd of our companions." We had scarcely sat down when a darkness came that was not like a moonless or cloudy night, but more like the black of closed and unlighted rooms. You could hear women lamenting, children crying, men shouting. Some were calling for parents, others for children or spouses; they could only recognize them by their voices. Some bemoaned their own lot, others that of their near and dear. There were some so afraid of death that they prayed for death. Many raised their hands to the gods, and even more believed that there were no gods any longer and that this was one last unending night for the world. Nor were we without people who magnified real dangers with fictitious horrors. Some announced that one or another part of Misenum had collapsed or burned; lies, but they found believers. It grew lighter, though that seemed not a return of day, but a sign that the fire was approaching. The fire itself actually stopped some distance away, but darkness and ashes came again, a great weight of them. We stood up and shook the ash off again and again, otherwise we would have been covered with it and crushed by the weight. I might boast that no groan escaped me in such perils, no cowardly word, but that I believed that I was perishing with the world, and the world with me, which was a great consolation for death. . . .

1. What dangers did Pliny and his mother face in Misenum?

2. What was the reaction of the people around them?

NAME _____ **DATE** _____

A. MULTIPLE CHOICE

Circle the letter of the best answer for each question.

1. What kind of town was Pompeii in 79 CE?
   a. a poor town of shepherds.
   b. a town of priests and priestesses.
   c. a wealthy town of farmers and traders.
   d. a military town.

2. Why did Pliny the Elder sail toward the volcano?
   a. to save his ships.
   b. to try to save his friends.
   c. to calm the frantic people.
   d. to show his courage.

3. How do we know so much detail about the day Mt. Vesuvius erupted?
   a. Pliny the Younger predicted that the volcano would erupt.
   b. Pliny the Elder took firsthand notes that Pliny the Younger rewrote.
   c. Pliny the Younger was a careful scientist.
   d. Pliny the Elder survived to write a full report on the eruption.

4. The overwhelming reaction of Pompeians to the eruption was to
   a. run away.
   b. save their most precious items.
   c. wait until help arrived.
   d. hope the gods would help them.

5. The cavities that archaeologists found in the volcanic remains of the city were
   a. holes made by gases in the lava.
   b. rocks that were disintegrated by the heat.
   c. columns of buildings.
   d. where bodies of the dead had been.

B. SHORT ANSWER

Write one or two sentences to answer each question.

6. What made Pompeii a popular city for visitors?

   _____

   _____

7. Why were so many people buried at Pompeii?

   _____

   _____

8. How did the eruption of Mt. Vesuvius "save" Pompeii?

   _____

   _____

C. ESSAY

On a separate sheet of paper, write an essay summarizing the events on the day that Mt. Vesuvius erupted. Include what was happening in Pompeii as well as the actions of Pliny the Elder.

ALL THE EMPEROR'S MEN: TRAJAN AND THE ARMY

PAGES 114–120

CAST OF CHARACTERS

Nerva (NERV-uh) emperor (96–98 CE); began tradition of choosing qualified successor

Trajan (TRAY-jun) emperor (98–117 CE); extended empire's borders; reigned fairly and with common sense

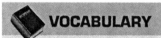

VOCABULARY

legacy something passed down from one person, generation, or civilization to another

THEN and NOW

Like the Roman Empire, the United States maintains a significant military presence abroad. The United States has about 1,000 military bases in other countries.

CHAPTER SUMMARY

The Roman Empire grew to its greatest extent during the reign of Trajan. Maintaining control of such a territory demanded a highly disciplined military. Rome had just such an organization. At the empire's height, an army of only 350,000 protected 60 million people in an area 2,000 miles long.

PERFORMANCE OBJECTIVES

▶ To explain the structure and importance of Rome's army
▶ To describe the life of the average soldier
▶ To understand the qualities that made Trajan a successful emperor

BUILDING BACKGROUND

Ask students to think of places in the world where American servicemen and women are deployed. Discuss with the class reasons why the United States might take military actions abroad. Explain to students that they will read about Rome's powerful military organization. Ask them what they already know about the Roman army through movies or books.

WORKING WITH PRIMARY SOURCES

Trajan's column itself is a wonderful primary source showing the operations of the army in the Dacian campaigns, what soldiers wore, and images of Trajan himself. There are numerous websites devoted to the column, with details of the carvings that students may study; for example, *http://cogaionon.home.ro/trajan.htm*.

GEOGRAPHY CONNECTION

Regions   Using a map of modern Europe, have students find Romania. Point out that this region was known as Dacia in Roman times. Trace the outlines of the Roman Empire under Trajan, naming the regions as you move your hand over the map. Then invite volunteers to point to the regions as you name them.

READING COMPREHENSION QUESTIONS

1. What were *centuries* in the Roman army, and who commanded them? (*Centuries were groups of about 100 men. An officer called a centurion commanded a century.*)
2. When Roman soldiers were not fighting, what was one of their principal occupations? (*They built walls, roads, bridges, aqueducts, canals, baths, and temples.*)
3. What rewards did an auxiliary soldier receive upon retirement? (*He and his family became citizens of Rome. He also received a bronze diploma, or plaque, outlining the benefits of citizenship.*)
4. How was Trajan different from emperors who had come before him? (*He was chosen to rule because of his practical qualities, he was concerned about the welfare of his people, and he was not born in Italy.*)
5. Distribute copies of the blackline master for Chapter 17 so students can see the Roman Empire at its greatest extent.

CRITICAL THINKING QUESTIONS

1. What qualities of the Roman army might be true of a successful army today? *(Possible answer: The Roman army was highly organized and disciplined. Soldiers were promoted for courage and loyalty. They received rewards for making the army a career.)*

2. What does the fact that Roman roads are often "arrow-straight" suggest about Roman values? *(Possible answer: The Romans were practical. They valued speed and efficiency.)*

3. What was there about Trajan's background that might explain his generosity to his people? *(Possible answer: Trajan was not an "insider." He came from Spain and knew how people lived and felt outside the capital.)*

4. How might Rome have benefited by granting citizenship to auxiliary soldiers when they retired? *(Possible answer: This created a group of citizens outside of Italy who were loyal and grateful to Rome.)*

SOCIAL SCIENCES

Science, Technology, and Society   Many Roman soldiers and administrators lived and worked in provinces far from Italy. What was daily life like for these men and women who lived on the outskirts of the empire? Encourage students to find out about Roman society in Britain, Gaul, Spain, North Africa, and other regions under Rome's control.

READING AND LANGUAGE ARTS

Reading Nonfiction   On pages 117–118, the text talks about the difference between Trajan and his predecessors as emperor. Have students pick out the main idea of this section and list the details used to support it.

Using Language   Point out the word *cavalryman* in the second line of page 114. Elicit that this is a compound word. As students read, have them pick out other compound words and determine their meanings by breaking the words apart.

SUPPORTING LEARNING

English Language Learners   Have students read pages 116–117, about daily life for Roman soldiers, to partners. Have partners ask each other questions to review the material.

Struggling Readers   Have students make a diagram showing the divisions of the army and the different soldiers in the units.

EXTENDING LEARNING

Enrichment   Roman armies also employed machinery such as catapults, giant crossbows, and assault towers. Encourage students to investigate the technology that helped Rome's armies control the empire. Students could begin their research in the Time-Life book *When Rome Ruled the World: The Roman Empire 100 BC to 200 AD.*

Extension   Have students make cardboard copies of Roman armor and shields. They can use them to act out scenes, such as the one reported by Cassius Dio on page 116.

WRITING

○ **Panegyric** Draw students' attention to the quotation from Pliny the Younger on page 118. Explain that this is from a *panegyric*, a composition written in praise of a person.

○ Point out that panegyrics were addressed to the subject (referred to as "you"). Have students write a panegyric of their own to someone they admire—a friend,

○ family member, or role model.

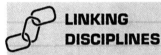

LINKING DISCIPLINES

Art Draw students' attention to the detail on Trajan's Column. Point out that memorials celebrating military victories or personal achievements were popular in Roman days. Have students design a memorial of their own, commemorating a historical or modern event of their own choosing.

NAME   **DATE**

THE ROMAN EMPIRE UNDER EMPEROR TRAJAN

Directions

Follow the directions below to complete the map of the Roman Empire at its greatest extent after the conquests of the Emperor Trajan.

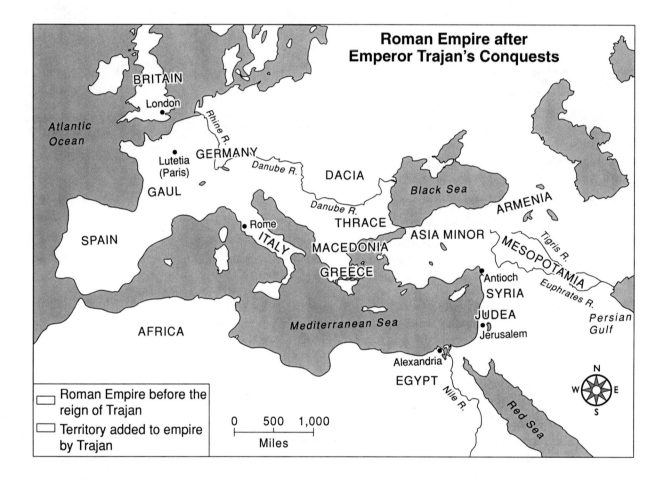

1. Use a colored pencil to show the territory of the Roman Empire before the reign of Trajan.

2. Use a different colored pencil to show the territory added to the empire by Trajan.

3. Complete the map by filling in the map legend.

4. Use the mileage scale to understand how large the empire was at this point. Approximately how far did it extend from north to south? How far did it extend from east to west?

_____.

A. MULTIPLE CHOICE

Circle the letter of the best answer for each question.

1. The backbone of the Roman army were the
   - **a.** centurions.
   - **b.** senators.
   - **c.** legionaries.
   - **d.** auxiliaries.

2. One key to the Roman army's success in battle was
   - **a.** always outnumbering the enemy.
   - **b.** its preparation in times of peace.
   - **c.** the enemy's poor organization.
   - **d.** the forts it had built.

3. Which was **not** a reason why Trajan was different from the emperors before him?
   - **a.** He was chosen emperor because of his abilities.
   - **b.** He was a close relative of the emperor Nerva.
   - **c.** He treated his subjects with fairness and justice.
   - **d.** He came from the provinces, and was concerned with the whole empire.

4. Why was Trajan's conquest of Dacia important to Rome?
   - **a.** It doubled the size of the empire.
   - **b.** It added rich gold and silver mines to the empire.
   - **c.** It made the empire's borders safer.
   - **d.** It led to the construction of Trajan's column.

5. Why did auxiliary soldiers fight in the Roman army?
   - **a.** They received poor pay.
   - **b.** They were forced into service.
   - **c.** They could become Roman citizens.
   - **d.** Roman armor was the best in the world.

B. SHORT ANSWER

Read this excerpt from the diploma of Reburrus, an auxiliary from Spain. Then use the information in the excerpt and in the chapter to answer each question in one or two sentences. Explain why Reburrus would have stayed so long in the Roman army just to get this diploma.

The emperor Trajan . . . has granted citizenship to [the soldiers] themselves, their children and descendents and the right of legal marriage with the wives they had when citizenship was granted them. . . .

6. How many years did auxiliaries have to serve in the Roman army before they could get a diploma?

_____

_____

7. Who was granted citizenship by this diploma?

_____

_____

8. What effect would this diploma have on future generations?

_____

_____

C. ESSAY

Write an essay on a separate sheet of paper discussing the benefits that Rome's army gave to the empire. Include details about construction projects, creation of new citizens, and improving the

6

BUSINESS AND PLEASURE

PAGES 121–137

Chapter 18 Pleasing the Rowdy Romans: Gladiators and Circuses
Chapter 19 How to Get Rich in Rome: Business and Trade
Chapter 20 The Restless Builder: The Emperor Hadrian

UNIT OBJECTIVES

Unit 6 continues the look at life in the Roman Empire begun in Unit 5. It details the entertainments that Romans loved, doing business in the empire, and the military life in the provinces. In this unit, your students will learn

▶ the life of gladiators and other performers.
▶ how trade within the empire and with other peoples enriched the lives of Romans.
▶ how the emperor Hadrian rebuilt Rome and secured the borders of the empire.

PRIMARY SOURCES

Unit 5 includes excerpts from the following primary sources:

▶ Martial, *On the Games*
▶ Fronto, *Elements of History*
▶ Sidonia Apollinaris, *Poems*
▶ Catullus, *Poems*
▶ Roman records of chariot drivers
▶ Graffiti from Pompeii
▶ Seneca the Younger, *Letters*
▶ Aelius Aristides, *In Praise of Rome*
▶ Anonymous, *Augustan History*
▶ Inscription from Africa

Pictures of artifacts from this period can also be analyzed as primary sources. Students can use them to complete their picture of life in Rome at this time:

▶ Ruins of Roman Colosseum
▶ Relief sculpture of gladiators and wild animals
▶ Statuette of armored gladiator
▶ Statue of woman from Pompeii
▶ Painting of clothworkers
▶ Painting of winemaking from Pompeii
▶ Bust of Hadrian
▶ Statues from Hadrian's villa

BIG IDEAS IN UNIT 6

Lifestyle is the big idea of Unit 6. These chapters concentrate on the lives of three groups of people who are not often featured in histories of the ancient world: gladiators and other performers, merchants and traders, and soldiers.

You may want to introduce this idea by having students preview the chapters in the unit. Have students scan the chapter titles, side notes, and graphic aids to predict what the chapters will discuss. Elicit that, except for the emperor Hadrian, the people in these chapters are not great historical personalities; they are everyday people. Taking a closer look at their lifestyle gives us a better understanding of what it was like to be a Roman in this period.

GEOGRAPHY CONNECTION

Have students compare the map on page 132 with the map on page 115. Elicit that the empire was no longer increasing its size. Instead, at this time, the empire was trying to secure its borders. As students will read, this was a relatively peaceful period, and trade within the empire and between Rome and neighboring empires increased dramatically. Talk about the significance of greater security within the empire, and the advantages of security and peace (for example, allowing trade with faraway regions).

TIMELINE

117 CE	Hadrian becomes emperor
118 CE	Construction of Pantheon begins
122 CE	Construction of Hadrian's Wall begins
138 CE	Hadrian dies

UNIT PROJECTS

Chronology

Have students distinguish the time spans represented in each chapter. Chapter 18: earliest Roman times–2nd century CE; Chapter 19: 1st century CE–present; Chapter 20: 117 CE–138 CE. Ask students to compute the time spans for each chapter. Students could create century timelines to illustrate the years encompassed by each century.

Roman Architecture

Help students understand that much of our knowledge of ancient Rome comes from a study of Roman architecture. Point out that guidebooks and Internet sites often provide detailed information about the structure and history of Roman buildings. Assign each student a building to research. Have them locate one useful website and one print source for their building. Ask students to print out or copy information from their source material and to present their findings to the class.

Roman Gladiators

Have small groups investigate the life of a gladiator. They can use the Historian at Work feature on pages 126–127 as a jumping-off point. One good source of information is *http://ablemedia.com/ctcweb/consortium/gladiators.html*. Have groups make displays of their information for their classmates to view.

Map of the Empire

The Roman Empire reached its largest size at this point. Have small groups create various maps of the empire. One could be an historical map showing how the empire grew. Another could be a map showing all of the subject peoples who were part of the empire. Still another could show threats to the empire from beyond its borders. Have groups display their maps in the classroom.

ADDITIONAL ASSESSMENT

For Unit 6, divide the class into groups and have them all undertake the Roman Architecture project so you can assess their understanding of Roman architecture and its influence on the modern world as well as their online and library/media room research skills. Use the scoring rubric at the back of this guide to assess students' work, and have students rate their own work with the self-assessment rubric.

LITERATURE CONNECTION

The poet Martial is famous for his epigrams—short, satiric lyrics that usually make a point about a subject or have a moral. Many of his epigrams have been revised and repeated through the centuries. One source of his works is *Martial: Epigrams* edited by Craig Williams (New York: Oxford University Press, 2004). Carefully select samples of Martial's work for students to read aloud. Have them relate the epigrams to modern life or to modern epigrams that they know. Students may also enjoy reading the following books that will extend their understanding of life in Rome during this period.

▶ Amery, Heather, and Patricia Vanagas. *Rome and Romans*. Tulsa, OK: EDC Publishing, 1998. Nonfiction. EASY
▶ Macaulay, David. *City: A Story of Roman Planning and Construction*. Boston MA: Houghton Mifflin, 1983. Nonfiction. AVERAGE
▶ Scieszka, Jon. *See You Later, Gladiator.* New York: Viking, 2000. Fiction. AVERAGE
▶ Time-Life Editors. *When Rome Ruled the World: The Roman Empire 100 BC to 200 AD (What Life Was Like* series*)*. New York: Time-Life Books, 1997. Nonfiction. ADVANCED

UNIVERSAL ACCESS

The following strategies are designed to cover a range of learning styles and reading, language, and skill levels.

Reading Strategies

▶ Preview the chapters by reading some of the primary sources aloud. Have students say what they can tell about each chapter from your readings.

▶ Have students scan the first sentences of the paragraphs in each chapter looking for main ideas. They can use these main ideas as section heads around which to organize the information.

Writing Strategies

▶ Have students make a three-column chart, with headings representing the three groups of people discussed in this unit: soldiers; gladiators and entertainers; merchants and traders. Have them fill in details in each column as they read.

▶ Before students read each chapter, have them write on index cards questions that they think the chapter will answer. Collect the cards. When they are finished reading, review some of the questions and have students answer them or state that the question was not answered by the chapter.

Listening and Speaking Strategies

▶ Partners can create a dialogue to show interactions between two people discussed in these chapters; for example, traders from different parts of the Roman Empire. Students should practice their dialogues and present them to their classmates.

▶ There are a number of opportunities for students to practice reading aloud. Have them read the primary source material to their classmates. They will learn from playing different roles and characters

▶ Ask students to help you read aloud the "Historian at Work" feature (pages 126–127). Read the questions, and students will read the answers. The rest of the class should take notes.

UNIT VOCABULARY LIST

The following words that appear in Unit 6 are important for your students' understanding of the social studies content as well as for development of literacy. Use these words for vocabulary study or to reinforce language arts skills (e.g., synonyms, compound words, prefixes and suffixes, and related words). The words are listed below in the order in which they appear in the chapters.

Chapter 18	**Chapter 19**	**Chapter 20**
mingle	prominent	strenuous
tantalizing	gratitude	sniper
gory	investment	villa
uproarious	capsize	relic
groom	summon	catacombs
artificial	infantryman	consecration
agility	artifact	
	peddler	
	caravan	
	monsoon	

PLEASING THE ROWDY ROMANS: GLADIATORS AND CIRCUSES
PAGES 121–127

FOR HOMEWORK

STUDENT STUDY GUIDE
pages 45–46

 VOCABULARY

ludi Roman games, or public entertainments

gladiator trained slave who fought to entertain Romans

arena large open area, surrounded by seating, where contests and entertainments take place

 **LINKING DISCIPLINES**

Art Chariot racing was so popular that Roman children practiced in carts pulled by sheep and goats. The poet Horace described boys "harnessing mice to a little cart." Students can make and display their own toy chariots out of found objects, cardboard, and paper.

CHAPTER SUMMARY

People love to be entertained, and Rome's leaders were expert in exploiting this human desire for their own purposes. They understood that staging extravagant shows featuring wild beasts and gladiators—and charging no admission—would win over a rowdy public. The violence featured in many of these spectacles reflected Rome's celebration of military conquest.

PERFORMANCE OBJECTIVES

▶ To describe the nature of public entertainment in ancient Rome
▶ To explain the reasons for staging these displays
▶ To understand the public values that made such entertainments popular

BUILDING BACKGROUND

Initiate a class discussion about violence in popular entertainment. Ask students what they think about professional wrestling and boxing, extreme sports, or brawls during sporting events. Invite the class to consider why such displays are popular. Challenge students to define how much violence a society should accept in the name of entertainment.

WORKING WITH PRIMARY SOURCES

The excerpts from Martial on page 121 and Sidonius Apollinaris on page 124 are especially useful to show students vivid description. Have students describe a sporting event, emulating the style of these writers.

GEOGRAPHY CONNECTION

Interaction The Colosseum was one of the greatest structures of imperial Rome. Its massive ruins still stand today. Distribute copies of the blackline master for Chapter 18 so students can learn more about this architectural wonder.

READING COMPREHENSION QUESTIONS

1. What kinds of shows were popular in Rome during the empire? (*wild animal shows, staged hunts, plays, chariot racing, footraces, mock sea battles, gladiatorial matches*)
2. What were the origins of Rome's *ludi*? What were some of the major festivals? (*The* ludi *started out as religious festivals honoring certain gods who controlled the harvest, the weather, and the hunt. The Ludi Cereales honored Ceres, goddess of grain, and the Saturnalia honored Saturn, god of agriculture.*)
3. Describe what the popular *ludi* were like. (*They were bloody and colorful, loud, and free.*)
4. How were successful performers (gladiators and chariot racers) treated? (*They were like rock stars. They had many devoted fans. They had the opportunity for fame, money, and an exciting life.*)

CRITICAL THINKING QUESTIONS

1. "The Roman people are devoted to two things: food and free shows," wrote one Roman politician. What was his opinion of the average Roman? (*Possible answer: He thought that the average Roman was concerned with the necessities of everyday life and just wanted to be entertained.*)

2. How does entertainment today compare to entertainment in Roman days? (*Possible answer: Entertainment today is often fast-paced and dangerous, as it was in Roman days. However, people today can usually avoid physical injury when they perform.*)

3. How might a slave react upon learning that he had been chosen to become a gladiator? (*Possible answer: He might be frightened at the thought of being killed. He might also be happy at the thought of being treated well or becoming a star.*)

SOCIAL SCIENCES

Civics   Public entertainment was an important aspect of Roman culture. Encourage students to explore this subject. Assign areas of research to individuals or partners, such as gladiatorial training, wild animal displays, chariot races, and public reaction to such events.

READING AND LANGUAGE ARTS

Reading Nonfiction   Have students read the excerpt from the play *The Mother in Law* in *The World in Ancient Times Primary Sources and Reference Volume* to get an idea of what it was like to stage a play in ancient Rome.

Using Language   Romans not only attended sporting events, they vividly described them. Discuss what makes good sports reporting. Have a volunteer prepare and read aloud Sidonius Apollinaris's description of the chariot race (page 124), using the style of a modern race announcer.

SUPPORTING LEARNING

English Language Learners   Have students write short descriptions of entertainment that they enjoy. Ask volunteers to read their descriptions to a small group.

Struggling Readers   Have students summarize sections of the chapter, paraphrasing key descriptions of the *ludi*.

EXTENDING LEARNING

Enrichment   Thousands of wild animals died to entertain the Romans. As a result, elephants disappeared from North Africa and lions from Mesopotamia. Have students learn about other animals facing extinction because of human activities.

Extension   Show selected scenes from the movie *Spartacus* (Chapter 8), including the chariot race. Screen the scenes for age appropriateness first.

WRITING

Persuasion Draw students' attention to the comment by Seneca the Younger that ends the chapter (page 127). Point out that debate continues over whether violent entertainment encourages similar behavior in spectators. Discuss this issue with the class. Then ask them to express their opinions about the effect of violent entertainment in a paragraph of their own. Encourage students to refer specifically to entertainment that they consider violent.

THEN and NOW

The Colosseum remains a substantial ruin, but only the outline of the Circus Maximus is visible today.

THAT'S ROMAN ENTERTAINMENT!

Directions

Study the diagram of the Colosseum. Then answer the questions.

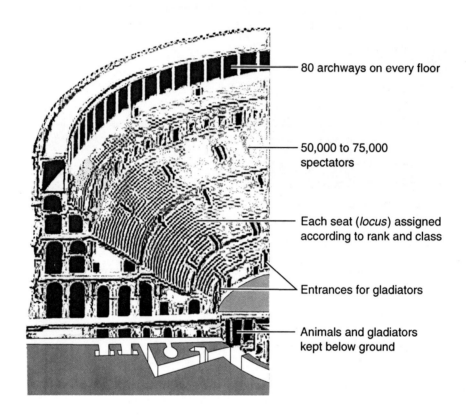

80 archways on every floor

50,000 to 75,000 spectators

Each seat (*locus*) assigned according to rank and class

Entrances for gladiators

Animals and gladiators kept below ground

1. How many spectators could the Colosseum hold?

_____

2. Where did gladiators stay while awaiting their matches?

_____

3. Where do you think you would sit if you were a plebeian? Where would you sit if you were a senator?

_____

NAME _____ **DATE** _____

A. MULTIPLE CHOICE

Circle the letter of the best answer for each question.

1. Entertainments that were **not** popular in ancient Rome were
   a. staged hunts.
   b. chariot races.
   c. sailboat races.
   d. gladiatorial shows.

2. Chariot racing dated back to the time of the founding of
   a. Rome.
   b. the Republic.
   c. the Empire.
   d. the Circus Maximus.

3. Most of the popular Roman entertainments
   a. were quiet and disciplined.
   b. were bloody, colorful, and loud.
   c. were musicals.
   d. charged admission.

4. Gladiatorial shows were held
   a. throughout the empire.
   b. only at the Circus Maximus.
   c. only at the Colosseum.
   d. only in the city of Rome.

5. The Roman *ludi* was a chance for politicians to
   a. make speeches to the people.
   b. gain favor with the people.
   c. cheer for their favorite gladiators.
   d. pay back their supporters.

B. SHORT ANSWER

Write one or two sentences to answer each question.

6. Why did people put their lives on the line as chariot drivers?

   _____

   _____

7. How were gladiators treated between battles?

   _____

   _____

8. How were gladiators like modern rock stars?

   _____

   _____

C. ESSAY

Imagine you are a citizen of the Roman Empire. On a separate sheet of paper, write an essay telling which of the public entertainments described in this chapter you like the best. Give details to support your opinion.

VOCABULARY

patron someone who
helps others, usually
with money

import product
brought into a country
from another country

LINKING
DISCIPLINES

Math Students can
use the information in
this chapter to create
word problems for
their classmates to
solve. For instance, if
45 million quarts of
Spanish olive oil
reached Rome every
year from 15 BCE to
255 CE, how many
quarts reached Rome
altogether in those
years? (270 years x
45 million quarts =
12,150,000,000
quarts)

CHAPTER SUMMARY

A vibrant economy maintained and enriched Rome's great empire. Roman
citizens grew to depend upon goods from all over the world. These included
essentials, such as grain from North Africa, as well as luxuries such as ivory,
perfumes, and silk from the East. In return, Rome's currency brought prosperity
to the lands under its control.

PERFORMANCE OBJECTIVES

▶ To explain the importance of business and trade in Roman society
▶ To understand how ancient evidence shed light on Rome's trading empire
▶ To describe some of the goods bought and sold by Roman merchants

BUILDING BACKGROUND

Write *exports* and *imports* on the board and ask students what these words mean.
Point out that successful economies export and import many goods. Brainstorm
with students a list of products and raw materials that the United States exports
and imports. Explain that the Roman Empire—like the United States—depended
upon trade for its prosperity and stability.

WORKING WITH PRIMARY SOURCES

This chapter provides an opportunity for students to work with artifacts as
primary sources, as much of the evidence of trade and trade goods around the
Roman Empire comes from finds of the articles traded. Brainstorm with students
the judgments that archaeologists and historians made to figure out that the
100,000 jugs of wine found at Pompeii, for example, were meant for shipment
throughout Italy and beyond (page 131).

GEOGRAPHY CONNECTION

Place   Ask students to review the description of monsoon winds on page 132.
Point out that monsoons still affect people living in India and Southeast Asia.
Encourage students to find out more about these powerful wind and rain systems
and to share their information with the class.

READING COMPREHENSION QUESTIONS

1. What did the wool makers of Pompeii do? (*They owned the sheep and the shops
   that processed the wool. They sold their products to shippers who took them to
   faraway ports.*)
2. Why are finds of Roman ships important to historians? (*The ships have been
   found far from Rome. Historians can use this information to track the paths of
   ancient ships, armies, and traders. From that, they can build a picture of Roman
   trade.*)
3. How did the monsoon influence Roman trade? (*Because of the monsoon,
   Egyptian traders could sail to India. This opened the way for trade between India
   and Rome. Rome also opened a land route to China.*)

4. According to the map on page 132, what trade goods would Rome get from the Monsoon Route? (*Answers should include myrrh, ivory, spices, and pepper. Although spices are not on the route itself, they probably would have been traded to India, and then passed on to the Egyptians, who took them back to Rome.*)

5. Distribute copies of the blackline master for Chapter 19 so students may learn more about the goods produced by the various regions of the empire.

CRITICAL THINKING QUESTIONS

1. From what you read about Eumachia, the priestess of Pompeii, what can you conclude about the role of Roman women at the time? (*Possible answer: Women could become wealthy and respected members of society.*)

2. Describe how Roman coins could have been discovered in India. (*Possible answer: A merchant might have purchased pepper in India and paid for it with Roman coins.*)

3. How would the discovery of a Roman aqueduct in Turkey help historians learn about Roman trade? (*Possible answer: The imperial government paid its workers in Roman coins. The workers would spend those coins on local products. If the workers returned to Italy, they would have a desire for the Turkish products, which would increase imports from that area.*)

SOCIAL SCIENCES

Science, Technology, and Society   On page 130, the text discusses how the ancient port of Pisa was lost. Elicit from students a definition for *silt*, and discuss with them how a harbor can get filled up with silt over many years.

READING AND LANGUAGE ARTS

Reading Nonfiction   Have students study the map of Roman trade on page 132. Lead students to understand that imports from distant regions were generally costly luxury items. Inexpensive staples, such as grain and oil, came from closer lands.

Using Language   The chapter explains the difference between *imports* and *exports* (page 131). Be sure students understand the Latin root *portare* and the prefixes *im-* and *ex-*. Elicit other words that have the same or similar prefixes (*inhale, exhale; implode, explode*), and define them.

SUPPORTING LEARNING

English Language Learners   Have students role-play a series of traders involved in bringing goods from a faraway land to Italy.

Struggling Readers   Have students use the outline graphic organizer at the back of this guide to organize the main ideas and details related to business and trade in Rome.

EXTENDING LEARNING

Enrichment   Have students conduct an Internet search using the key phrase *Roman coins*. Have them print out images and information to share with classmates.

Extension   One of the most common Roman artifacts is the clay amphora, a two handled, wide-bodied jar for transporting oil or wine. Show students a picture of an amphora and have them create one of their own out of modeling clay.

WRITING

Expository Composition Have students look at the map on page 132. Ask them to find out more about one of the products imported to Rome (tin from Britain, silk from China, amber from the Baltic, etc.). Have students write two or three paragraphs about the product they have chosen.

NAME

DATE

FAR-FLUNG TRADE

Directions

Study the map of trading products in the Roman Empire and surrounding regions. Then answer the questions.

1. From which regions did Rome get food products (grain, wine, fruit, honey)?

_____

_____

2. The text says that Romans traded a lot of Roman silver for foreign goods. Where did Rome get gold and silver to make its coins?

_____

_____

3. If you were a trader living in Germany, what deals might you have to make to get marble from Numidia?

_____

_____

NAME _____ **DATE** _____

A. MULTIPLE CHOICE

Circle the letter of the best answer for each question.

1. In ancient Rome, the safest investment was land, but the biggest profits were in
   a. medicine.   **c.** the army.
   b. trade.   **d.** government.

2. Archaeologists could pinpoint the origin of the ancient cargo ship found at Pisa because of the
   a. stones in the ship's hold.   **c.** surviving ship's log.
   b. trade goods in the ship's hold. **d.** silt that covered the boat.

3. How did trade goods get to Rome if few Italians took part in foreign trade?
   a. All of the boats on the Mediterranean Sea were Roman.
   b. Rome exported a lot of products.
   c. Traders from all over the world used Rome as a marketplace.
   d. Roman roads were the best in the world.

4. What opened up trade between Rome and the far countries of Asia?
   a. the need for pepper.   **c.** the discovery of the monsoon winds.
   b. too much gold in Rome.   **d.** adventurous Roman traders.

5. The Silk Route to China was
   a. an overland route.   **c.** a short route.
   b. a sea route.   **d.** a little-traveled route.

B. SHORT ANSWER

Write one or two sentences to answer each question.

6. Why was transporting goods by ship risky?

_____

_____

7. Where have sunken Roman ships been found?

_____

_____

8. What did Romans use coins for?

_____

_____

C. ESSAY

On a separate sheet of paper, use information from the Roman Trade map on page 132 in your book to write an essay describing the trade goods that Rome received from Europe, Africa, and Asia.

THE RESTLESS BUILDER: THE EMPEROR HADRIAN

PAGES 133–137

CAST OF CHARACTERS

Hadrian emperor (117–138 CE); strengthened army; built wall across England

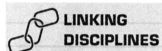 **LINKING DISCIPLINES**

Science Point out that the dome spanning Hadrian's Pantheon remains one of Rome's most remarkable landmarks. But what is a dome? Have students research the structure of a dome. Invite volunteers to explain how a typical dome is constructed, what gives it strength, and why it remains an important architectural feature. Create a classroom gallery of great domes in world architecture.

CHAPTER SUMMARY

The emperor Hadrian did not fit the mold of a Roman ruler. He loved the arts more than war and did not attempt to hide his admiration of Greek civilization. Yet this eccentric man brought peace and security to Rome's territories for more than 20 years.

PERFORMANCE OBJECTIVES

▶ To understand the complex character of the emperor Hadrian
▶ To identify the qualities that made Hadrian a successful leader
▶ To describe some of Hadrian's great building projects

BUILDING BACKGROUND

Ask students what grand buildings they know about. Invite them to describe impressive churches, libraries, museums, theaters, tombs, or school buildings that they have seen or read about. Point out that architecture serves both a practical and an artistic purpose. Explain that the chapter they are about to read concerns one of the world's great builders.

WORKING WITH PRIMARY SOURCES

Hadrian wrote poems, although they are not well-remembered. One website that has copies of a few that have survived is *www.forumromanum.org/literature/hadriane.html*. Have volunteers read the poems aloud to classmates.

GEOGRAPHY CONNECTION

Location   On a map of Britain, point out the approximate route of Hadrian's Wall (an east-west course terminating just north of Newcastle-upon-Tyne on the North Sea and Carlisle on the Irish Sea). Point out how this structure is well placed to define and fortify a border where Britain is at its narrowest. Talk about the threat that the wall was designed to protect against.

READING COMPREHENSION QUESTIONS

1. Why did some people refer to the young Hadrian as the "Little Greek"? (*because he loved Greek literature, art, and music*)
2. Why did Hadrian take two tours of the empire? (*He toured the empire to lead his armies and handle official business, but he also was curious and wanted to experience the world.*)
3. What famous structure did Hadrian build that showed his desire to defend the empire's borders? (*a wall stretching 74 miles across northern England*)
4. What is unusual about the buildings Hadrian built on his retreat 20 miles outside Rome? (*Each was an exact copy of some place that Hadrian admired from his travels.*)

CRITICAL THINKING QUESTIONS

1. How was Hadrian like his predecessor Trajan? How were they different? (*Possible answer: They were both successful emperors. Unlike Trajan, Hadrian tried to avoid unnecessary wars.*)
2. Why did Hadrian climb Mount Etna? What does that suggest about his character? (*He climbed Mount Etna to see the sunrise. This suggests that he appreciated beauty.*)
3. What do you think is a more important accomplishment, Hadrian's successful strengthening of the empire or the many buildings he left behind? Explain your answer. (*Possible answer: The buildings, because they are still here for people to admire.*)

SOCIAL SCIENCES

Civics   Explain to students that Hadrian was the third of five rulers traditionally known as "the five good emperors": Nerva, Trajan, Hadrian, Antoninus Pius, and Marcus Aurelius. Encourage students to find out more about these rulers and to explore what made them "good" (e.g., maintained peace, developed trade, provided jobs, expanded empire, provided justice, and so on).

READING AND LANGUAGE ARTS

Reading Nonfiction   Use a copy of David Macaulay's book *City: A Story of Roman Planning and Construction* to give students practice in reading cross-section diagrams of Roman buildings.

Using Language   Have students carefully read the second paragraph on page 133. Point out the single and double quotation marks. Explain that when certain words in a quotation require quotation marks, they are surrounded with single quotation marks.

SUPPORTING LEARNING

English Language Learners   Have partners read the poems of Florus and Hadrian (page 134) aloud. Have them write similar rhymed verses to each other.

Struggling Readers   Have students list the construction projects that Hadrian completed and categorize the structures as military, religious, or personal.

EXTENDING LEARNING

Enrichment   Many of Hadrian's structures are still standing. Have students find pictures of Hadrian's Wall, the Pantheon, or the Castel Sant'Angelo. Ask them to create drawings or models of these buildings.

Extension   Display interior and exterior pictures of the Pantheon so that students can see the size of the dome. One source for pictures is the website *http://web.kyoto-inet.or.jp/org/orion/eng/hst/roma/pantheon.html*.

 **WRITING**

Personal Letter
Review with students the location and purpose of Hadrian's Wall. Point out that the weather and isolation made this an unpopular posting for Roman soldiers. Then have students write a letter from a legionary about life along Hadrian's Wall to a friend or family member back in the more southerly provinces of the empire.

 **THEN** and **NOW**
The remains of Hadrian's Wall have long been popular with walkers. A footpath running its entire length opened in 2003.

VOCABULARY

pagan follower of traditional religion with many gods

BORDERS OF THE EMPIRE

Directions

Study the maps showing two artificial borders built by the Roman army. One is Hadrian's Wall, built in Britain starting in 122 CE. The other is the Limes, built in Germany starting about 80 CE. Then answer the questions.

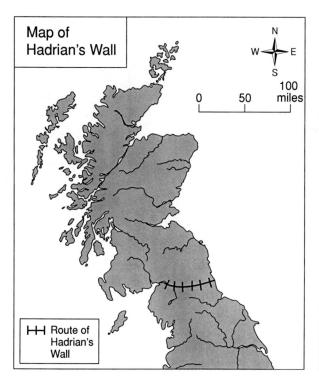

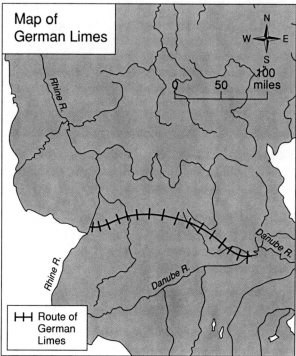

1. Use the mileage scale to figure out the approximate length of each wall.

_____

_____

2. Describe the location of each wall. Why do you suppose a wall was needed at these places?

_____

_____

3. Both walls were built to control the flow of barbarians into and out of the empire, rather than to stop them completely. Why was this necessary?

_____

_____

NAME   **DATE**

A. MULTIPLE CHOICE

Circle the letter of the best answer for each question.

1. One reason that the Roman senators disliked Hadrian was
   a. he did not listen to them.
   b. he seemed to like Greek culture more than Roman culture.
   c. he was a cruel ruler.
   d. he didn't try to expand the empire.

2. Hadrian used the army to
   a. keep order in the city of Rome.
   b. attack Rome's neighbors.
   c. be his personal bodyguards.
   d. safeguard the empire's borders.

3. Hadrian's frontier policy was to
   a. give the empire easily defended borders.
   b. stir up the barbarians against each other.
   c. let the barbarians control the borders.
   d. build walls around the entire empire.

4. Although Rome was mostly at peace during his rule, Hadrian enforced strict discipline in the army because
   a. he didn't want the army to threaten his rule.
   b. an efficient army might be needed at any time to counter a threat.
   c. traders needed protection when they ventured outside the empire.
   d. there was little else for him to do.

5. The Pantheon survived when other Roman buildings were destroyed because
   a. it was too beautiful to be destroyed.
   b. it was re-used as a Christian church.
   c. the concrete used in its construction made it difficult to destroy.
   d. it was owned by a single family.

B. SHORT ANSWER

Write one or two sentences to answer each question.

6. What started Hadrian on the road to becoming emperor?

_____

_____

7. What buildings did Hadrian order to be built?

_____

_____

8. Why did Hadrian pull back the army from the farthest frontiers?

_____

_____

B. ESSAY

Write an essay on a separate sheet of paper in which you state your opinion on whether Hadrian was a good Roman emperor. Use details from the chapter to support your opinion.

UNIT 7
IMPACT OF AN EXPANDING EMPIRE

Chapter 21   Magic and the Cults of the Near East: New Religious Ideas
Chapter 22   Taxes and Tactics in the Provinces: Administering the Empire
Chapter 23   One God or Many? The Jews of the Roman Empire
Chapter 24   From Jesus to Constantine: The Rise of Christianity

UNIT OBJECTIVES

Unit 7 takes a look at new religious ideas that transformed the Roman Empire, as well as the way in which the Romans administered their far-flung territories. In this unit, your students will learn

▶ how Romans borrowed new religious ideas from other cultures.
▶ the relationship of the provinces and conquered peoples to Rome.
▶ the reasons for Roman success in administering such a large empire.
▶ the development of the monotheistic religions Judaism and Christianity.
▶ how Christianity grew to be the favored religion of the Roman Empire.

PRIMARY SOURCES

Unit 7 includes excerpts from the following primary sources:

▶ Pliny the Elder, *Natural History*
▶ Curse found in North Africa
▶ Cato, *On Agriculture*
▶ Suetonius, *Life of Augustus*
▶ Suetonius, *Life of Vespasian*
▶ Livy, *From the Founding of the City*
▶ Tacitus, *The Life of Agricola*
▶ Tacitus, *Histories*
▶ Tacitus, *Annals*
▶ Synesius, *Letters*
▶ The Book of Genesis
▶ The Book of Exodus
▶ The First Book of Maccabees
▶ The Gospel of Matthew
▶ The Gospel of Luke
▶ The Book of Isaiah
▶ The Book of Zechariah
▶ The Book of Micah
▶ Eusebius, *Ecclesiastical History*

Pictures of artifacts from this period can also be analyzed as primary sources. They can help students evaluate the impact of new religions on Rome:

▶ Relief sculpture of Rome's port
▶ Wall painting of Bacchanalians, Pompeii
▶ Statuette of Cybele
▶ Bronze rattle used in religious ceremonies
▶ Relief sculpture of Germans paying taxes
▶ Mosaic of Egyptian scene
▶ Tax collector's tablet
▶ Roman aqueduct

- ▶ Relief sculpture from Arch of Titus
- ▶ Roman coins of Vespasian
- ▶ Wailing Wall in Jerusalem
- ▶ Jewish fortress of Masada
- ▶ Christian tombs
- ▶ Statue of Constantine

BIG IDEAS IN UNIT 7

Religion, change, exchange, and **movement** are the big ideas of Unit 7. These chapters concentrate on major changes in religious life that were taking place in the Roman Empire in the first centuries CE. They talk about how the Romans appropriated religious ideas that they liked from other cultures. They also discuss how the Romans persecuted peoples who believed in religions that could not be assimilated into the Roman world view.

You may want to introduce these ideas by having students preview the chapters in the unit. Have students scan the chapter titles, side notes, and graphic aids to predict what the chapters will discuss. Elicit that, although the map of the Roman Empire didn't change much in this period, internal changes were happening that would mean much more for the future of the empire.

GEOGRAPHY CONNECTION

Have students look at the map on page 161. Elicit that the light green area indicates roughly the area of the Roman Empire. Help students understand that this is an historical map that shows changes over time. Compare and contrast different kinds of maps.

TIMELINE

1000 BCE	David unites Jewish tribes, creating Israel
950 BCE	Solomon builds first temple in Jerusalem
587 BCE	Babylonians destroy temple and exile Jews
538 BCE	Returning Jews build second temple in Jerusalem
200 BCE	Cult of Cybele becomes popular in Rome
164 BCE	Judas Maccabeus defeats Antiochus IV of Syria
40 BCE	Reign of Herod in Judea begins
6–4 BCE	Jesus is born
62 CE	Paul is martyred in Rome
64 CE	Nero begins brutal persecution of Christians
70 CE	Titus destroys second temple in Jerusalem
71 CE	Agricola becomes governor of Britain
100 CE	Cult of Mithras becomes popular in Rome
135 CE	Final Jewish revolt and diaspora
212 CE	Majority of provincials in empire (except slaves) were Roman citizens
312 CE	Constantine becomes emperor; ends persecution of Christians in empire
330 CE	Constantine builds new capital for empire in Constantinople
337 CE	Death of Constantine; Christianity is the favored religion of the empire

UNIT PROJECTS

Chronology

Point out that this unit deals with ideas from outside of Rome that changed the empire. Have students create a timeline for the religions discussed in this unit, and a parallel timeline showing what was happening in Rome at the same time.

Superstitions

Point out that the best resources for finding out about superstitions are often superstitious people themselves! Explain to students that interviewing people for their beliefs and experiences is a form of research known as oral history. Encourage students to ask adult friends or family members to share with them superstitions that they believe in or have heard about. Invite students to share their oral histories with the class.

Adaptability

Much of Rome's strength lay in its willingness to borrow from the countries it conquered. Have small groups compare this with the way that foreign elements are adopted by the people of the United States. Students can make a bulletin board display of foreign ideas and objects that have become part of American culture.

Jewish Origins

The Book of Genesis in the Hebrew Bible presents the Judeo-Christian beliefs about how God created the earth and of the early history of humankind. Have small groups read parts of Genesis and create a report on the Jewish idea of creation.

Original Christian Sources

Explain that the Christian Bible is the primary source for studying the life and teachings of Jesus and his followers. Point out that this book is available in several translations, many with notes to aid the reader. Encourage students to locate and read the original versions of passages about the life of Jesus and Paul summarized in their texts and to orally report their findings to the class.

ADDITIONAL ASSESSMENT

For Unit 7, divide the class into groups and have them all undertake the Jewish Origins and Original Christian Sources projects so you can assess their understanding of early Jewish and Christian history and beliefs. Use the Group Project rubric at the back of this guide to assess students' work, and have students rate their own work with the self-assessment rubric.

LITERATURE CONNECTION

The most important source for the Judeo-Christian tradition is the Bible. As there are many translations, and different religions use different Bibles, you may need to be careful in addressing this subject. Ask students to bring in copies from home, or make copies from one particular version available in your resource center. Use the Bible both as a supplement to historical writings about the Jewish and Christian religions and as a literary source. The example of the Beatitudes on pages 156–157 shows the power of the writing.

Students will also enjoy reading the following books that will extend their understanding of life in Rome during this period.

- ▶ Cowell, F. R. *Life in Ancient Rome.* Perigee Books, 1976. Nonfiction. ADVANCED
- ▶ Sheehan, Sean, and Patricia Levy. *The Ancient World of Rome.* Raintree Steck-Vaughan, 1999. Nonfiction. AVERAGE
- ▶ Simpson, Judith. *Ancient Rome.* New York: Time-Life Books, 1997. Nonfiction. EASY
- ▶ Speere, Elizabeth George. *Bronze Bow.* Boston: Houghton Mifflin, 1972. Fiction. ADVANCED

UNIVERSAL ACCESS

The following strategies are designed to cover a range of learning styles and reading, language, and skill levels.

Reading Strategies

▶ To facilitate reading, help students preview chapter titles and artwork in each chapter to make predictions of what they will learn about. This will help them concentrate on the important ideas presented in the chapter.

▶ This unit has a strong chronological component, as it deals with the change in religion in the Roman Empire from the second century BCE to 337 CE. You may wish to have students keep track of the sequence of events in their journals as they read.

Writing Strategies

▶ Have students make a chart in their journals, using the unit's big ideas as column headings. As they read the unit, they can jot down notes in each category.

▶ Have students use concept webs to record information about the different religions described in this unit.

Listening and Speaking Strategies

▶ Partners can create a dialogue between a Roman administrator of a faraway province, such as Syria or Britain, and a local leader. The local leader is questioning why the people must pay taxes to Rome. The administrator argues that taxes are necessary to pay for the Roman army and Roman government in the area, to protect the people from foreign invasions. Students should practice their dialogues and present them to their classmates.

▶ Have a small group prepare a panel discussion about why the Roman authorities considered some religions, particularly Judaism and Christianity, a threat to their authority. Each panel member can represent a religion— Judaism, Christianity, the cult of Isis or Mithras—and present a presentation about how this religion might or might not challenge Roman authority. Panel members would then answer questions from the class.

UNIT VOCABULARY LIST

The following words that appear in Unit 7 are important for your students' understanding of the social studies content as well as for development of literacy. Use these words for vocabulary study or to reinforce language arts skills (e.g., synonyms, compound words, prefixes and suffixes, and related words). The words are listed below in the order in which they appear in the chapters.

Chapter 21	Chapter 22	Chapter 23	Chapter 24
pregnancy	haven	diaspora	prophet
misfortune	tyranny	persecute	Messiah
evil eye	bristle	suspicious	disciple
astrology	census	extremist	sermon
meteorite	technology		parable
self-mutilation			missionary
depiction			martyr
			bishop
			incentive

LINKING DISCIPLINES

Science Point out that many traditional religions offer an explanation of why things in nature appear to die in winter and then come back to life in spring. Explain that this story often involves a god or goddess dying and returning to earth every year. Point out that science provides a simpler explanation based on what actually happens in nature. Have students research the cause of the seasons. Encourage them to copy or print out illustrations and to present their explanation to the class.

THEN and NOW

The eagle was the sacred symbol of Rome's powerful army. Nearly two thousand years later, another world power—the United States of America—chose the eagle as its national symbol.

CHAPTER SUMMARY

Rome's religion was a hodgepodge of superstitions, nature worship, and rituals borrowed from other cultures. Wherever Romans traveled, they returned with new beliefs and gods. These were often assimilated into Roman life, adding to the empire's cosmopolitan atmosphere.

PERFORMANCE OBJECTIVES

▶ To describe some of the superstitions and rituals that ruled Roman life
▶ To understand the way Rome borrowed beliefs from other cultures
▶ To identify three specific cults Romans adopted from the Near East

BUILDING BACKGROUND

Write *superstition* on the board. Brainstorm with the class a list of common superstitions. Help students understand that the word refers to an illogical belief that one action influences another. Encourage students to discuss the difference between superstition and religion. Explain that the Roman Empire was a great melting pot of beliefs from all over the world.

WORKING WITH PRIMARY SOURCES

Have students read what Pliny the Elder has to say about Roman superstitions (page 139). Ask them to compare these Roman beliefs to beliefs that they have or know about.

GEOGRAPHY CONNECTION

Regions   On a map of the Roman Empire, have students identify where the cults of Isis and Cybele originated. (*Egypt, Asia Minor*)

READING COMPREHENSION QUESTIONS

1. Why did Romans use magic? (*They used magic to control people, either negatively or positively. A good charm was thought to make good things happen, an evil charm to make evil things happen.*)
2. What kinds of gods did the traditional Roman religion have? (*It had traditional gods like Jupiter and Mars and lesser gods like Ceres and Bacchus; it also created gods, such as the deified emperors.*)
3. Who was Cybele supposed to be? What did her story explain? (*Cybele was thought to be the mother of all the gods. Her story explained the mystery of the seasons—the cold of winter and the new life of spring.*)
4. Distribute copies of the blackline master for Chapter 21 so students can learn about the reaction of official Rome to various religious practices.

CRITICAL THINKING

1. Pliny the Elder and Cato were superstitious and believed in magic. Why do people still have these beliefs despite scientific evidence? (*Possible answer: There are always some things that science cannot explain. Superstition and magic fill that need.*)

2. Why might magic, charms, and curses seem to work? (*Possible answer: Coincidentally, the person who is the subject of the charm may act as if he or she were charmed. Or, something bad might happen to someone who has been cursed.*)

3. What did the goddesses Cybele and Isis have in common? What does this say about the Romans of the time? (*Both goddesses loved a man who was dead. When they brought him back to life, spring came to the land. This explained the seasons and rebirth in spring. It also expressed a desire for life after death.*)

SOCIAL SCIENCES

Science, Technology, and Society   Use this chapter to contrast the scientific method with the belief that gods or other powers can control natural events. Have students research the steps of the scientific method.

READING AND LANGUAGE ARTS

Reading Nonfiction   The chapter divides easily into six sections: superstitions, astrology, Roman gods, Cybele, Isis, Mithras. Have students identify the main idea and details of each section.

Using Language   Point out the simile in the first sentence of paragraph 2 on page 141: *religion was like a huge basket filled with gods.* Define *simile*, and elicit the unlike subjects in this example. Ask how this comparison explains Roman religion. Have students make up their own similes describing Roman religion.

SUPPORTING LEARNING

English Language Learners   Have students ask their family members about superstitions, and write a short paragraph describing one or more of them.

Struggling Readers   Have students complete a two-column chart with the headings *Roman Superstition* and *Modern Equivalent.*

EXTENDING LEARNING

Enrichment   Romans had their own beliefs about the origins of the seasons. Have students investigate the myth of Persephone (Proserpina in Latin) and compare it to that of Cybele and Isis.

Extension   Have students find pictures relating to the gods and goddesses discussed in this chapter, and display them in class.

 VOCABULARY

superstitious believing in magic and witches

fertility able to produce life, as a mother or farmland

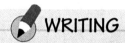 **WRITING**

Personal Narrative Point out that most people have some superstitious habits or beliefs, even if they know them to be untrue. Ask students to write a short narrative about a superstition of their own that they have or used to have.

LAWS ABOUT THE BACCHANALIA

Directions

With a partner, read the excerpt from Livy's *History of Rome* about the limits that the Roman Senate placed on Bacchanalian religious practices. Then answer the questions.

Regarding the Bacchanalia, it was resolved to give the following directions to those who are in alliance with us:

1. No one of them is to possess a place where the festivals of Bacchus are celebrated; if there are any who claim that it is necessary for them to have such a place, they are to come to Rome. . . .

2. No man is to be a Bacchantian, neither a Roman citizen, nor one of the Latin name, nor any of our allies unless they come to the praetor urbanus [the consul in charge of the city of Rome], and he in accordance with the opinion of the Senate . . . shall have given leave. . . .

3. No man is to be a priest; no one, either man or woman, is to be an officer (to manage the affairs of the organization); nor is anyone of them to have charge of a common treasury; . . . henceforth they shall not form conspiracies among themselves, stir up any disorder, make mutual promises or agreements, or interchange pledges.

4. No one shall carry out the sacred rites either in public or private or outside the city, unless he comes to the praetor urbanus, and he, in accordance with the opinion of the senate . . . shall have given leave.

See that you declare it in the assembly for not less than three market days; that you may know that this was the opinion of the Senate and their judgment: if there are any who have acted contrary to what was written above, the Senate has decided that a proceeding for a capital offense should be instituted against them. . . .

---

1. The decree regulates Bacchanalian practices, but it does not forbid them. What do people have to do to be able to practice the Bacchanalian rites?

_____

_____

2. What does the third point of the decree seem to be concerned with?

_____

_____

3. What is the penalty for breaking the rules of this decree?

_____

_____

NAME _____ **DATE** _____

A. MULTIPLE CHOICE

Circle the letter of the best answer for each question.

1. The Romans believed in the power of the "evil eye," which was
   a. a large eye in a monument at the center of every town.
   b. the ability of some people to cause misfortune by looking at someone else.
   c. a power of certain gods.
   d. an early form of television.

b

2. Supernatural beliefs that were part of Roman medical treatment included using
   a. home remedies.   **c.** chants.
   b. plants and roots.   **d.** medicines.

c

3. All of the following show how Rome's early religion was tied to a place **except**
   a. people worshiping spirits that lived in a river.
   b. people worshiping spirits that lived in a woodland.
   c. people worshiping an emperor after his death.
   d. people worshiping gods that protected certain cities.

c

4. Cybele's worshipers celebrated the coming of spring with
   a. plays and contests.   **c.** feasts and prayer.
   b. speeches and demonstrations.   **d.** wild dancing and animal sacrifices.

d

5. The worship of gods and goddesses like Cybele, Isis, and Mithras became popular
   a. in the city of Rome.   **c.** throughout the eastern empire.
   b. in the city of Pompeii.   **d.** throughout the whole empire.

d

B. SHORT ANSWER

Write one or two sentences to answer each question.

6. Why were chariot drivers especially superstitious?

_____

_____

7. Why can the Roman religion be likened to a huge basket?

_____

_____

8. Why did Romans worship Isis?

_____

_____

C. ESSAY

Write an essay on a separate sheet of paper comparing and contrasting the cults of Cybele and Isis.

CHAPTER 22

TAXES AND TACTICS IN THE PROVINCES: ADMINISTERING THE EMPIRE
PAGES 144–148

FOR HOMEWORK

STUDENT STUDY GUIDE
pages 53–54

 VOCABULARY

enemy someone seeking to harm or conquer another

ocher red or yellow clay used for makeup

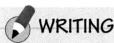 **WRITING**

○ **Dialogue** Discuss with the class the reasons Roman provincials might have had for supporting or opposing the Roman
○ occupation. Then have students form pairs and write "silent dialogues" between a supporter and an opponent of Roman rule.
○ Students should pass a piece of paper back and forth, responding to each other in writing. Invite pairs to perform their dialogues.

CHAPTER SUMMARY

Maintaining Rome's sprawling empire required thousands of men and a constant supply of money. Collecting taxes to pay for officials and soldiers was an endless task for administrators and a burden for citizens. Even the most reluctant taxpayer, however, appreciated the paved roads, clean water, and public order that often accompanied Roman occupation.

PERFORMANCE OBJECTIVES

▶ To understand Rome's need for taxes and means of collecting them
▶ To describe the relationship between taxes and the census
▶ To appreciate the long-lasting influence of Roman occupation

BUILDING BACKGROUND

Ask students what they know about taxes—what they are and how governments collect them. Then brainstorm with the class ways in which tax revenue—local, state, and national—is spent. Explain that Rome's empire had many of the same needs for tax money that modern countries have.

WORKING WITH PRIMARY SOURCES

Read the first page of the chapter with students. Discuss the effect of a historian making up words for real historical people to say. What are the advantages? (*makes history come to life*) What are the disadvantages? (*may change the reality of the historical situation*) Elicit that historians generally have to interpret events from long ago and write about them in a way that appeals to readers. Good historians balance the desire to tell a good story and the need to present facts correctly.

GEOGRAPHY CONNECTION

Region   Have students turn to the map of the ancient Roman world at the beginning of their books and identify the different provinces of the empire. Elicit that such far-flung lands would have widely differing cultures and practices, but that under the Roman Empire, they all had a similar government.

READING COMPREHENSION QUESTIONS

1. What argument does Tacitus say the Roman general Cerialis used to persuade the Britons that imperial taxes were necessary? (*Taxes paid the soldiers who kept the peace.*)
2. What was the "genius" of the way Rome ruled the provinces? (*Although the Romans brought in governors, tax collectors, and troops, it let the provinces mostly govern themselves, even choosing local people to be governors and military commanders.*)
3. What was the purpose of the census? (*to count the number of taxpayers and calculate how much they should pay*)
4. What effects did Roman rule have on people in the provinces? (*Not only did they benefit from the peace that Roman rule brought them, but they began to imitate Roman ways in education, fashion, architecture, town planning, and so on.*)

5. Distribute copies of the blackline master for Chapter 22 so students can learn more about becoming a Roman citizen.

CRITICAL THINKING QUESTIONS

1. Review the opposing arguments of Calgacus and Cerialis on page 144. Which do you find most persuasive? Explain your answer. (*Possible answer: I find Calgacus most persuasive. The Romans had invaded his country and taken over. Nothing can make that right.*)

2. The philosopher Synesius claimed that the people had no clear idea of who the emperor was. Would you say this is similar to the attitude of Americans toward their president? Explain your answer. (*Possible answer: No. We see a lot of the president on TV and in the newspapers. Every four years there is a presidential campaign.*)

3. Why do you suppose the Roman governor Agricola was successful in winning over the Britons? (*Possible answer: He allowed them to live like Romans and to get ahead in the world. The Britons probably enjoyed the benefits of education and modern cities.*)

SOCIAL SCIENCES

Civics   Have students explore the tax system of your state and local community. Encourage them to contact local municipal offices for a breakdown of how town or city taxes are spent.

READING AND LANGUAGE ARTS

Reading Nonfiction   Ask what fact is given in the fourth paragraph on page 145, and how we know it is a fact. (*that soldiers were stationed at Fishbourne; the words "We know" precede the fact, and details follow it*) Point out the paragraph on page 147 beginning "People must have complained . . ." Ask: Is this statement a fact or an opinion? Elicit that it is an opinion supported by what we know about people in general.

Using Language   Have students find synonyms for *leader* in the chapter, such as *king, emperor, commander, chief, general, governor*. Have students distinguish shades of meaning between the synonyms.

SUPPORTING LEARNING

English Language Learners   Have students find examples of figurative language; for instance, the first sentence of the paragraph on page 148 beginning "Just as Rome . . ." Have them explain to partners what the figurative language means.

Struggling Readers   Have students complete a two-column chart about Roman rule of the provinces labeled *Advantages* and *Disadvantages*. Have students evaluate whether Roman rule was positive or negative for the provinces.

EXTENDING LEARNING

Enrichment   Point out that Roman aqueducts were designed for their function but are admired for their beauty. Have students find pictures of aqueducts. Ask them to redraw the pictures on poster board, adding labels of the various parts.

Extension   Have students role-play Calgacus and Cerialis from Tacitus's account (page 144).

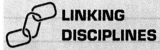
Math Distribute to partners copies of U.S. income tax tables (available on many websites). Explain how the charts work, and then have partners make up word problems about imaginary citizens and the income taxes they have to pay. Partners can exchange their problems with others for solving. After students have solved problems, you may wish to discuss whether the tax system is fair (i.e., people who make more money are supposed to pay more in taxes).

WHAT DID IT MEAN TO BE A ROMAN CITIZEN?

Directions

With a partner, read the following paragraphs about Roman citizenship. The first paragraph was inscribed on a bronze tablet from 168 CE. It commemorates the granting of Roman citizenship to Julianus, a member of the Zegrenses, a tribe living in North Africa in what is now Morocco. The second paragraph is an excerpt from the *Roman Oration* written around 144 CE, by Publius Aelius Aristides, a Greek who became a Roman citizen, philosopher, and champion of Roman rule. After you have finished reading, answer the questions.

> Copy of the letter of our Emperors Marcus Aurelius and Verus, Augusti, to [the governor]: We have read the petition of Julianus the Zegresian attached to your letter. It is not usual to give Roman citizenship to men of that tribe except when very great services prompt the Emperor to show this kindness. Nevertheless, since you say he is one of the leading men of his people and is very loyal and ready to be of help to us—and since we think there are not many families among the Zegrenses who can make equal boasts about their services—although we hope that many of them will imitate Julianus because of the honor we confer on him and his family—we do not hesitate to grant Roman citizenship, without impairment to the law of the tribe, to himself, to his wife Ziddina, likewise to their children Julianus, Maximus, Maximinus, Diogenianus.

> You [Romans] have caused the word "Roman" to be the mark, not of membership in a city, but of some common nationality. . . . For the categories into which you now divide the world are Romans and non-Romans. . . . Many in every city are fellow-citizens of yours . . . though some of them have never set eyes on Rome. There is no need of garrisons to hold . . . the empire. The men of greatest standing and influence in every city guard their own fatherlands for you. . . . What previously seemed impossible has come to pass in your time: maintenance of control over an empire—a vast one too—and at the same time firmness of rule without severity.

1. How did Julianus qualify to become a Roman citizen?

_____

_____

2. What effect did the Romans hope Julianus's citizenship would have on other members of his tribe?

_____

_____

3. Julianus and his family became Roman citizens "without impairment to the law of the tribe." This meant that they were expected to obey local laws and customs as well as the laws of Rome. Do you think this "dual citizenship" strengthened or weakened the Roman Empire? Why?

_____

_____

4. In *Roman Oration*, Aristides says, "The men of greatest standing and influence in every city guard their own fatherlands for you." Explain how the Roman citizens he is talking about kept the empire strong.

_____

_____

NAME   **DATE**

A. MULTIPLE CHOICE

Circle the letter of the best answer for each question.

1. Disadvantages of Roman rule in the provinces included all of the following **except**
   a. forced labor.
   b. taxes.
   c. cruelty of the Romans.
   d. tyranny of local kings.

2. Advantages of Roman rule in the provinces included all of the following **except**
   a. paying taxes.
   b. greater safety.
   c. local rulers.
   d. schools and aqueducts.

3. For people living in the provinces, the Roman emperor
   a. had a major effect on everyday life.
   b. was mostly unknown.
   c. was well liked.
   d. had no control.

4. Roman censuses were designed to gather information to
   a. create voting lists.
   b. collect taxes.
   c. write government reports.
   d. make people move to their hometowns.

5. The governmental practices of Agricola in Britain had the effect of
   a. angering the provincials.
   b. educating all the Britons.
   c. making provincials more like Romans.
   d. raising more tax revenue.

B. SHORT ANSWER

Write one or two sentences to answer each question.

6. How did Rome manage to rule its huge empire so successfully?

7. In order to be counted in a Roman census, what did people have to do?

8. What were the most long-lasting effects of Roman rule on the provinces?

C. ESSAY

On a separate sheeet of paper, write an essay explaining what Rome got from the provinces and what the provinces got from Rome.

FOR HOMEWORK

**STUDENT
STUDY GUIDE**
pages 55–56

**CAST OF
CHARACTERS**

Judas Maccabeus
leader of successful
Jewish revolt against
Antiochus

THEN and NOW

"His Majesty's
Government view with
favour the establishment
in Palestine of a national
home for the Jewish
people." These simple
words—written in 1917
by the British foreign
secretary—signaled the
beginning of the Jewish
people's return to their
homeland after an exile
of 1,800 years.

 VOCABULARY

kosher laws about food
followed by certain Jews

Yahweh (YAH-way) the
name for the Jewish
God

client a state that relies
on another state for
protection

CHAPTER SUMMARY

In attempting to unify the diverse cultures under its rule, Rome faced an uphill battle. The Jews of Judea proved impossible to assimilate. They could be crushed in warfare and scattered throughout the world, but their unifying faith and defining cultural memories assured survival for the Jewish people.

PERFORMANCE OBJECTIVES

▶ To explain the fundamental principles of Judaism
▶ To trace the key events in early Jewish history
▶ To describe Rome's struggle with the Jews

BUILDING BACKGROUND

Write the term *anti-Semitism* on the board, and elicit from students what they know about it. (You might introduce Germany's treatment of the Jews prior to and during World War II or a current issue involving anti-Semitism.) Point out that the Jewish people have struggled throughout their history—and continue to struggle—to live an unthreatened existence.

WORKING WITH PRIMARY SOURCES

Many students will be familiar with the Christian Bible, known as the New Testament, represented in this chapter by the Gospel of Matthew. Students may also be familiar with the Hebrew Bible, often referred to as the Old Testament. Relevant passages include stories about the Exodus, the Ten Commandments, and King David. Help students understand that, besides being holy books of Judaism and Christianity, these books are full of references that historians use to corroborate other sources and fix dates in antiquity.

GEOGRAPHY CONNECTION

Movement   Since ancient times described in this chapter, the history of the Jewish people has been one of *diaspora* (dispersal) and attempts to return to Palestine (or Jerusalem or Israel). Explain to students that, although the Jewish people have spread to all regions of the globe, they are held together by their common religion and their belief in a special relationship with a single god, Yahweh. Distribute copies of the blackline master for Chapter 23 so students can learn more about the Jewish diaspora in Roman times.

READING COMPREHENSION QUESTIONS

1. Why is the Sabbath day important in the Jewish faith? (*That was the seventh day of creation, when God rested. Every seventh day is a holy day for the Jews.*)
2. Why would the Jews not bow down to a Roman emperor and call him a god? (*They believed there was only one God—Yahweh. To worship the state gods of Rome would be a sin in their religion.*)
3. Why is Judas Maccabeus a hero to the Jewish people? (*He drove King Antiochus of Syria out of Jerusalem and rebuilt the temple.*)

4. What caused the tradition of rabbinic Judaism to arise? (*With the temple in Jerusalem destroyed and sacrifices no longer allowed, priests no longer led the Jewish community. Instead, rabbis led the study of the ancient religious texts and became the new community leaders.*)

CRITICAL THINKING QUESTIONS

1. What makes the Ten Commandments particularly important to the Jewish people? (*They were believed to have been written by Yahweh and given directly to Moses. Because they came straight from God, these laws were sacred.*)

2. According to the text, Antiochus of Syria disliked the Jews because they were different. What was the difference? (*The Jewish people believed in a single god, whereas the Syrians believed in many gods. Antiochus wanted to make the Jews be more like the Greeks, and therefore less "suspicious."*)

3. Why do you suppose the Romans crushed the Jews and didn't let them practice their own customs? (*Possible answer: The Romans wanted all of their conquered peoples to become like Romans—worship their gods, give allegiance to the emperor, and so on. The Jews had a powerful religion that would never permit them to become good Roman citizens. They obeyed their God first, not the emperor.*)

SOCIAL SCIENCES

Science, Technology, and Society   Point out that modern-day Jerusalem has special meaning to Judaism, Christianity, and Islam. Have students research the major holy sites in Jerusalem of each of these religions. Students can make bulletin board displays of their work. A useful website is *www.md.huji.ac.il/vjt.*

READING AND LANGUAGE ARTS

Reading Nonfiction   Draw attention to the Jewish creation story (page 150). Many peoples have their own versions of how the world began. Encourage students to research a creation story from another culture and present it orally to the class.

Using Language   Write *monotheist* and *polytheist* on the board. Elicit the meanings of *mono-* ("one") and *poly-* ("many"). Have students name and define other words that begin with these prefixes.

SUPPORTING LEARNING

English Language Learners   Have students write an organized list of religious practices that their families or relatives follow.

Struggling Readers   Have students use a Venn diagram (found in the back of this guide) to compare and contrast the religious beliefs and practices of the Romans and the Jews.

EXTENDING LEARNING

Enrichment   Have students use an encyclopedia to investigate the founding of the modern state of Israel and report to their classmates.

Extension   Have volunteers draw a picture of the tablets on which Moses is said to have inscribed the Ten Commandments. Display the picture, and discuss the meaning of each commandment.

WRITING

Research Report
Hanukkah, the Festival of Light, is one of the best-known Jewish holidays. Have students research Hanukkah at the library or online and ask them to tell about this festival's unique traditions.

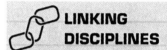

LINKING DISCIPLINES

Art Have students examine the coin pictured on page 150. Point out that throughout history coins have commemorated historical events. Ask students to design a coin celebrating an event of their own choosing.

THE JEWISH DIASPORA

Directions

Study the map and read the information. Then answer the questions on a separate sheet of paper.

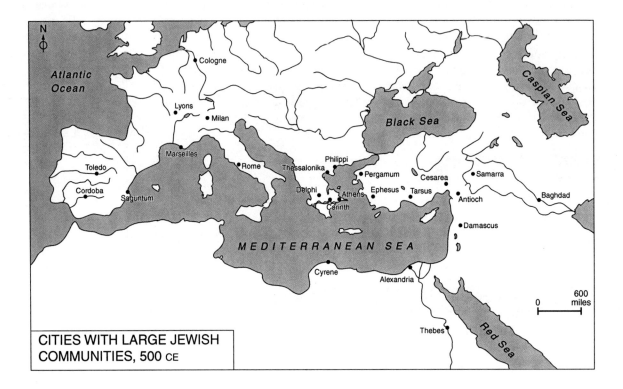

CITIES WITH LARGE JEWISH COMMUNITIES, 500 CE

Many people were displaced by invaders in the ancient world and forced to move to new locations. This movement of a whole people united by religion and custom is called a *diaspora*. The word is usually applied to the forced movement of Jews out of Judea and Jerusalem.

Many Jews were brought to Rome as slaves. In Rome the Jewish slaves were ransomed by free Jews living in Rome. In addition to Jews who arrived as slaves, many Jews emigrated from Judea to Rome. Roman writers describe some Roman Jews as poor and some as beggars, but there were also Jewish merchants, craftsmen, actors, and scholars.

In the later Roman Empire, cities in southern Italy became important Jewish centers, and large settlements appeared in western North Africa and in Spain. Jewish communities were also established in Gaul. The Greek geographer Strabo wrote, "This people [Jewish] has already made its way into every city, and it is not easy to find any place in the habitable world which has not received the nation and in which it has not made its power felt."

1. Jerusalem is on the eastern shore of the Mediterranean Sea, south of Damascus. Which Jewish communities were farthest from the Jews' original homeland?

2. Why isn't Jerusalem shown on the map?

3. Why do you think Jews would have voluntarily moved to Rome from Judea?

NAME   **DATE**

A. MULTIPLE CHOICE

Circle the letter of the best answer for each question.

1. Jewish law, found in the Hebrew Bible, set strict rules for
   a. daily life.
   b. relations with other countries.
   c. warfare.
   d. education.

2. The major difference between the Jews and other people in the region was that Jews
   a. had special rules about food.
   b. had priests.
   c. worshiped only one God.
   d. worshiped many gods.

3. The Jewish festival of Hanukkah celebrates
   a. Judas Maccabeus's defeat by Antiochus IV.
   b. Judas Maccabeus's defeat of Antiochus IV.
   c. the building of the temple in Jerusalem by Solomon.
   d. the uniting of the Jewish tribes under David.

4. The Jews hated Herod because
   a. he was only half Jewish.
   b. he tried to force Greek and Roman ways on them.
   c. he didn't eat pork.
   d. he crushed their rebellion.

5. The rebellion of Simon Bar-Kochbar resulted in
   a. the founding of a strong Jewish state.
   b. the destruction of the temple in Jerusalem.
   c. the scattering of the Jews throughout the Roman Empire.
   d. the return of the Jewish priests to Jerusalem.

B. SHORT ANSWER

Write one or two sentences to answer each question.

6. What were some religious rules that the Jews followed?

_____

_____

7. How did Antiochus IV try to force the Jews to be more like Greeks?

_____

_____

8. What is the tradition of Rabbinic Judaism?

_____

_____

C. ESSAY

Write an essay on a separate sheet of paper explaining why the Jews were despised and persecuted by the Romans, and how they were able to remain as a united people.

CAST OF CHARACTERS

Jesus Christ Jewish prophet thought to be the Messiah; his disciples founded Christianity

Herod cruel king of Judea (37–4 BCE)

Paul disciple of Jesus who spread Christianity beyond Palestine

Constantine emperor who made Christianity favored religion of Roman Empire

 WRITING

Modern Parables
Provide the class with copies of the original parables of the Good Samaritan and the Prodigal Son (summarized on pages 157 and 159). Read and discuss them with the class. Then have students rewrite the parables, setting them in the modern world.

CHAPTER SUMMARY

The humble life of Christ and the struggles of the early Christian church gave no suggestion that Christianity would become one of the major spiritual and political forces of the world. By the fourth century CE, however, Christians were in control of the Roman Empire and determining the course of world history.

PERFORMANCE OBJECTIVES

▶ To summarize the life and teachings of Jesus
▶ To describe the development of the early Christian church
▶ To understand the church's rise to political power

BUILDING BACKGROUND

Elicit details that students know about early Christianity—who founded it, where did it begin, what were its teachings.

WORKING WITH PRIMARY SOURCES

Help students understand which of the sources used in this chapter are from the Christian Bible (Gospels of Luke and Matthew), which are from the Hebrew Bible (Isaiah, Zechariah, and Micah), and which are from other sources (Tacitus and Eusebius). Have students recognize that the sources from the two bibles were written specifically for adherents of those religions, whereas the works of Tacitus and Eusebius were general histories. Have students infer how the religious texts differ from the history texts.

GEOGRAPHY CONNECTION

Movement Have students study the map of the spread of Christianity on page 161. Ask them what they notice about the extent of Christianity in 300 CE versus its extent from 300–600 CE. Have them predict what caused the entire empire to become Christianized so quickly.

READING COMPREHENSION QUESTIONS

1. Why did the Jews look forward to the coming of the Messiah? (*They believed that the Messiah would save them from enemy rule.*)
2. According to Matthew, why did Mary and Joseph escape to Egypt with the baby Jesus? (*King Herod ordered the slaughter of all newborn babies in Bethlehem.*)
3. What did followers of Jesus believe happened after his death? (*After three days in the tomb, he rose from the dead.*)
4. What did Constantine see in the sky and how did it change his life? (*He saw a cross in the sky before a battle. He became a supporter of the Christians.*)
5. Distribute copies of the blackline master for Chapter 24 so students can learn more about the Roman treatment of Christians in the second century CE.

CRITICAL THINKING QUESTIONS

1. Why did many Jews expect the Messiah to be a warrior king? (*Possible answer: They must have thought that he would have to be a warrior in order to drive out the Romans.*)

2. By telling the world that Jesus came back to life, what message were his followers sending to the authorities? (*Possible answer: A man who can conquer death really is the Messiah.*)

3. Why might the Roman emperors have permitted Christians to worship Jesus if they had worshiped the emperor as well? (*Possible answer: Romans were polytheists. They didn't mind people worshiping many gods.*)

SOCIAL SCIENCES

Civics   Point out that Constantine's choice of Constantinople for his Christian capital was no accident. Have students research the location of Constantinople and find out why it was an ideal site for "the new Rome."

READING AND LANGUAGE ARTS

Reading Nonfiction   Have students reread the excerpt from the Beatitudes. Invite volunteers to read the passage aloud as if they were addressing a large crowd. Point out how repetition gives extra power to the words.

Using Language   Have students read the Prodigal Son parable in *The World in Ancient Times Primary Sources and Reference Volume*, and then have partners write their own parables. Elicit universal themes about which the parables will teach, and write them on the board. Have partners read their parables to the class.

SUPPORTING LEARNING

English Language Learners   Call on volunteers to read aloud the excerpts from the primary sources in the chapter. Discuss what they think the sources mean, and how the style of writing is different from the way people write and speak today.

Struggling Readers   Have students make a comparison-contrast chart to show how the teachings of Jesus differed from Roman culture.

EXTENDING LEARNING

Enrichment   Ask students to research the historical aspects of the life of Jesus Christ. Students can create a timeline of events in his life.

Extension   Discuss the idea that, in early Rome, Christians were seen to be different and dangerous. Elicit modern instances of misconceptions between people of different cultures. Ask how people can deal with this problem peacefully.

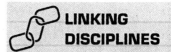

THEN and **NOW**

From its difficult early years, Christianity emerged to become the world's largest religion. About a third of the world's population (over 2 billion people) call themselves Christians.

LINKING DISCIPLINES

Art Draw students' attention to the painting reproduced on page 158. Point out that scenes from the life of Christ—from birth to resurrection—were among the favorite subjects of great European artists for centuries. Have students print out images of scenes from Christ's life from reproductions of fine art available on the Internet. Students may choose to make their own paintings in imitation of those they find.

NAME   DATE

ROMAN TREATMENT OF CHRISTIANS

Directions

With a partner, read the following selections. The first is a letter from Pliny the Younger, governor of Bithynia (Turkey) in 112 CE to Emperor Trajan. Pliny was faced with determining the guilt or innocence of people accused of being Christians. Unsure of how to deal with them, he wrote to Trajan for advice. The second selection is Trajan's reply to Pliny. When you are finished reading, answer the questions.

Pliny to Trajan

Since I have had no experience with questioning or punishing Christians . . . I have done the following with those who have been brought before me as Christians. I asked them whether they were Christians or not. If they confessed that they were Christians, I asked them again, and a third time, intermixing threats with the questions. If they continued to confess, I ordered them to be executed. . . . There have been some of this mad sect who are Roman citizens, and they were sent to that city.

After some time . . . many more cases came before me. . . . An unsigned message was sent to me accusing many people by name of being Christians. . . . They were called in but denied that they were Christians now, or ever had been. They called upon the gods, and prayed to your image, which I caused to be brought to me for that purpose. . . . Since they did things that people say Christians cannot be compelled to do, I let them go. . . .

This superstition [Christianity] is spreading like a contagious disease, not only into cities and towns, but into country villages. . . . Yet there is reason to hope it may be stopped and corrected.

Trajan to Pliny

You have used the correct method in examining . . . those . . . accused as Christians, for indeed no certain and general form of judging can be ordained in this case. These people are not to be sought for; but if they be accused and convicted, they are to be punished; but with this caution, that he who denies himself to be a Christian, and makes it plain that he is not by praying to our gods, . . . even if he had been a Christian at one time, may be pardoned, upon his repentance. As for libels [messages accusing others of crimes] sent without an author, they ought to have no place in any accusation whatsoever, for that would be a thing of very ill example, and not agreeable to my reign.

---

1. Pliny says he questions the accused in a particular manner. Why do you suppose he uses this technique?

_____

_____

2. What is Pliny's attitude toward Christians? How can you tell?

_____

_____

3. What does Trajan's response tell you about his major concerns?

_____

_____

NAME _____ DATE _____

A. MULTIPLE CHOICE

Circle the letter of the best answer for each question.

1. According to the Gospel of Luke, Jesus was first recognized as the Messiah
   a. when he was a baby.
   b. when he and his parents escaped to Egypt.
   c. when he returned to Jerusalem.
   d. when he preached the Sermon on the Mount.

2. Through his teachings, Jesus made enemies among the Jews because he
   a. demanded the overthrow of Roman rule.
   b. advised that Jewish holidays not be observed.
   c. had ideas that were different from traditional Jewish teachings.
   d. was taking students away from other teachers.

3. After Jesus' death, his teachings were spread throughout the Roman world by
   a. his disciple Paul and other missionaries.
   b. Roman soldiers.
   c. the emperor Nero.
   d. people who sold his books.

4. In the Roman Empire, early Christians were persecuted because
   a. they worshiped Jesus.
   b. they had originally been Jews.
   c. they wanted to overthrow the government.
   d. they wouldn't worship the emperor.

5. The course of Christian history changed in 312 CE when
   a. the Christians won a major battle.
   b. Constantine, who later became emperor, began to worship Jesus.
   c. the Roman emperor became a Christian.
   d. a new version of the Gospels was published.

B. SHORT ANSWER

Write one or two sentences to answer each question.

6. What signs did the followers of Jesus believe showed that he was the Messiah?

   _____

   _____

7. What were some of the values emphasized by the Beatitudes?

   _____

   _____

8. Why was Emperor Constantine's reign important for the growth of Christianity?

   _____

   _____

C. ESSAY

Rome had conquered the Mediterranean world militarily. It can be said that Christianity conquered the Roman Empire through its teachings. On a separate sheet of paper, write an essay comparing and contrasting these two conquests.

DECLINE AND FALL OF THE EMPIRE PAGES 163–176

UNIT OBJECTIVES

Unit 8 deals with the final fall of the Roman Empire and the legacy that the empire left behind. In this unit, your students will learn

► the problems that plagued the later empire.
► the attempt to rule the empire better by splitting it in two.
► the disastrous results for the western empire of this split.
► the influence that Rome has had on Europe and the world after the fall of the empire.

PRIMARY SOURCES

Unit 8 includes excerpts from the following primary sources:

► Tacitus, *The Annals*
► Suetonius, *Life of Augustus*
► Lactantius, *Divine Institutes*
► Anonymous, *The Life of Leo the Great*
► Symmachus, *Dispatches to the Emperor*
► Cassiodorus, *Variae*
► Cicero, *On Duties*

Pictures of artifacts from this period can also be analyzed as primary sources:

► Statue of wounded soldier
► Relief sculpture on Constantine's victory arch
► Pantheon
► Painting of emperors with Jesus and Mary
► Hagia Sophia
► Statue of George Washington
► U.S. Capitol
► Los Angeles Coliseum

BIG IDEAS IN UNIT 8

Religion, change, conflict, and **movement** are the big ideas of Unit 8. These chapters concentrate on the major changes in Europe that occurred in the later part of the Roman Empire. The empire was becoming Christianized at the same time it was being overrun by barbarians. When the government of the empire was split, the western half could no longer support itself, which accelerated losses to barbarian invaders. Eventually, the Germanic and Central Asian barbarians took over all of the lands of the western empire, and placed one of their own on the throne of Rome.

The decline and fall of Rome suggests that civilizations, like living creatures, have life spans of their own. Rome's legacy to the modern world in politics, art, and philosophy argues that great ideas also have independent lives. Studying Roman history casts a revealing light upon our own civilization.

You may want to introduce these ideas by having students preview the chapters in the unit. Have students scan the chapter titles, side notes, and graphic aids to predict what the chapters will discuss. Have them look at the map on page 165 to see a graphic portrayal of how power slipped away from Rome.

GEOGRAPHY CONNECTION

Have students look at the map on page 165. Point out the location of Constantinople, near the small neck of land that connects Asia to Macedonia by the Black Sea. Use the map to discuss why the eastern empire was not subject to barbarian invasions. (*Barbarians could not get past the defenses of Constantinople; deserts blocked their advance in Africa and Syria.*)

TIMELINE

9 CE	Arminius's Germans massacre Roman legions under Varus
235 CE	Beginning of 50 years of governmental chaos
284 CE	Domitian becomes emperor
312 CE	Constantine becomes emperor
330 CE	Constantinople built; power shifts to eastern empire
392 CE	Theodosius the Great outlaws pagan worship in Rome
395 CE	Theodosius dies; empire splits into eastern and western halves
407 CE	Last Roman soldiers leave Britain
410 CE	Sack of Rome by Goths
429 CE	Barbarians gain control of almost all of Rome's western provinces
450 CE	Huns invade Italy
476 CE	Last Roman emperor forced from throne by Odoacer, King of Italy

UNIT PROJECTS

Chronology

Students can finish the class timeline begun in earlier units to show the sequence of events in this unit. As a review of the book, you may want to have students condense all of the unit timelines into one that shows the most important points in Rome's history.

Sketching History

Draw students' attention to the painting reproduced on page 167. Point out that before photography, paintings and sketches were the only way important moments could be visually preserved. Have small groups sketch their vision of important events in this unit. (They may want to do an online search to find pictures of these events to copy.) Students can put their artwork together into a booklet for display.

Roman-Style Architecture

Point out that physical evidence of Rome's influence is all around us in the architecture of our public buildings. Many state capitol buildings, for example, are built in a Roman style. Have students research Roman architecture and find American buildings constructed in the Roman tradition. Encourage students to bring illustrations of their buildings to class.

ADDITIONAL ASSESSMENT

For Unit 8, divide the class into groups and have them all undertake the Sketching History project so you can assess their understanding of events in this unit. Use the scoring rubric at the back of this guide to assess students' work, and have students rate their own work with the self-assessment rubric.

LITERATURE CONNECTION

Remind students of the literary sources they have used in connection with studying ancient Rome: the great historians, the dramatists and humorists, the biographers, and the philosophers. Help them understand that part of the Roman heritage is its fine literary tradition. Have volunteers read aloud excerpts from these works from the pages of their book.

Students may also enjoy reading the following books that will extend their understanding of life in Rome during this period.

▶ Chrisp, Peter. *Revealed: Ancient Rome*. New York: Dorling Kindersley, 2003. Nonfiction. AVERAGE
▶ Nardo, Don. *The Decline and Fall of the Roman Empire*. San Diego, CA: Lucent, 1998. Nonfiction. ADVANCED
▶ Sutcliffe, Rosemary. *The Lantern Bearers*. New York: Farrar, Straus & Giroux, 1994. Fiction. EASY

UNIVERSAL ACCESS

The following strategies are designed to cover a range of learning styles and reading, language, and skill levels.

Reading Strategies

▶ This unit deals with the decline and fall of the Roman Empire. Students can keep track of the events by creating a downward-trending line graph in their notebooks and adding labels for the different events. Positive events can cause a slight upturn in the line, but then it will continue its downward movement.

▶ The Epilogue can serve as a jumping-off point for a review of the book. Read the chapter aloud with your students, and use the points brought out in the chapter to review information in the book.

Writing Strategies

▶ Review with students the skills of summarizing and paraphrasing. Have students write a summary of a section of a chapter in a few sentences, including only the main ideas. Then have them paraphrase what they wrote, using their own words. Students can work in pairs, paraphrasing each other's work and reinforcing their understanding of the material.

▶ Have students create an outline to organize information about the decline and fall of the Roman Empire. Major headings could include *Barbarians, Government Turmoil, Revenues,* and *Christianity.*

Listening and Speaking Strategies

▶ Small groups can create skits showing important events in the unit: the defeat of Varus's legions, the meeting of Attila the Hun and Pope Leo, and so on. Students can create simple props and perform their skits for the class.

▶ Encourage groups of students to prepare a debate about the legacy of Rome. Each group should put forth and support the idea that a certain aspect of Rome's legacy—architecture, government, culture, military, for example—is the most important.

UNIT VOCABULARY LIST

The following words that appear in Unit 8 are important for your students' understanding of the social studies content as well as for development of literacy. Use these words for vocabulary study or to reinforce language arts skills (e.g., synonyms, compound words, prefixes and suffixes, and related words). The words are listed below in the order in which they appear in the chapters.

Chapter 25	**Chapter 26**	**Epilogue**
massacre	humble	ambassador
kinsman	reorganize	cement
flattery	tetrarchy	concrete
ambush	devastate	tangible
underestimate	vulnerable	civic
disorganized	manufacture	
catapult	adapt	
cannibalism		
dull witted		
crucial		
hordes		
nomadic		
ransack		
traumatic		
beggar		

ROME'S POWER SLIPS AWAY: THE BARBARIANS
PAGES 163–167

CAST OF CHARACTERS

Varus Roman general who suffered terrible defeat by Germans (9 CE)

Arminius (ar-MIN-ee-us) leader of Germans who defeated Varus

Marcus Aurelius (ow-REL-ee-us) 2nd-century CE emperor who defended the Rhine and Danube borders

VOCABULARY

barbarian foreigner; someone who did not share Roman culture

THEN and NOW

Because of Attila the Hun's fearsome reputation, today people who are seen as having no mercy in a competition may be called "Attila"

CHAPTER SUMMARY

Rome's "eternal" empire was never entirely secure. Even at the height of its power, barbarians constantly threatened the unstable borderlands. By the 5th century CE, Germanic tribes were making regular incursions into Roman territory. Divided within and attacked from without, Rome lost its centuries-old grip on the empire.

PERFORMANCE OBJECTIVES

▶ To describe an early attack by barbarians upon Rome
▶ To understand the relationship between Rome and the barbarians
▶ To summarize attacks on the empire by the Goths and the Huns

BUILDING BACKGROUND

Ask students if the world is ever totally at peace. Lead them to understand that even in times of relative stability, there are tensions and flare-ups throughout the world. Discuss with students dangers that currently threaten the United States and other nations. Point out that the Roman Empire was constantly on guard against enemy attack.

WORKING WITH PRIMARY SOURCES

Distribute copies of the blackline master for Chapter 25 so students can read a firsthand account of Attila the Hun and conditions at his court.

GEOGRAPHY CONNECTION

Movement   Have students form pairs and ask them to examine the map of Germanic invasions on page 165. Partners should then formulate and answer questions based on the map. (Examples: *Which tribes invaded Britain? Which tribes directly threatened Rome?*)

READING COMPREHENSION QUESTIONS

1. How did the Germanic barbarians under Arminius surprise and defeat the Roman legions under Varus? (*Arminius fooled Varus, who thought of the Germans as slaves and underestimated Arminius's skills. Arminius tricked Varus into sending his legions into a trap from which few escaped.*)
2. How did the Roman attitude to barbarians change over time? (*At first, Romans thought the barbarians were simply savages. Later they learned that barbarians could be clever and capable.*)
3. What happened in 410 CE that shocked the city of Rome? Why was this so shocking? (*The sack of Rome by the Goths; no barbarian army had captured Rome in 800 years.*)
4. What saved Rome from being captured by Attila the Hun? (*Pope Leo met with Attila and convinced him—or bribed him—not to take the city.*)

CRITICAL THINKING QUESTIONS

1. What caused wave after wave of barbarians to push against the borders of the Roman Empire? (*Hungry, poor people were coming from eastern Europe in search of more fertile lands near the Mediterranean. A long drought forced the Huns to migrate westward, uprooting other people and forcing them to push into the empire.*)

2. How did the idea of "Eternal Rome" contribute to the shock after the "Sack of Rome" in 410 CE? (*Possible answer: People believed that Rome would last forever. Seeing the city invaded was unbelievable and terrible to them.*)

3. Given the evidence in this chapter, do you think it was possible for Rome to keep the barbarians out of the empire? (*Possible answer: No, the Roman army did not have the power to stop the immigration of huge masses of people into western Europe.*)

SOCIAL SCIENCES

Science, Technology, and Society Consider why the Roman army, which had over the centuries defeated the best armies of the civilized world because of better weapons, discipline, training, and leadership, could not control the barbarian incursions. Have students investigate the Huns and why they were able to sweep almost all resistance before them.

READING AND LANGUAGE ARTS

Reading Nonfiction Have students use the cause and effect chart (found in the back of this guide) while they read to identify the causes of the decline of the Roman Empire.

Using Language Write *barbarian* and *Vandal* on the board. Ask students how history defines these words. Then ask them for modern meanings of these words, and have them use the words in original sentences.

SUPPORTING LEARNING

English Language Learners Point out the expression *smoothly buttered words* on page 164, and have students figure out its meaning. Do the same for *dull witted* on pages 165–166.

Struggling Readers Have students list reasons why Roman citizens would think that the fall of Rome would mean the end of the world.

EXTENDING LEARNING

Enrichment Students will use encyclopedias to investigate Arminius to learn about his role in German rebellions against Roman rule and the ultimate Roman decision to abandon the conquest of Germany.

Extension Have students act out the meeting between Attila the Hun and Pope Leo.

WRITING

Persuasive Letter Review with students the trick Arminius played on Varus, described on page 164. Ask how they think Arminius would have persuaded Varus to put his legions in harm's way. Have students write the letter Arminius might have sent to Varus.

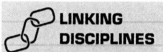

LINKING DISCIPLINES

Art Roman carvings often represented scenes from real life, as shown in the photograph on page 166. Ask students what they would include on an arch dedicated to themselves. Have them design a panel for this imaginary arch based upon an experience of their own.

ROMANS AT ATTILA'S COURT (449 CE)

Directions

Read this firsthand account of meeting Attila the Hun by Priscus, an eastern Roman politician. Then answer the questions.

> The next day we came to the station of Agintheus . . . to receive five of those seventeen deserters, about whom Attila had written to the Emperor. . . .
>
> As we were considering what to say to Attila, and how to present the Emperor's gifts, Scottas came to fetch us, and we entered Attila's tent, which was surrounded by a multitude of barbarians. We found Attila sitting on a wooden chair. We stood at a little distance and Maximin advanced and saluted the barbarian, to whom he gave the Emperor's letter, saying that the Emperor prayed for the safety of him and his. The king replied, "It shall be unto the Romans as they wish it to be unto me," and immediately addressed Bigilas [one of the Romans], calling him a shameless beast, and asking him why he ventured to come when only some of the deserters had been returned. . . .
>
> [After making peace with Attila and being asked to dine with him] The places on the right of Attila were held chief in honor, those on the left, where we sat, were only second. . . . When all were arranged, a cup-bearer came and handed Attila a wooden cup of wine. He took it, and saluted the first in precedence, who, honored by the salutation, stood up, and might not sit down until the king, having tasted or drained the wine, returned the cup to the attendant. All the guests then honored Attila in the same way. . . .
>
> After more toasts the attendant of Attila first entered with a dish full of meat, and behind him came the other attendants with bread and viands, which they laid on the tables. A luxurious meal, served on silver plate, had been made ready for us and the barbarian guests, but Attila ate nothing but meat on a wooden trencher. In everything else, too, he showed himself temperate; his cup was of wood, while to the guests were given goblets of gold and silver. His dress, too, was quite simple, affecting only to be clean. The sword he carried at his side, the latchets of his Scythian shoes, the bridle of his horse were not adorned with gold or gems or anything costly. . . . When evening fell torches were lit, and two barbarians coming forward in front of Attila sang songs they had composed, celebrating his victories and deeds of valor in war. . . .

1. How does Attila live? What details tell you this?

_____

_____

2. What kind of host is Attila? What evidence can you find for your answer?

_____

_____

3. Write a brief description of Attila's character traits based on this account.

_____

_____

_____

A. MULTIPLE CHOICE

Circle the letter of the best answer for each question.

1. Arminius was a German leader who
    a. was an ally of the Romans.
    b. wiped out three Roman legions.
    c. invaded Rome.
    d. invaded Gaul.

2. Varus infuriated the German tribes that he governed by
    a. taxing them too much.
    b. imprisoning their leaders.
    c. not helping them against Rome.
    d. treating them as if they were slaves.

3. Romans first believed that barbarians were all
    a. educated.
    b. savages.
    c. slaves.
    d. gladiators.

4. Very often, barbarians pushed into Roman territory not as invaders but as
    a. immigrants.
    b. individuals.
    c. infidels.
    d. inferiors.

5. The Roman who negotiated with Attila the Hun to save Rome was
    a. Marcus Aurelius.
    b. Lactantius.
    c. Pope Leo.
    d. Hannibal.

B. SHORT ANSWER

Write one or two sentences to answer each question.

6. Why did the Romans have little fear of the barbarians for hundreds of years?

_____

_____

7. Why did barbarians want to enter the Roman Empire?

_____

_____

8. Why was the Sack of Rome by the Goths in 410 CE such a shock?

_____

_____

C. ESSAY

Study the map on page 165. Of all the invading peoples, only the Huns are shown to have turned back toward where they came from. On a separate sheet of papeer, write an essay telling what you think the other invading peoples did after they moved into Roman lands. Support your opinion with details from the chapter.

CHAPTER 26

THE EMPIRE, DIVIDED AND DEFEATED: THE FALL OF ROME

PAGES 168–172

STUDENT STUDY GUIDE

pages 61–62

CAST OF CHARACTERS

Theodosius emperor who outlawed pagan worship in the empire (392 CE)

Diocletian emperor who split Roman empire into eastern and western halves (284 CE)

 VOCABULARY

horrified struck with horror

Vandals a powerful, destructive tribe that invaded the western Roman Empire

magnificent great, beautiful, and impressive

Renaissance rebirth of interest in ancient Greek and Roman culture in 15th-century Europe

et cetera (etc.) and other things

circus round arena

auditorium hall or building used for public gatherings

video electronic recording of a performance with sound and images

CHAPTER SUMMARY

Plagued by corruption, foreign invasions, and civil wars, the Roman Empire had a long, slow death. The emperor Diocletian briefly restored order, but the stability he brought did not outlast him. The empire was split in 395 CE. When a German invader became king of Rome in 476, Roman control of western Europe was ended, although the legacies of Rome still affect us in the present.

PERFORMANCE OBJECTIVES

▶ To understand the causes that led to Rome's fall
▶ To describe Diocletian's attempts to restore stability to the empire
▶ To explain the survival of Rome's Eastern Empire
▶ To recognize the legacies of Rome

BUILDING BACKGROUND

Suggest to students that groups of people—whether nations, political parties, or school clubs—live and die just as individual people and animals do. Ask students to consider the "physical condition" of the United States. Is it young, middle-aged, or old? Explain that they are going to read about the death of a very old empire.

WORKING WITH PRIMARY SOURCES

Use the quote from Cicero on page 175 of the Epilogue to discuss what our modern conception of a good citizen is, and how close it is to the ideal of ancient Rome.

GEOGRAPHY CONNECTION

Location   When reading the explanation for the survival of the Eastern Empire (page 171), indicate its location on a map of Europe and Asia. Explain the importance of Constantinople's strategic location and its access to eastern trade.

READING COMPREHENSION QUESTIONS

1. How did Diocletian change the way the empire was governed? Why did he do this? (*After 50 years of chaos, Diocletian realized how hard it was to rule the entire empire. Knowing that he had to reorganize the army and increase tax collections, he divided the empire into two parts with four rulers.*)
2. What role did Constantinople play in the empire after the death of Theodosius in 395 CE? (*It became the capital of the separate Eastern Empire, with its own emperor.*)
3. Why is 476 CE often given as the official date for the end of the Roman Empire? (*That is when Odoacer, a German invader, became king of Rome, replacing the last Roman emperor, Romulus Augustulus.*)
4. What was the effect of Rome's fall on most people in the former empire's territory? (*Life went on as usual for most people. Most government officials stayed the same. Latin was still used for official business. The Christian Church grew more powerful, making Rome the leading city in Europe for many centuries.*)

5. What are some of the legacies of Rome? (*roads, architecture, legal ideas, governmental systems, idea of civic duty, literature, alphabet, and words*)

CRITICAL THINKING QUESTIONS

1. Do you think the writer Symmachus had good reason to be horrified when the emperor Gratian removed the Altar of Victory from the Senate House? Explain. (*Possible answer: Yes. The altar had been there for hundreds of years. It was a part of Roman history. Moving it was like saying the past was worthless.*)

2. Of the reasons given for the fall of Rome, which strikes you as the most important? Explain your answer. (*Possible answer: Foreign invasions were the most important. Because of them, Rome lost control of vast territories, lost tax revenues, couldn't maintain its armies, and became too weak to survive.*)

3. Distribute copies of the blackline master for Chapter 26 so students can compare and contrast the eastern and western Roman empires.

4. Why do you suppose the legacy of Rome is so strong more than 1,500 years after its fall? (*Possible answer: The ideas handed down to us from Roman times are good, practical ideas that are still useful today.*)

SOCIAL SCIENCES

Civics   Draw students' attention to the passage on civic duty in the Epilogue (page 175). Compile with the class a list of voluntary projects that Cicero would approve of. Encourage students to find local community service opportunities that are available to people of their age.

READING AND LANGUAGE ARTS

Reading Nonfiction   Have students make a timeline to summarize the events leading up to the fall of Rome.

Using Language   Help students understand the importance of Latin in our everyday vocabulary. Have them use the Internet or dictionaries to discover Latin roots to English words. Encourage students to create posters of words they find interesting.

SUPPORTING LEARNING

English Language Learners   For students whose first language is one of the Romance languages, you may want to have them list words from their first languages that have their origins in Latin. Compare these with words they have learned in this chapter.

Struggling Readers   Have students work in pairs to reread the quote from Theodoric on page 172. Have students explain his meaning, using details and examples from the text.

EXTENDING LEARNING

Enrichment   Latin words are used in many state mottoes in the United States. Students can use an almanac to find state mottoes, list the ones that are in Latin, and give their translations.

Extension   Remind students of the previous work they did with Roman numerals. (See blackline master for Chapter 15.) Brainstorm with students where they might see Roman numerals used today.

WRITING

Obituary Explain to students that an obituary is a death notice, telling about a person's life. Chapter 26 refers to Rome as an old woman named Roma. Have students write an obituary of Roma.

THEN and NOW

The Roman Forum is still in ruins, but today there is not a cow in sight.

LINKING DISCIPLINES

Science Some people would name concrete as the most important of Rome's contributions to western civilization. Have students discover more about this versatile building material and the Romans' use of it. Invite interested students to undertake a miniature Roman building project using ready-mix concrete and homemade forms.

NAME **DATE**

COMPARING THE WESTERN AND EASTERN EMPIRES

Directions

Imagine you are interviewing the emperors of the Western Empire and the Eastern Empire in about 400 CE. Ask them the following questions, and then use the information in Chapter 26 to write the answers they would give.

Question	Western Emperor	Eastern Emperor
1. What religion do you follow? Why?		
2. Whom did the name *Romans* apply to in your realm?		
3. Is your economy mostly agricultural, or do you manufacture and trade goods? Why?		
4. Who pays the taxes in your realm? What is the money used for?		
5. Is your army able to defend your borders? Why or why not?		
6. Is your population growing? Why or why not?		
7. Who, if anyone, attacked you? Why?		

NAME   DATE

A. MULTIPLE CHOICE

Circle the letter of the best answer for each question.

1. The emperor Gratian took the Altar of Victory out of the Senate house because
  a. there was no room for it.
  b. it did not have a picture of the emperor on it.
  c. it was symbolic of the old Roman gods.
  d. it was symbolic of the Christian religion.

2. The emperor Diocletian changed the government of the empire by
  a. dividing the empire into two parts with four rulers.
  b. dividing the empire into three parts with six rulers.
  c. going back to the Republican form of government.
  d. ruling the empire by himself.

3. The empire finally split into two separate parts after the death of
  a. Diocletian.
  b. Constantine.
  c. Theodosius.
  d. Romulus Augustulus.

4. When the empire split, the government in Rome could not pay its bills because
  a. all of the tax collectors were in the east.
  b. it could no longer tax the rich eastern provinces.
  c. the Germanic invaders paid taxes to the eastern empire.
  d. it could not borrow enough money.

5. The end of the Western Empire was marked in 476 CE when
  a. the barbarians controlled all the western provinces.
  b. the Irish and Scots overran Britain.
  c. the Vandals devastated Gaul.
  d. the German king Odoacer forced the Roman emperor from his throne.

B. SHORT ANSWER

Write one or two sentences to answer each question.

6. How did the geography of the Western Empire contribute to its fall?

_____

_____

7. How did Rome's reliance on agriculture contribute to its fall?

_____

_____

8. What are some of the lasting influences of the Roman Empire?

_____

_____

C. ESSAY

Write an essay on a separate sheet of paper telling which part of the Roman heritage you think is most important to the modern world. Support your opinion with details from the chapter.

NAME   **DATE**

Directions

On a separate sheet of paper, answer each of the following questions.

1. Write a paragraph summarizing one of the legends of the founding of Rome and the archaeological evidence that supports it.

2. In the 5th century BCE, the Greek poet Euripides wrote, "When laws are written, rich and poor get equal justice." Write a paragraph evaluating how true this was in Rome during the Republic.

3. Write one or two paragraphs describing slavery in ancient Rome. Tell who the slaves were, how they were treated, and why they were feared by the Romans.

4. Cicero was a loyal Roman whose greatest desire was to save the Republic in the 1st century BCE. However, his cause seemed doomed to fail. Write a list of the political, social, and military conditions that worked against Cicero caused the downfall of the Roman Republic.

5. Write a two-paragraph reaction to Cleopatra. In the first paragraph, describe her character, using details from the textbook. In the second paragraph, state and support your opinion of how she ruled, given the power struggles of that time.

6. The expansion of the Roman Empire brought benefits and changes to Rome. It also brought benefits and changes to the people of the provinces who came under Roman rule. Make a two-column chart with the headings *Effects of Empire on Rome* and *Effects of Empire on Provinces*. Fill in the chart with details from your textbook.

7. Imagine you are a Roman during the empire. Write a two-paragraph reaction to the entertainments held in the Colosseum. In the first paragraph, describe the entertainments. In the second paragraph, describe how you feel after going to see them.

8. The Roman religion often added gods from other cultures. Write a paragraph explaining why this did not happen with the Jewish and Christian God.

9. Near the end of its life, the Roman Empire was beset by internal problems as well as external problems. Make lists of both types of problems. Then write a paragraph stating whether you think the empire could have survived if one or the other type of problem did not exist. Support your opinion with details from the textbook.

10. Write a paragraph describing the echoes of Rome that are found in the United States government.

GRAPHIC ORGANIZERS

GUIDELINES

Reproducibles of seven different graphic organizers are provided on the following pages. These give your students a variety of ways to sort and order all the information they are receiving in this course. Use the organizers for homework assignments, classroom activities, tests, small group projects, and as ways to help the students take notes as they read.

1. Determine which graphic organizers work best for the content you are teaching. Some are useful for identifying main ideas and details; others work better for making comparisons, and so on.

2. Graphic organizers help students focus on the central points of the lesson while leaving out irrelevant details.

3. Use graphic organizers to give a visual picture of the key ideas you are teaching.

4. Graphic organizers can help students recall important information. Suggest students use them to study for tests.

5. Graphic organizers provide a visual way to show the connections between different content areas.

6. Graphic organizers can enliven traditional lesson plans and encourage greater interactivity within the classroom.

7. Apply graphic organizers to give students a concise, visual way to break down complex ideas.

8. Encourage students to use graphic organizers to identify patterns and clarify their ideas.

9. Graphic organizers stimulate creative thinking in the classroom, in small groups, and for the individual student.

10. Help students determine which graphic organizers work best for their purposes, and encourage them to use graphic organizers collaboratively whenever they can.

11. Help students customize graphic organizers when necessary; e.g., make more or fewer boxes, lines, or blanks, if dictated by the exercise..

OUTLINE

MAIN IDEA: _____

_____

_____

DETAIL: _____

_____

DETAIL: _____

_____

DETAIL: _____

_____

MAIN IDEA: _____

_____

_____

DETAIL: _____

_____

DETAIL: _____

_____

DETAIL: _____

_____

Name _____ Date _____

MAIN IDEA MAP

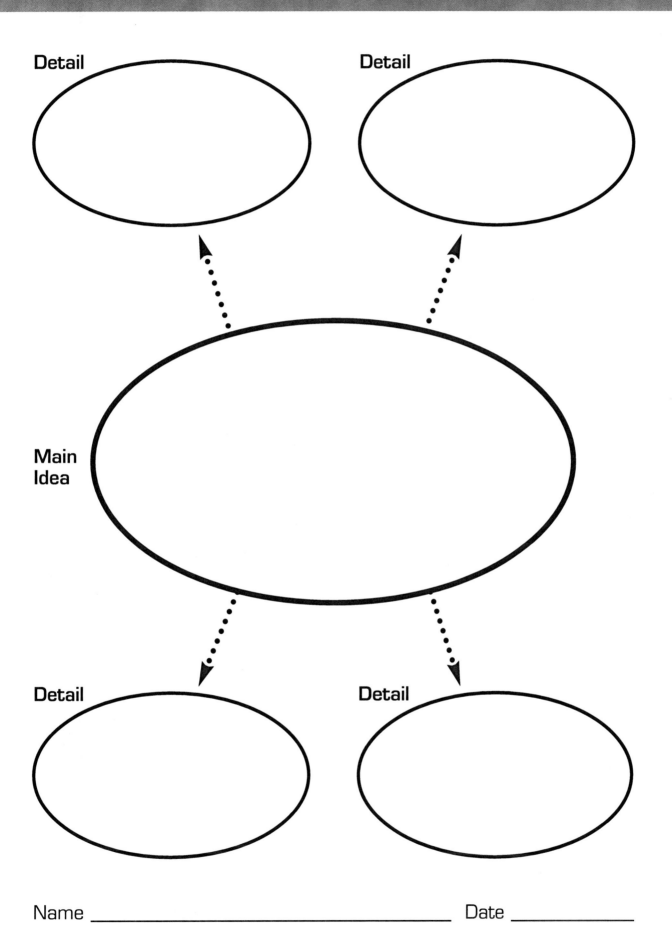

Detail

Detail

Main
Idea

Detail

Detail

Name _____ Date _____

K-W-L CHART

K	W	L
What I Know	What I Want to Know	What I Learned

Name _____   Date _____

VENN DIAGRAM

Write differences in the circles. Write similarities where the circles overlap.

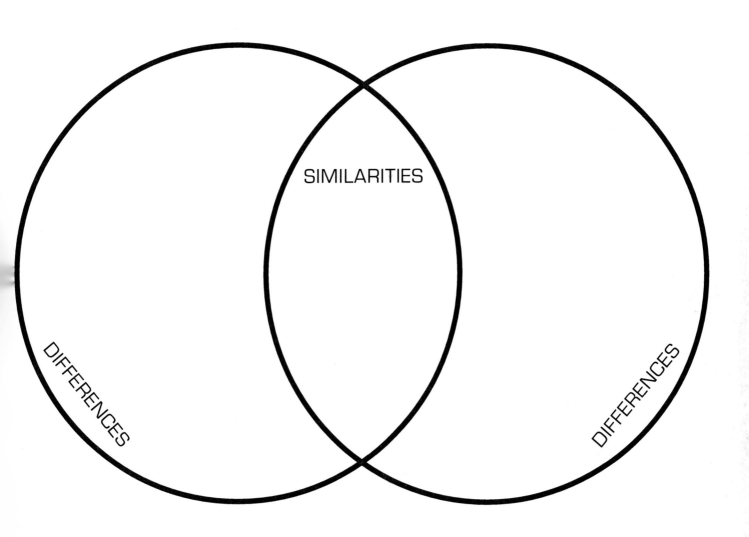

Name _____ Date _____

TIMELINE

DATE

EVENT Draw lines to connect the event to the correct year on the timeline.

Name _____ Date

SEQUENCE OF EVENTS CHART

Event

Next Event

Next Event

Next Event

Next Event

Name _____ Date _____

T–CHART

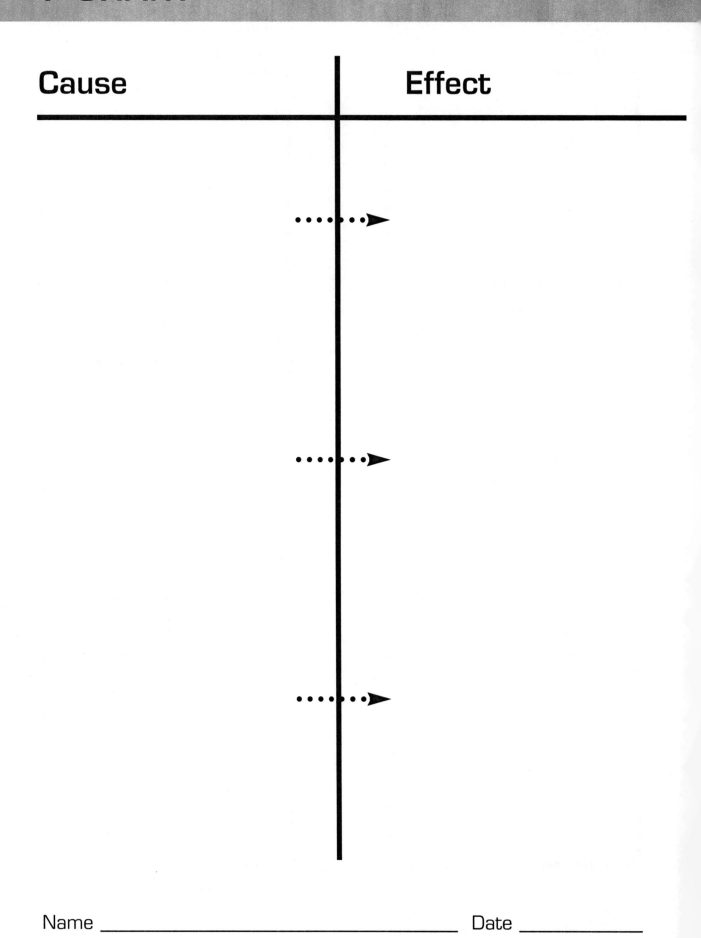

Cause | Effect

Name _____ Date _____

SCORING RUBRIC

The reproducibles on the following pages have been adapted from this rubric for use as handouts and a student self-scoring activity, with added focus on planning, cooperation, revision and presentation. You may wish to tailor the self-scoring activity—for example, asking students to comment on how low scores could be improved, or focusing only on specific rubric points. Use the Library/Media Center Research Log to help students focus and evaluate their research for projects and assignments.

As with any rubric, you should introduce and explain the rubric before students begin their assignments. The more thoroughly your students understand how they will be evaluated, the better prepared they will be to produce projects that fulfill your expectations.

	ORGANIZATION	CONTENT	ORAL/WRITTEN CONVENTIONS	GROUP PARTICIPATION
4	• Clearly addresses all parts of the writing task. • Demonstrates a clear understanding of purpose and audience. • Maintains a consistent point of view, focus, and organizational structure, including the effective use of transitions. • Includes a clearly presented central idea with relevant facts, details, and/or explanations.	• Demonstrates that the topic was well researched. • Uses only information that was essential and relevant to the topic. • Presents the topic thoroughly and accurately. • Reaches reasonable conclusions clearly based on evidence.	• Contains few, if any, errors in grammar, punctuation, capitalization, or spelling. • Uses a variety of sentence types. • Speaks clearly, using effective volume and intonation.	• Demonstrated high levels of participation and effective decision making. • Planned well and used time efficiently. • Demonstrated ability to negotiate opinions fairly and reach compromise when needed. • Utilized effective visual aids.
3	• Addresses all parts of the writing task. • Demonstrates a general understanding of purpose and audience. • Maintains a mostly consistent point of view, focus, and organizational structure, including the effective use of some transitions. • Presents a central idea with mostly relevant facts, details, and/or explanations.	• Demonstrates that the topic was sufficiently researched. • Uses mainly information that was essential and relevant to the topic. • Presents the topic accurately but leaves some aspects unexplored. • Reaches reasonable conclusions loosely related to evidence.	• Contains some errors in grammar, punctuation, capitalization, or spelling. • Uses a variety of sentence types. • Speaks somewhat clearly, using effective volume and intonation.	• Demonstrated good participation and decision making with few distractions. • Planning and used its time acceptably. • Demonstrated ability to negotiate opinions and compromise with little aggression or unfairness.
2	• Addresses only parts of the writing task. • Demonstrates little understanding of purpose and audience. • Maintains an inconsistent point of view, focus, and/or organizational structure, which may include ineffective or awkward transitions that do not unify important ideas. • Suggests a central idea with limited facts, details, and/or explanations.	• Demonstrates that the topic was minimally researched. • Uses a mix of relevant and irrelevant information. • Presents the topic with some factual errors and leaves some aspects unexplored. • Reaches conclusions that do not stem from evidence presented in the project.	• Contains several errors in grammar, punctuation, capitalization, or spelling. These errors may interfere with the reader's understanding of the writing. • Uses little variety in sentence types. • Speaks unclearly or too quickly. May interfere with the audience's understanding of the project.	• Demonstrated uneven participation or was often off-topic. Task distribution was lopsided. • Did not show a clear plan for the project, and did not use time well. • Allowed one or two opinions to dominate the activity, or had trouble reaching a fair consensus.
1	• Addresses only one part of the writing task. • Demonstrates no understanding of purpose and audience. • Lacks a point of view, focus, organizational structure, and transitions that unify important ideas. • Lacks a central idea but may contain marginally related facts, details, and/or explanations.	• Demonstrates that the topic was poorly researched. • Does not discriminate relevant from irrelevant information. • Presents the topic incompletely, with many factual errors. • Did not reach conclusions.	• Contains serious errors in grammar, punctuation, capitalization, or spelling. These errors interfere with the reader's understanding of the writing. • Uses no sentence variety. • Speaks unclearly. The audience must struggle to understand the project.	• Demonstrated poor participation by the majority of the group. Tasks were completed by a small minority. • Failed to show planning or effective use of time. • Was dominated by a single voice, or allowed hostility to derail the project.

NAME _____ **PROJECT** _____

DATE _____

ORGANIZATION & FOCUS	CONTENT	ORAL/WRITTEN CONVENTIONS	GROUP PARTICIPATION

COMMENTS AND SUGGESTIONS

UNDERSTANDING YOUR SCORE

Organization: Your project should be clear, focused on a main idea, and organized. You should use details and facts to support your main idea.

Content: You should use strong research skills. Your project should be thorough and accurate.

Oral/Written Conventions: For writing projects, you should use good composition, grammar, punctuation, and spelling, with a good variety of sentence types. For oral projects, you should engage the class using good public speaking skills.

Group Participation: Your group should cooperate fairly and use its time well to plan, assign and revise the tasks involved in the project.

NAME _____   **GROUP MEMBERS** _____

_____

_____

_____

Use this worksheet to describe your project by finishing the sentences below.
For individual projects and writing assignments, use the "How I did" section.
For group projects, use both "How I did" and "How we did" sections.

The purpose of this project is to :

Scoring Key =   **4** – extremely well
3 – well
2 – could have been better
1 – not well at all

HOW I DID

I understood the purpose and requirements for this project...

I planned and organized my time and work...

This project showed clear organization that emphasized the central idea...

I supported my point with details and description...

I polished and revised this project...

I utilized correct grammar and good writing/speaking style...

Overall, this project met its purpose...

HOW WE DID

We divided up tasks...

We cooperated and listened to each other...

We talked through what we didn't understand...

We used all our time to make this project the best it could be...

Overall, as a group we worked together...

I contributed and cooperated with the team...

LIBRARY/ MEDIA CENTER RESEARCH LOG

NAME _____

DUE DATE _____

What I Need to **Find**

I need to use:

☐ primary
☐ secondary

sources.

Places I **Know** to Look

Brainstorm: Other Sources and Places to Look

WHAT I FOUND

Title/Author/Location (call # or URL)

How I Found it

☐ Suggestion
☐ Library Catalog
☐ Browsing
☐ Internet Search
☐ Web link

☐ Primary Source
☐ Secondary Source

☐ Book/Periodical
☐ Website
☐ Other

Rate each source
from 1 (low) to 4 (high)
in the categories below

helpful   relevant

CHAPTER 1   Blackline Master

Seven Hills: high land good for defensive positions. *Lake and stream:* transporting goods and people. *Tiber River:* transporting goods and people, large river blocks invading forces. *Inland and coastal routes nearby:* trade and travel throughout peninsula. *Route along Tiber and coast:* can travel to coastal as well as inland cities, can send army on different routes.

Students' opinions about the most important of these features will vary, but should be supported by a logical argument.

Chapter Test   A. 1. b 2. c 3. b 4. b 5. a

B. 6. They dated everything from the founding of Rome in 753 BCE. 7. Evidence of different burial customs has been found in Roman cemeteries. 8. Roman heroes were thought to be the children of the gods.

C. Students' essays will compare and contrast the myths of Aeneas and Romulus.

CHAPTER 2   Blackline Master

1. Draining the marshy land made the land dry, and created the *Cloaca Maxima,* which became Rome's sewer.

2. the Tiber floods, and presses against the walls of the sewers; houses fall against them due to conflagration or spontaneous falling to ruins; earthquakes shake them

3. The Tiber backs up into the sewers when it floods, so heavy rain or melting snow might cause this.

Chapter Test   A. 1. a 2. c 3. c 4. b 5. a

B. 6. Women were much more involved in public life in Etruscan society. They went out with their husbands to public events, and ate dinner with them. 7. The Etruscans lived in independent cities that handled their own affairs but worked together in times of war or other crises. 8. The Etruscans believed that many gods and demons ruled the world. The gods showed their power in nature.

C. Essays should discuss similarities in religion; features such as the arch and vault, city planning, and waterworks; and the Etruscan rulers of Rome.

CHAPTER 3   Blackline Master

Temple of Juno: priests making sacrifices, people praying. *Senate House:* senators arguing over and voting on decrees. *Prison:* wails of prisoners, prisoners being punished. *Forum:* people gathered to discuss news and do business. *Food Market:* smells of different fruits, meats, bread, wines, and so on. *Tuscan Street, Cloaca Maxima:* smells of the sewer. *Cattle Market:* sounds, smells of cattle being sold or butchered. *Tiber River:* boats, calls of captains, fish, birds.

Chapter Test   A. 1. d 2. b 3. b 4. c 5. b

B. 6. The Assembly was made up of all citizens who could vote—landowning men. 7. The Senate controlled how money was spent and had nearly all the experienced ex-magistrates. 8. Dictators were supposed to give up their power when the crisis passed.

C. Essays should tell about Horatius's bravery, selflessness, and devotion to duty.

CHAPTER 4   Blackline Master

1. Tables 1–3 deal with legal matters. The Romans took their legal system very seriously. If people didn't show up when they were supposed to, they could be forced to appear.

2. Tables 4 and 10 concern public health matters.

3. Tables 5 and 11 concern the society's structure. They tell us details about a woman's place in Roman society and that the social classes did not mix with each other.

4. Answers will vary; it may be to prevent secret plots from being hatched.

5. Judges or arbiters who take bribes could be killed, which means that the Romans of this time valued fairness in their judges.

Chapter Test   A. 1. b 2. a 3. a 4. d 5. c

B. 6. The plebeians moved from the farms to the cities, and were no longer dependent on the patricians. 7. Everybody can know the laws, and the laws remain constant. 8. They could appeal the death sentence to the Assembly.

C. Essays should discuss the self-interest of each group, and should note that the conflict was never truly resolved.

CHAPTER 5   Blackline Master

1. Since gods and goddesses controlled life, Romans would want them on their side in war.

2. The Romans held onto their beliefs in their gods for hundreds of years. After a while, the words would become traditional.

3. Romans believed deeply that their gods and goddesses affected their lives, and so should be treated well.

Chapter Test   A. 1. c 2. c 3. b 4. c 5. a

B. 6. The Roman father would bang on the threshold of the home with an ax and a broom to drive away wild spirits. 7. The job was first handled by the king, but as society grew more complex, it was handled by the consuls and then priests and priestesses. 8. Older Roman gods were tied to a place. Later Roman gods that were thought to be useful were borrowed from other places.

C. Essays should detail the similarities between the structure of the Roman gods, state, and family.

CHAPTER 6   Blackline Master

Fearful soldiers: Hannibal spoke to soldiers, reminding them of their goal. *Attacked by natives:* Fought them off, scared them off with elephants. *Army exhausted:* Soldiers got two days to rest. *Path slippery and steep:* Cut through rock to build track. *Exhausted men and starving animals:* Men given three days' rest, animals put out to pasture.

Chapter Test   A. 1. c 2. a 3. d 4. c 5. a

B. 6. His father made him swear to be Rome's enemy. When his father died, Hannibal became general of Carthage's army in Spain. 7. Hannibal won the battles of Trebia, Trasimene, and Cannae. 8. Romans started to support their army more. Roman strategy changed to making Hannibal wear himself out in small battles.

C. Essays should tell that Rome won control of the entire Mediterranean while Carthage was completely destroyed.

CHAPTER 7   Blackline Master

1. The doctor found something wrong even though the patient wasn't sick.

2. A gladiator might put out someone's eyes. The doctor probably wasn't a very good eye doctor.

3. Doctors don't make very good medicines.

4. An undertaker is someone who buries dead people. When he was a doctor, Diaulus killed his patients rather than curing them.

Chapter Test   A. 1. b 2. b 3. d 4. b 5. b

B. 6. Romans may not speak well, but they speak the truth. Greeks speak well, but their words can't be trusted. 7. They treated the Greeks brutally, crushing any resistance and taking thousands of Greeks as slaves. 8. Cato's duties included recording the ages and property of citizens, directing building projects, and watching over the morals of the people.

C. Essays should note that Cato emphasized traditional Roman values, which the common people liked but the patricians found limiting.

CHAPTER 8   Blackline Master

Slave: could be bought and sold; could be forced to wear metal collar; could not own land; could not marry; children were slaves, too; master would choose his work; treated cruelly; household slaves treated better; would get gifts from master; could buy freedom. *Freedman:* usually educated people or household workers; could legally marry; could own property; could live anywhere, but often stayed with former masters; needed to work to make a living; were paid for their work; could not be bought and sold. *Both:* were poor; worked very hard; were servants.

Chapter Test   A. 1. d 2. d 3. c 4. d 5. d

B. 6. to inspire his men to defeat the Roman army 7. He was a skilled fighter, who could defeat two centurions at the same time.
C. Essays should follow the slave's life, and discuss the lack of freedom of such a life.

CHAPTER 9   Blackline Master

Reforms of Tiberius Gracchus: No one could own more than 300 acres of state land; the rest would be given to the poor. *Reforms of Gaius Gracchus:* Allow non-senators to be on juries. Allow non-Roman Italians to be Roman citizens.
1. Possible answer: Tiberius's land reform was best for Rome because it would solve the problems of poor, landless people, stop mobs from roaming through Rome, and result in more soldiers available for the army. 2. Possible answer: Allowing non-Roman Italians to be citizens was best, because it decreased tension between the people in Italy, extended rights to more people, and supplied more people to the army. 3. Possible answer: The poor people eventually sold their land to the wealthy, and conditions returned to where they were before the reforms.

Chapter Test   A. 1. b 2. c 3. b 4. a 5. b

B. 6. He got a law passed limiting anyone's holdings of public land to 300 acres, which meant that poor Romans could own land, too. 7. It kept the price of grain low enough so that poor people could afford it. 8. They thought he was trying to promote his own power, and that he was going to be a tyrant.
C. Essays should show that the Gracchi tried to make Rome's laws fairer to common people, but also intended to strengthen all aspects of Roman society.

CHAPTER 10   Blackline Master

7 led to 3, which led to 5, which led to 6, which led to 4, which led to 1, which led to the end of the Roman Republic.

Chapter Test   A. 1. b 2. a 3. c 4. c 5. b

B. 6. Cicero was best known for his letters and passionate speeches. 7. Pompey was a great general. Caesar was a popular politican. Crassus was a millionaire. 8. He was not able to achieve his life's goal of saving the Republic.
C. Students' essays will vary, but should state that Cicero probably would have tried to do what he did no matter who was against him.

CHAPTER 11   Blackline Master

1. Praising someone else (third-person) doesn't sound like boasting; praising yourself (first-person) sounds like boasting.
2. Caesar treated civilians brutally. If they weren't killed in the fighting, they were captured and held as prisoners.
3. During the siege of Avericum, the soldiers were starving, but they refused to end the siege and begged Caesar not to do so.
4. Students should state that Caesar was an effective leader. His troops were loyal to him, and they won many battles under his leadership.

Chapter Test   A. 1. b 2. c 3. b 4. b 5. a

B. 6. The plebeians believed he understood and cared about their needs. 7. He became consul and then governor of Gaul, where he established himself as a major power. 8. Ptolemy had killed Pompey and cut off his head, which disgusted Caesar.
C. Students' opinions will differ, but should be supported with details from the chapter.

CHAPTER 12   Blackline Master

Cleopatra becomes co-ruler of Egypt at age 18. Plot to overthrow Cleopatra; she escapes to Syria. Julius Caesar comes to Egypt; puts Cleopatra back on throne. Cleopatra returns to Rome with Julius Caesar; son Caesarion is born. Julius Caesar is assassinated; Cleopatra returns to Egypt. Cleopatra meets Mark Antony at Tarsus. Cleopatra gives birth to Mark Antony's children. Mark Antony returns to Cleopatra in Egypt. Octavian declares war on Mark Antony and Cleopatra. Octavian defeats Mark Antony at Actium. Mark Antony's troops desert at Alexandria. Mark Antony dies in Cleopatra's arms; Cleopatra commits suicide.

Chapter Test   A. 1. d 2. c 3. c 4. a 5. a

B. 6. She was highly educated and could speak nine languages. She was charming, and had a forceful character. 7. She had made everyone in Rome hate her. 8. She was trying to get them to help her save Egypt from collapse.
C. Students' opinions will vary, but should be supported by details from the chapter.

CHAPTER 13   Blackline Master

Students' paragraphs will vary. They should recognize that Augustus accomplished many things in his long reign, but that his personal opinion of those accomplishments can be viewed in different lights by different people.

Chapter Test   A. 1. b 2. a 3. a 4. c 5. d

B. 6. He gave them land to settle on. 7. He built an elaborate Altar of Peace and closed the doors of the temple of Janus. 8. He didn't seem to be able to settle on a good successor.
C. Students' essays will vary.

CHAPTER 14   Blackline Master

Tiberius: believed in free speech, left treasury 20 times larger; became suspicious and ordered executions of innocent men. *Caligula:* reduced taxes, put on many entertainments; became mad, killed senators to steal their property or take their wives, gave provinces to boyhood friends, insisted that people worship him as god Jupiter. *Claudius:* established strong system of government, invaded Britain, gave citizenship to provincials, passed laws requiring more lenient treatment of slaves; foolish in choosing wives. *Nero:* attacked corruption, returned power to Senate, made careful decisions in law and government; became more interested in performing on stage, killed his mother and wife, loved luxury, neglected the army. *Vespasian:* practical and thrifty, restored the economy, kept soldiers loyal, built the Colosseum. *Titus:* launched Colosseum's opening games. *Domitian:* successful general; brutal reign marked by book burnings, plots, and executions.

Chapter Test   A. 1. b 2. a 3. d 4. d 5. a

B. 6. Tiberius allowed free speech and increased the treasury. He believed the gossip of malicious men and executed many innocent people. 7. The army rebelled and chose a new emperor, and Nero committed suicide. 8. Vespasian's second son Domitian was a cruel tyrant who was killed in a palace conspiracy. He had no other sons.
C. Students' opinions will differ, but should be supported by details from the chapter.

CHAPTER 15   Blackline Master

Students' problems will vary.

Chapter Test   A. 1. b 2. c 3. a 4. b 5. b

B. 6. A matriarch is a mother and a patriarch is a father. Both are strong people who wield control over their families. 7. They did not have enough money to rent or buy rooms for their classes. 8. Livia advised and had great influence over Augustus during his reign.
C. Essays should note that the influence of these three women increased: Livia had the least open power and Julia Mammaea had the most.

CHAPTER 16   Blackline Master

1. They faced collapsing buildings, earthquakes, darkness, ash and dust, being trampled by the crowd. 2. The people around them tried to escape, prayed to the gods to save them, and told lies about the destruction of Misenum.

Chapter Test   A. 1. c 2. b 3. b 4. a 5. d

B. 6. It was a market center with many hotels, taverns, bars, and other attractions. 7. Many people were killed by poisonous gases in their homes. Others were overtaken by fast-moving lava and flying rocks and ash. 8. It preserved the town in its normal state for later archaeologists.

C. Students' essays will vary.

CHAPTER 17   Blackline Master

Students should color most of the Roman Empire in one color, and the provinces of Dacia and Mesopotamia in a second color. The map legend should reflect these colors. The empire stretched about 3,500 miles from east to west and about 2,500 miles from north to south.

Chapter Test   A. 1. a 2. b 3. b 4. b 5. c

B. 6. They had to serve for 20 years. 7. Reburrus was granted citizenship, as well as his wife and children and their descendants. 8. Future generations had all the rights of Roman citizens. They could become legionaries instead of auxiliaries.

C. Students' essays will vary.

CHAPTER 18   Blackline Master

1. 50,000–75,000 spectators
2. in rooms below ground
3. Plebeians probably sat in the seats farthest away from the action, whereas patricians sat closer down.

Chapter Test   A. 1. c 2. c 3. b 4. a 5. b

B. 6. They became chariot drivers for the excitement, money, and fame. 7. They were treated like professional athletes, and were fed and trained well. 8. They had fans who adored them and managers who took care of them, and could earn a lot of money.

C. Students' opinions will vary and should be supported with details from the chapter.

CHAPTER 19   Blackline Master

1. Spain, Gaul, Scythia, Thrace, Macedonia, Asia Minor, Egypt, Greece, Sicily, Sardinia
2. Spain, Gaul, Dalmatia, Dacia
3. The trader might trade amber in Gaul for gold, then go to Rome and pay for Numidian marble with the gold.

Chapter Test   A. 1. b 2. a 3. c 4. c 5. a

B. 6. The ship could capsize in the storm, causing great monetary loss to the owner. 7. Sunken Roman ships have been found in Pisa, Italy and in Britain. 8. Romans used coins to pay taxes, buy food and services, and all sorts of other transactions.

C. Essays should include the types of trade goods that came from various places.

CHAPTER 20   Blackline Master

1. Hadrian's Wall was approximately 75 miles long; the Limes was approximately 330 miles long.
2. Hadrian's Wall ran from sea to sea. The Limes ran from the Rhine River to the Danube River. There were no natural lines of defense in either area.
3. Barbarians needed to move back and forth over the lines for trade.

Chapter Test   A. 1. b 2. d 3. a 4. b 5. b

B. 6. Hadrian's father died, and his distant relative, the emperor Trajan, adopted him. 7. Hadrian built a villa for himself, the Pantheon, and the Castel Sant'Angelo. 8. He pulled back the army to more easily defended borders because he didn't want to fight unnecessary wars.

C. Students' essays will vary. They should acknowledge that Hadrian did many good things for Rome, although he may have been too interested in Greek culture.

CHAPTER 21   Blackline Master

1. They must get permission from the *praetor urbanus*.
2. The third point is concerned with bacchanalians using their meetings to join conspiracies or disturb the public order.
3. The penalty was capital punishment, or death.

Chapter Test   A. 1. b 2. c 3. c 4. d 5. d

B. 6. Their job was very dangerous, and they wanted whatever edge they could get over their competitors. 7. The Romans borrowed gods of all kinds from all over. They also added gods by deifying deceased emperors. 8. The worship of Isis was about death and rebirth.

C. Essays should show the similarities and differences between the cults of Cybele and Isis.

CHAPTER 22   Blackline Master

1. He had to prove he had performed very great services to the empire.
2. His citizenship would hopefully cause others of the tribe to emulate Julianus's offer of service to the empire.
3. Possible answer: It strengthened the empire because it allowed provincials to follow their laws, which would please them, while also making them loyal to the empire.
4. By making the provincials Roman citizens, they guarded the empire by guarding their own homes.

Chapter Test   A. 1. d 2. a 3. b 4. b 5. c

B. 6. It sent governors and tax collectors to the provinces, but also allowed the provincials to govern themselves. 7. To be counted, people had to return to the place where they were born. 8. Long-lasting effects on the provinces were Roman language, technology, and customs.

C. Essays should give details about what the provinces and Rome got from each other.

CHAPTER 23   Blackline Master

1. The Jewish communities in Spain and Gaul were farthest from Jerusalem.
2. Jerusalem isn't shown because the Jewish community there was dispersed throughout the empire.
3. Jewish merchants and craftsmen could find work in Rome. Other Jews lived there, so they would have a community.

Chapter Test   A. 1. a 2. c 3. b 4. b 5. c

B. 6. The Jews did no work on the Sabbath, they didn't eat certain foods, and they believed in one god. 7. Antiochus looted the temple at Jerusalem, built an altar to Zeus there, and tried to force the Jews to sacrifice swine. 8. This tradition centers Jewish communities around local rabbis, or teachers, rather than around the temple at Jerusalem.

C. Essays should tell why the Romans despised the Jews and the powerful customs that maintained Jewish communities.

CHAPTER 24   Blackline Master

1. Possible answer: He probably mixed questions with threats to weed out the people who were not true Christians, so that innocent people would not be executed.
2. Pliny is antagonistic toward Christians. He says the religion is spreading like a contagious disease, and has hopes of stopping it.
3. Trajan seems to be concerned with fairness and justice. He seems less concerned with the spread of Christianity.

Chapter Test   A. 1. a 2. c 3. a 4. d 5. b

B. 6. Simeon believed that Jesus was the Savior; Zechariah said the Messiah would be humble; Micah said he would be born in Bethlehem; a large star would appear when the Messiah was born. 7. Some of the values are comforting the sad, promoting justice, being merciful, being pure of heart, and being peacemakers.

8. Constantine stopped the persecution of Christians in the empire, allowing the religion to grow.

C. Students' essays will vary, but students should liken the way Roman influence spread throughout the Mediterranean world with the way Christian influence spread throughout the Roman world. Christian influence was spread by teaching and conversion, rather than by force of arms.

CHAPTER 25   Blackline Master

1. Attila lives simply in a tent with wooden furniture.

2. Attila is a reasonably good host who honors his guests at dinner and provides a lavish meal, but who has plain manners himself.

3. Paragraphs will vary, but should include details from the source.

Chapter Test   A. 1. b 2. d 3. b 4. a 5. c

B. 6. The barbarians were disorganized and easily defeated by the superior Roman army. 7. The barbarians were looking for fertile land near the Mediterranean, and were pushed out of their homelands by other warlike peoples. 8. Rome was the "Eternal City," and hadn't been captured in 800 years.

C. Essays should explain that the invaders probably settled down and started their own kingdoms.

CHAPTER 26/EPILOGUE   Blackline Master

1. *Western:* Christianity. *Eastern:* Christianity.

2. *Western:* all citizens of Rome, including people in the provinces. *Eastern:* Greek-speaking citizens.

3. *Western:* mostly agricultural. *Eastern:* manufacturing and trade goods.

4. *Western:* landowners, although many of them avoid paying. *Eastern:* merchants and traders in cities, as well as landowners.

5. *Western:* It can't defend our borders, because the borders are so long, we have so little tax money to supply the army, and so many barbarians are invading. *Eastern:* It can defend our borders, because we have enough tax money to supply the army and our borders are short.

6. *Western:* Our population is decreasing, as more of our lands are taken over by barbarians. *Eastern:* Our population is thriving.

7. *Western:* Barbarian tribes from Germany, such as the Vandals and the Goths, are attacking us. *Eastern:* We don't have any major enemies attacking us.

Chapter Test   A. 1. c 2. a 3. c 4. b 5. d

B. 6. The Western Empire had long borders that were difficult to defend. 7. Rome did not manufacture products, and so when it lost its land to barbarians, it had not tax funds coming in to pay for its army. 8. Lasting influences include the religious government of the Christian Church, its roads and aqueducts, cement, law, art, architecture, civic duty, literature, and foods.

C. Students' essays will vary, but their ideas should be supported with details from the book.

WRAP-UP TEST

1. Students' paragraphs will vary. They should describe the Aeneas or the Romulus and Remus legend, and include the archaeological evidence supporting the legend.

2. Students' paragraphs should say that although Rome had written laws, justice wasn't always equal for poor and rich in Rome.

3. *Who the slaves were:* originally Romans who couldn't pay their debts; later, prisoners taken in foreign wars. *How they were treated:* many treated cruelly, could be bought and sold, had to do what masters said; household and skilled servants were treated better, could buy their freedom. *Why they were feared by Romans:* Romans feared periodic slave uprisings in which thousands of slaves would fight for their freedom.

4. *Political conditions:* rise of the *populares*, corruption of government officials, outdated governmental ideas, use of mob violence in politics. *Social conditions:* mobs of poor, unemployed workers in Rome; loss of land by farmers; most work being done by slaves. *Military conditions:* soldiers who were loyal to generals, not to Republic; generals competing for power for themselves.

5. Students should describe Cleopatra as intelligent, charming, and politically clever. Students' opinions of her rule will vary.

6. *Effects of empire on Rome:* brought great wealth in gold and material goods; made Rome the center of the world; made Rome a great trading center; made Rome the largest city of its time; caused the construction of monumental buildings. *Effects of empire on provinces:* brought peace, a legal system, increased trade, and building projects such as aqueducts and roads; brought sometimes cruel treatment by Romans.

7. Students' descriptions of the entertainments should be vivid. Their reactions to the entertainments will vary.

8. The Jewish and Christian God could not be added to the Roman gods, because Jews and Christians believed there was only one true God. If the Romans accepted that God, they would have to do away with all of their other gods.

9. *Internal problems:* governmental chaos, civil unrest, lack of tax revenues, undue emphasis on agriculture instead of manufacturing and trade, corruption of officials, inability to keep up large army. *External problems:* long borders to defend, many barbarian invaders. Students should recognize that if the internal problems were fixed, the empire might have stood against the barbarian invasions. If there weren't barbarian invasions, the empire might have lasted longer, but the internal problems might have caused its collapse anyway.

10. Students' charts should include similarities between the Roman government and the U.S. government such as the following: powerful leader of central government, legislative body to make laws, judges to hear legal cases, juries to decide the legal cases, large group of public officials to do the daily business of government.

ANSWERS FOR THE STUDENT STUDY GUIDE

CHAPTER 1

Cast of Characters

Aeneas, legendary founder of Rome (Virgil)
Romulus, legendary founder of Rome (Livy)
Remus, brother of Romulus

What Happened When?

753 BCE   Traditional date for founding of Rome

Word Play   Immortal; mortal

Critical Thinking   1. f; 2. e; 3. a; 4. c; 5. b; 6. d

Write About It   c

CHAPTER 2

Cast of Characters

Etruscans, ancient people of Tuscany

What Happened When?

1000 BCE	Italic peoples arrive on Italian peninsula
900 BCE	Etruscans living in central Italy
750 BCE	Greek colonies founded in southern Italy
616 BCE	Etruscan kings rule Rome
509 BCE	Roman army expels last Etruscan king

Word Bank   1. peninsula; 2. immigrant; 3. architect; 4. omen;
Word Play immigrant

All Over the Map   Suggested "push" words: war, hunger, poverty, drought; suggested "pull" words: wealth, land, freedom

Primary Sources   Circled word: famine.

CHAPTER 3

Cast of Characters

Tarquin, last king of Rome, about 500 BCE
Brutus, Roman citizen credited with driving out Tarquin
Horatius, Roman soldier famed for bravery
Cincinnatus, Roman dictator who defeated the Aequi, 458 BCE
Lucreta, legendary figure known for her virtue

What Happened When?

509 BCE	Roman army expels last Etruscan king
475 BCE	Etruscans attack Rome
458 BCE	Cincinnatus named dictator; defeats Aequi
266 BCE	Rome controls entire Italian peninsula

Word Bank 1. aedile; 2. magistrates; 3. praetor; 4. Senate; 5. consuls; 6. Assembly, citizens; 7. republic; 8. dictator

Critical Thinking (columns checked) Senate: men; Assembly: men; consul: men, highest official, elected; dictator: men, appointed, absolute power; magistrate: men, appointed, official.

CHAPTER 4

Cast of Characters
Agrippa Menenius, patrician who ended plebeian rebellion, 493 BCE

What Happened When?
493 BCE First plebeian rebellion
450 BCE Second plebeian rebellion; Twelve Tables written

Do the Math 43 years

Word Bank patrician; plebian; *status quo*; tribunes; veto

Word Play rebellion

Compare and Contrast Patricians: lead troops; collect taxes; pass laws; own land Plebeians: serve as soldiers; work in fields; make sandals; weave cloth; sell fish; build temples.

Primary Sources Roman Code of Law
1. No; 2. *malice* means "hatred"; "before"; 3. b

CHAPTER 5

Cast of Characters
Scipio Hispanus, member of Rome's leading family
Vestal Virgins: women who conducted rituals to honor the oddess Vesta

Word Bank 1. ancestor, *toga virilis*; 2. paterfamilias, Lares. *Think Word Play* Janus looks back to the old year and forward to the coming year.

Classification Household spirits: throw flour into a fire; toss salt onto the hearth; carry masks in funerals. Powerful gods: pray for help in ruling Rome; give thanks for victory; pray for a good harvest.

CHAPTER 6

Cast of Characters
Hamilcar Barca, Carthaginian general in First Punic War; father of Hannibal
Hannibal, Carthaginian general in Second Punic War; greatest enemy of Rome
Scipio Africanus, Roman general who defeated Hannibal

What Happened When?
264 BCE Start of First Punic War
218 BCE Start of Second Punic War
217 BCE Hannibal's army invades Italian peninsula

Word Bank 1. cavalry; 2. fertile; 3. alliances; 4. cavalry, ambushed

Critical Thinking 1. f; 2. a; 3. g; 4. e; 5. d; 6. b; 7. c

All Over the Map 1. about 150 miles; 2.–5. check students' work

CHAPTER 7

Cast of Characters
Cato, Roman general and senator who supported Roman culture
Alexander the Great, creator of Greek empire in 4th century BCE
Antiochus III, Greek king defeated by Rome, 2nd century BCE

What Happened When?
336 BCE Alexander the Great begins his conquests
190 BCE Romans defeat Macedonians
149 BCE Romans conquer Greece

Do the Math Before

Word Bank 1. reign; 2. censor; 3. remedies; 4. oration; 5. aqueducts

CHAPTER 8

Cast of Characters
Spartacus, leader of Roman slave revolt, 73 BCE
Crassus, Roman general who finally defeated Spartacus

What Happened When?
135 BCE Slave rebellion in Sicily
73 BCE Slave rebellion led by Spartacus

Word Bank 1. rebellion, crucified; 2. freedman; 3. aristocrat

Word Play plebeian, patrician

Sequence of Events (top to bottom) 2; 6; 5; 7; 1; 4; 3. *Think About It* to warn them what would happen if they lost (discuss other answers)

Primary Sources Discuss students' responses

CHAPTER 9

Cast of Characters
Tiberius and Gaius Gracchus, 2nd-century BCE tribunes; fought against power of nobles and to improve life of plebeians

What Happened When?
133 BCE Tiberius Gracchus elected tribune
123 BCE Gaius Gracchus elected tribune
90 BCE Rome's Italian allies rebel (War of the Allies)

Word Bank importance; infuriated; revolutionary; *populares*; Mediterranean

Word Play popular, population; discuss other words

Critical Thinking 1. a and c; 2. a, b, and d.

All Over the Map Check students' maps against map on page 60.

CHAPTER 10

Cast of Characters
Cicero, 1st-century BCE consul and orator; tried to save Republic
Pompey, general, First Triumvirate member; took part in civil wars that destroyed Republic
Julius Caesar, statesman, general, First Triumvirate member
Mark Antony, politician and soldier who ordered Cicero murdered

Word Bank orator; innate; civil; triumvirate

What Happened When?
75 BCE Cicero elected quaestor
63 BCE Cicero elected consul
43 BCE Cicero killed

Critical Thinking Fact: 2, 4, 8. Opinion: 1, 2, 5, 6, 7

CHAPTER 11

Cast of Characters
Pompey, political rival of Caesar's
Julia, Julius Caesar's daughter; married to Pompey
Brutus, leader of senators who killed Caesar

What Happened When?
60 BCE First Triumvirate formed: Julius Caesar, Pompey, Crassus
48 BCE Caesar defeats Pompey; gains absolute power in Rome
44 BCE Caesar declared dictator for life
March 15, 44 BCE Caesar assassinated

Sequence of Events 1. before; 2. after; 3. before; 4. before; 5. after; 6. before; 7. before; 8. after; 9. after

Primary Source 1. Suetonius wrote many years after Caesar's death and could not have seen him alive; 2. well-dressed; 3. Baldness was considered unattractive in Roman times.

CHAPTER 12

Cast of Characters
Cleopatra, 1st-century BCE pharaoh of Egypt; made alliances with Caesar and Mark Antony
Mark Antony, partner, then enemy, of Octavian after Caesar's death
Octavian, Caesar's heir; avenged his death, then gained control of Rome

Word Bank 1. pharaoh; 2. consort

What Happened When?
51 BCE Cleopatra takes throne
46 BCE Cleopatra follows Caesar back to Rome
44 BCE Caesar assassinated; Cleopatra returns to Egypt
31 BCE Mark Antony and Cleopatra defeated at Actium
30 BCE Antony defeated by Octavian at Alexandria

Compare and Contrast

Caesar circle: defeated Ptolemy; was assassinated
Antony circle: lost to Octavian
Cleopatra circle: hid in a carpet; had child by Caesar; had children by Antony
Antony/Caesar: was married; lived with Cleopatra; ruled Rome
Antony/Cleopatra: committed suicide; went to Tarsus; dressed as servant
Caesar/Antony/Cleopatra: lived in Rome; lived in Alexandria

CHAPTER 13

Cast of Characters

Augustus Caesar, first emperor of Rome; reigned 41 years; established *Pax Romana*
Julia, Augustus's daughter
Lepidus, member of Second Triumvirate with Antony and Octavian
Tiberius, Augustus's stepson and heir

Word Bank   1. legitimate; 2. conspirator; 3. confiscate

What Happened When?

30 BCE   Octavian achieves victory over his rivals
27 BCE   Octavian becomes "Augustus"
14 CE   Death of Augustus; Tiberius becomes emperor

Do the Math   1 CE (there was no year zero)

Sequence of Events   (top to bottom) 4; 7; 5; 3; 1; 6; 2.

CHAPTER 14

Cast of Characters

Tiberius, Caligula, Claudius, Nero, emperors who followed Augustus
Vespasian ended civil wars in 69 CE; restored good government to empire (69–79 CE)
Titus, emperor who continued Vespasian's reforms (79–81 CE)
Domitian, tyrant who brought reign of fear to Rome (81–96 CE)

Word Bank   1. successor; 2. tyrant

What Happened When?

14–37 CE Tiberius; 37–41 CE Caligula; 41–54 CE Claudius; 54–68 CE Nero; 68 CE marked the beginning of the Civil War of the Four Emperors.

Fact or Opinion?   1. opinion; 2. Suetonius;
3. Dio Cassius says "several days and nights"; Suetonius says "six days and seven nights"; 4. Discuss answers. Key point: Suetonius says Nero set the fire "openly;" Dio Cassius says Nero "sent out men" to start the fires.

CHAPTER 15

Cast of Characters

Livia, influential wife and advisor of Augustus
Julia Domna, wife of 3rd-century emperor Septimius Severus who ran government when husband was away
Julia Mammaea, niece of Domna; ruled for her son

Drawing Conclusions   1. Livius, Julius; 2. she was the second daughter

Word Bank   1. education; 2. erased; 3. matriarch. *Word Play* the patriarch is the oldest male in a family, a man of great power

Critical Thinking   checked phrases: a girl marries at 14; a woman owns land; an infant girl is abandoned; a woman goes to a play; a girl works; a woman earns money; a woman works with her husband; a woman reads; a woman inherits her father's wealth

CHAPTER 16

Cast of Characters

Pliny the Elder, Roman fleet commander, writer, scientist, wrote about eruption of Mt. Vesuvius
Pliny the Younger, Roman writer and historian; witnessed eruption of Mt. Vesuvius

Word Bank   volcano, plumbing

Making Inferences   Caligula's actions resembled those of a person who suffered from extreme mental illness. He may well have consumed a great deal of lead in the wine and water mixture that he drank.

What Happened When?

August 24, 79 CE Mt. Vesuvius erupted, burying Pompeii and Herculaneum

Comprehension   1. Jewels and silver; 2. Romans first wore just one ring on the third finger; by Pliny's time they wore more than one ring on all of their fingers; 3. a; 4. he disapproves of "showing off"

CHAPTER 17

Cast of Characters

Nerva, Emperor (96–98 CE); began tradition of choosing qualified successor
Trajan, Emperor (98–117 CE); extended empire's borders; reigned fairly and with common sense; They were not related

Critical Thinking   1. b; 2. g; 3. c; 4. f; 5. e; 6. a

Primary Source   1. he disliked it; 2. exercising; 3. removing body hair; 4. discuss students' responses.

CHAPTER 18

Cast of Characters

Plautus, 2nd-century BCE writer of comedies
Diocles, chariot racer
The names are for men because the do not end in "a"

Word Bank   *ludi*; Saturnalia; arena; chariot, gladiators; sword, shield, net, trident, mercy.

Word Play   Saturday

Primary Sources   1. men were thrown to animals—Seneca is being sarcastic; 2. gladiators' fights were extremely bloody; 3. b

CHAPTER 19

Cast of Characters

Eumachia, wealthy businesswoman in Pompeii

Word Bank   1. patron; import

Critical Thinking   1. export wool; 2. import amber; 3. import marble, glass; 4. import silk; 5. import olives; 6. import paper; 7. import pepper; 8. export grain.

All Over the Map

1. about 3,600 miles; 2. about 2,600 miles; 3. about 800 miles; 4. silk and ivory; 5. wine and grain; compare students' maps with map on page 132

CHAPTER 20

Cast of Characters

Hadrian, emperor (117–138 CE); strengthened army; built wall across England

What Happened When?

117 CE   Hadrian becomes emperor
118 CE   Construction of Pantheon begins
122 CE   Construction of Hadrian's Wall begins
138 CE   Hadrian dies

Have students read sentences aloud. Comparison should point out the accomplishments of Hadrian contrasted to the destructive reigns of three of the four emperors following Augustus. Point out that Claudius was the exception.

Critical Thinking   1. A; 2. A; 3. L; 4. L; 5. L; 6. L; 7. B

Primary Sources   1. loved poetry, danced and sang extremely well, enriched his friends; 2. devoted . . . to the exercises of gladiators; growing suspicious of some put them to death; 3. he was a skilled leader in battle

CHAPTER 21

Cast of Characters

Cybele, Asian goddess; believed to be mother of the gods
Isis, Egyptian goddess of fertility
Mithras, Roman sun god

Drawing Conclusions   Life spans in Roman times were short. Myths about overcoming death offered great comfort.

Word Bank   1. superstitious; 2. fertility

Critical Thinking Superstitions: witches, evil eye, woodland spirits, omens, spiders, ringing ears, spells, charms. Religions: sacrifice, rebirth, black meteorite, life after death, planets and stars, sun, emperor, blossoming flowers, fertility

Primary Sources 1. he is making fun of those who believe in it; 2. fool; 3. b; 4. b.

CHAPTER 22

Cast of Characters
Agricola, governor of Britain (71 CE); extended Roman control and civilization

Word Bank
1. enemy; 2. ocher.

All Over the Map
1. England; 2. Northern Europe; 3. Israel; 4. It was the easiest way to gather non-Romans in areas where soldiers were stationed.

Sequence of Events
(top to bottom) 5; 8; 6; 3; 1; 4; 7; 2

CHAPTER 23

Cast of Characters
Titus, Roman general who captured Jerusalem and destroyed Jewish temple (70 CE)
David, first king of ancient Israel (about 1000 BCE)
Solomon, king of ancient Israel (about 950 BCE)
Antiochus IV, Syrian king (175 BCE) who outlawed Jewish customs
Judas Maccabeus, leader of successful Jewish revolt against Antiochus

Word Bank.
1. client; 2. kosher; 3. Yahweh

Critical Thinking
1. d; 2. f; 3. a; 4. b; 5. c; 6. e

Primary Sources 1. tasteless, low; 2. Masada had been destroyed, the Jewish people had been scattered across the empire. 3. Insulted—discuss other answers

CHAPTER 24

Cast of Characters
Jesus Christ, Jewish prophet thought to be the Messiah; his disciples founded Christianity
Herod, cruel king of Judea (37–4 BCE)
Pontius Pilate, Roman official who ordered Jesus crucified

Paul, disciple of Jesus who spread Christianity beyond Palestine
Constantine, emperor who made Christianity favored religion of Roman Empire

Word Bank Messiah; gospel; disciples; Beatitudes; persecuted.

Sequence of Events 1. before; 2. after; 3. after; 4. after; 5. before; 6. after; 7. before; 8. after; 9. before

Primary Sources 1. agree, falsely accused; 2. destructive superstition.

CHAPTER 25

Cast of Characters
Varus, Roman general who suffered terrible defeat by Germans
Arminius, leader of Germans who defeated Varus
Marcus Aurelius, 2nd-century emperor who defended the Rhine and Danube borders
Attila, leader of Central Asian tribes who invaded Italy about 450 CE

Word Play A sack in football occurs when the quarterback is tackled while attempting to pass the ball.

Critical Thinking 1. a, c; 2. b; 3. a, c; 4. a.

Primary Sources utterly cruel 1. inflamed; 2. they were fierce warriors; 3. horrible, over a large area; 4. its level was raised by the blood flowing into it.

CHAPTER 26/EPILOGUE

Cast of Characters
Theodosius, emperor who outlawed pagan worship in the empire (392 CE)
Diocletian, emperor who split Roman Empire into eastern and western halves (284 CE)
Odoacer, German king who ended the Roman Empire in the west

Word Bank horrified; Vandals; magnificent; Renaissance; circus; auditorium; video; et cetera; etc.

Do the Math 1,229 years

Compare and Contrast
Western Rome circle: capital: Rome; longer borders; agricultural economy; private armies; corrupt aristocrats
Eastern Rome circle controlled Egypt; capital: Constantinople; trade with Asia; larger population; manufacturing economy; larger army
Overlapping areas Christians spoke Latin; ruled by emperor

Primary Sources As Rome grew older, it became weaker, much like an aging person.

CPSIA information can be obtained at www.ICGtesting.com
Printed in the USA
242917LV00001B/8/P